Catharine Arnold read English at Cambridge and holds a further degree
in psychology. A journalist, academic and popular historian, Catharine's
previous books include her London quartet for Simon & Schuster,
comprising of *Necropolis*, *Bedlam*, *City of Sin* and *Underworld London*.

Also by Catharine Arnold

UNDERWORLD LONDON: Crime and Punishment in
the Capital City

THE SEXUAL HISTORY OF LONDON: From Roman
Londinium to the Swinging City

CITY OF SIN: London and Its Vices

BEDLAM: London and Its Mad

NECROPOLIS: London and Its Dead

GLOBE

Life in Shakespeare's London

CATHARINE ARNOLD

**SIMON &
SCHUSTER**

London · New York · Sydney · Toronto · New Delhi

A CBS COMPANY

First published in Great Britain by Simon & Schuster UK Ltd, 2015
This paperback edition first published in Great Britain by Simon & Schuster UK Ltd, 2016
A CBS COMPANY

1 3 5 7 9 10 8 6 4 2

Simon & Schuster UK Ltd
1st Floor
222 Gray's Inn Road
London WC1X 8HB

www.simonandschuster.co.uk

Simon & Schuster Australia, Sydney
Simon & Schuster India, New Delhi

The author and publishers have made all reasonable
efforts to contact copyright-holders for permission, and apologise
for any omissions or errors in the form of credits given.
Corrections may be made to future printings.

Jacket illustration © Panorama of London and the Thames, part two showing
St Paul's Cathedral and the Globe Theatre, 1600 (engraving) (see also 64730-32),
Visscher, Nicolaes (Claes) Jansz (1586-1652) / London Metropolitan Archives,
City of London / Bridgeman Images

A CIP catalogue record for this book
is available from the British Library

Paperback ISBN: 978-1-47112-570-6
Ebook ISBN: 978-1-47112-571-3

Typeset in the UK by Group FMG using Book Cloud
Printed and bound by CPI Group (UK) Ltd, Croydon, CR0 4YY

Simon & Schuster UK Ltd are committed to sourcing paper
that is made from wood grown in sustainable forests and supports the Forest
Stewardship Council, the leading international forest certification organisation.
Our books displaying the FSC logo are printed on FSC certified paper.

All the world's a stage,
And all the men and women merely players:
They have their exits and their entrances;
And one man in his time plays many parts.

As You Like It, Act 2 Scene 7

For my father, Robert Arnold

Remember thee?
Ay, thou poor ghost, while memory holds a seat
In this distracted Globe.

Hamlet, Act 1 Scene 5

Contents

Introduction		1
Acknowledgements		15
1	LONDON, THE FLOWER OF CITIES ALL	16
2	A FELLOWSHIP OF PLAYERS	33
3	THE FIRST THEATRE IN LONDON	61
4	THE UPSTART CROW	87
5	THE HOLLOW CROWN	123
6	ALL THE WORLD'S A STAGE	148
7	THE GREAT GLOBE ITSELF	171
8	GUNPOWDER, TREASON AND PLOT	197
9	CHIMES AT MIDNIGHT	228
10	THE GLOBE REBORN	257
Bibliography		277
Picture Acknowledgements		283
Notes		284
Index		299

Introduction

The life of William Shakespeare, Britain's greatest dramatist, was inextricably linked with the history of London. Together, the great writer and the great city came of age and confronted triumph and tragedy. Triumph came when Shakespeare's company, the Chamberlain's Men, opened the Globe playhouse on Bankside in 1599, under the patronage of the Queen herself. Tragedy came fourteen years later, when the Globe was burned to the ground after the thatched roof caught fire during an early performance of *King Henry VIII*. Tragedy touched the lives of many of Shakespeare's contemporaries, from fellow playwright Christopher Marlowe and actor Gabriel Spenser, to the disgraced Earl of Essex and Guido Fawkes. In 1601, Essex made a bid for power with an attempted coup, only to flounder as his supporters drifted away, while it was Fawkes who made the most spectacular attempt to remove the monarch. Had Fawkes and his fellow plotters succeeded in November 1605, King James I and his Court would have been blown to kingdom come during the State Opening of Parliament. These extraordinary characters and events not only inspired Shakespeare, and his fellow playwrights, but were reflected in his work.

Globe, Life in Shakespeare's London takes the reader on a virtual tour of the great city through Shakespeare's life and work, and the achievements of his exceptional fellow authors, actors and pioneers of the theatre. By focusing on the early life and career of James Burbage, father of the more famous Richard and builder of the first theatre in London, I set the stage for Shakespeare's entrance and the explosion of dramatic writing which characterised the closing years of the sixteenth century. Between the years 1576 and 1642, the year Parliament banned the staging of plays, theatre became England's principal art form, and Shakespeare its foremost exponent, although he had notable rivals in the form of Christopher Marlowe, Ben Jonson, Beaumont and Fletcher, John Webster and Thomas Middleton.

In the opening chapter I imagine a young Shakespeare encountering London for the first time. The chapters that follow explore the way in which acting came of age as a trade during the 1570s and 1580s, and how the troupes of touring players who roamed the country lanes were transformed from scruffy vagabonds playing outside village inns to the finely dressed 'strutters' of the Globe itself. Under the patronage of influential courtiers such as the Earl of Leicester and the Lord Chamberlain, companies of players performed at Court before Queen Elizabeth herself, in lavish productions characterised by rich costumes and glittering display. Strutting in rich velvet doublets bequeathed to the actors by their noble patrons, these men transformed themselves from humble players into mythical creatures: Romeo, Othello, Hamlet, Lear, Coriolanus, Prospero, 'good' King Henry V and 'bad' King Richard III.

The Elizabethan era was a time of great change, and acting just another way for young men to transform themselves. Shakespeare remains the supreme example of an ambitious provincial arriving in London and reinventing himself, but his journey from a small town to the London stage was replicated many times. In a city of deceptions, where appearance was all and nobody quite what they seemed, acting was the occupation to which attractive and resourceful young men were inexorably drawn. Whether fleet of foot and smooth of cheek, or built like a bear with a commanding bellow, whether beautifully dressed in clothes purloined from an aristocratic master, or wrapped in a cloak which masked a stained doublet and laddered hose, the resourceful individual with the gift of the gab gravitated to the profession most associated with outsiders and thieves. As Hamlet observes (*Hamlet*, Act 3 Scene 2), if all else fails there is always the theatre:

> If the rest of my fortunes turn Turk with me – with two Provincial roses on my razed shoes, get me a fellowship in a cry of players, sir?

In the theatre, two worlds collided, the shimmering mirage of the playhouse, with its scenes of mystery and imagination, and the criminal underworld, itself built on pretence and deception. Philip Henslowe, impresario of the Rose, made his fortune in pawnbroking and prostitution. Henslowe opened a brothel next door to his famous theatre, and his stepdaughter Joan, who married the eminent actor Edward Alleyn, was whipped at the cart's arse for running it.

Canny young drifters, more than capable of strutting and fretting their hour upon the stage, and sufficiently educated to ensure that they flung the dramatists' words so that they ring around the arena of the Globe or the Rose, found a vocation parading their skills before a paying audience. Many of these actors also turned their classical education to good account, drawing on Greek verse or Latin prose exercises to create towering melodramas and incisive political satires. However, such were the changing tides of fortune in Elizabethan London that it was very easy for a writer to find himself on the wrong side of the law. In an age where the distinction between petty crime and grand treason was decidedly indistinct, being a professional writer was a dangerous occupation and many an author found himself in prison, or worse, for penning a political satire. When in 1597 Ben Jonson completed Thomas Nashe's play *The Isle of Dogs,* the manuscript of which is now, sadly, lost, the play was deemed so seditious that Jonson and his cast were imprisoned in the Marshalsea. The Puritan and political commentator John Stubbe (*c.*1541–90) and his publisher William Page received an even more severe punishment in 1579, after Stubbe had criticised Elizabeth I's plans to marry the Duke of Anjou. Objecting on religious grounds (he feared that the Roman Catholic Duke might restore Catholicism to England), Stubbe added insult to injury by commenting that, at forty-six, the Queen was too old to have children, and that the union of the two was 'immoral, foul and gross'. Elizabeth was less than delighted by these remarks, and the pamphlet, *The Discoverie of a Gaping Gulf whereinto England is like to be Swallowed by another French Marriage*, was publically burned in Stationers' Hall. As for Stubbe and Page, they lost their right hands, the wrist being divided by a cleaver driven through the joint at the blow of a mallet. The historian William Camden recalled the scene in his *Historie III.* 'I remember, being then present, that Stubbs [*sic*], when his right hand was cut off, plucked off his hat with his left hand and said with a loud voice, "God save the Queen". The multitude standing about was deeply silent, either out of horror at this new form of punishment, or out of commiseration towards the man.'

For all its perks, an actor's life, and a writer's too, was a precarious one. The authorities were constantly looking for excuses to close the playhouses. Regular outbreaks of bubonic plague or even the threat of plague left playhouses dark for weeks at a time, while sedition became another weapon in the war against the theatres. When apprentices rioted following a production of Will Kemp's *A Knack to Know a Knave* in 1592, the Lord Mayor wrote to Queen Elizabeth demanding that the pestilential playhouses be plucked down.

While today the greatest professional threat faced by London's actors is that of unemployment, Elizabethan actors lived with the constant reality of violent death. Shakespeare was remarkable, and unusual, in escaping the clutches of the law throughout his professional life. A year after Ben Jonson and Gabriel Spenser were gaoled for appearing together in *The Isle of Dogs,* Jonson was attacked by his former cellmate in Hoxton. Spenser, embittered and drunk, resented his young rival's success, and challenged him to a duel. Jonson slew Spenser in self-defence, but only escaped with his life thanks to the legal loophole of the 'neck verse', which spared him from the gallows. Christopher Marlowe was stabbed to death in mysterious circumstances in Deptford, possibly because of his secondary occupation as a spy. If one did not die by the sword or plague, career failure also had deadly consequences in sixteenth-century London, as in the sad case of Robert Greene. London's first real professional writer, Greene drank himself to death after being eclipsed by a provincial nobody who had sold out the Rose with his historical epic, *Harey the Sixth*. With virtually his dying breath, Greene railed and ranted against this pretentious 'Shake-scene' with his 'Tiger's heart wrapped in a player's hide'. Who *was* this upstart?

Who indeed? While Greene is remembered in a footnote as an explanation of that puzzling reference in *A Midsummer*

Night's Dream to 'learning late deceased in beggary', Shakespeare himself played many parts, from actor to author, from upstart provincial to presiding genius of the London stage. At a time when history plays and tragedies proved most popular, Shakespeare possessed a unique talent for bringing the past to life. From the embers of myths and half-forgotten histories he conjured up unforgettable characters: Cleopatra, Queen of the Nile; the tormented Prince Hamlet; the magnificent Henry V. Year after year his dramas packed out London's theatres, appealing to poet and peasant alike. Shakespeare's is the authentic voice of London, wise-cracking, witty, insightful and humane. Political feuds are played out in the palaces of Westminster, Whitehall and Hampton Court; the Guildhall, Smithfield, Moorfields, Temple and the Savoy are backdrops to power struggles and deadly feuds; Henry V's victory parade brings loyal subjects pouring into the streets, the same streets that are hung with mourning when the great king dies. The Tower of London hangs over all, like the shadow of death. Comic relief is to be found in the Boar's Head Tavern, where Prince Hal drinks the nights away with Falstaff and Mistress Quickly.

Shakespeare himself seemed wholly absorbed in writing, performing and administration. With his fellow actors or 'sharers', who held a joint financial interest, he participated in a successful acting company and invested in property in London and Stratford. This appeared to consume his energies; he scarcely bothered to curate his own work, a task which was left to his fellow actors, Hemmings and Condell, who published his plays in one posthumous volume, known as the First Folio, in 1623. He was admired by and popular with his fellow dramatists as contemporary records attest, and yet we know so little of him, compared with other towering figures of the time, such as Christopher Marlowe, who was endlessly self-mythologising, the Tamburlaine of the stage and – in an age when homosexuality was forbidden – outrageous in his assertion that 'all who love not tobacco and boys are fools!' Ben Jonson emerges from the pages of history as a clever thug of a man, described by John Aubrey as a staring leviathan with a terrible mouth and a face like a battered warming pan. That Jonson eventually became Poet Laureate, despite two spells in prison and killing Gabriel Spenser, was a considerable achievement.

There are comic characters here, too. Philip Henslowe was proprietor of the Rose theatre on Bankside where many of Shakespeare's earliest plays were performed. It is thanks to Henslowe, and his famous diary, that we know so much about the economic realities of the Elizabethan theatre. From Henslowe, we learn that Edward Alleyn strode the stage as Tamburlaine in crimson velvet breeches trimmed with copper lace, and that if an actor turned up drunk, he would be fined ten shillings. Henslowe, who had begun his career in the Elizabethan entertainment industry running a bear garden, had no pretensions to artistry. He ended his days with the achievement of his greatest ambition: as the King's bear-warden. Tarlton the clown, discovered by a member of the Earl of Leicester's troupe while Tarlton was making his 'happy unhappy remarks' to his herd of pigs, looked so comical that he had only to walk across the stage to put the audience in stitches. Tarlton proved to be so popular with Elizabeth I that courtiers would visit him first to ascertain what sort of mood she was in. Tarlton proved inspiring in another way, too. He was the model for Hamlet's late jester, Yorick, who could set the table 'on a roar' with his flashes of merriment. Will Kemp, celebrated for his tumbling and dancing, swiftly became Tarlton's successor as clown by appointment to the crown. In February 1600 Kemp accepted

a bet that he would dance from London to Norwich, seen
off from the Lord Mayor's house at seven o'clock in the
morning in a hail of groats and sixpences from crowds of
well-wishers. This triumphant progress, the original 'Nine
Days' Wonder', saw Kemp dance his way through Essex and
Suffolk, resting at night in the houses of wealthy admirers,
until he eventually danced through St Stephen's Gate in
Norwich, squeezed through the crowds and was welcomed
with five pounds from the mayor and the freedom of the
city. His dancing shoes, left as a memento, were nailed up
in the Guildhall. Kemp's long-distance jig proved so popular
that he accepted a second bet, resigning from the Chamberlain's
Men to dance across the Alps to Rome.

The London stage, then as now, was populated with larger-
than-life characters. Edward Alleyn, Henslowe's son-in-law
and celebrated tragedian, was the first giant of English drama,
a tall man with a great vocal range who proved ideal for all
those roles which were 'a part to tear a cat in'. No actual cats
were harmed during such proceedings – this was merely a
term, pressed into service by Shakespeare in *A Midsummer
Night's Dream,* to indicate the extreme histrionics required of
a tragic role, such as Hieronimo in *The Spanish Tragedy.* Alleyn's
greatest legacy was the founding of Dulwich College as an act
of atonement after his performance as Dr Faustus proved so
convincing that he supposedly conjured up real devils on stage
during a performance in Dulwich. Alleyn's barnstorming
approach to acting was moderated by Richard Burbage, son of
James Burbage, who was capable of greater subtly and range.
An anonymous obituary following Burbage's death in 1619
extolled his outstanding performances as a leading man, in the
roles of King Lear, Romeo, Richard III, Brutus, Malvolio,
Shylock, Othello and 'young Hamlet, though but scant of breath
crying revenge for his dear father's death', continuing:

Oft have I seen him leap into a grave,
Suiting ye person (which he seemed to have)
Of a sad lover, with so true an eye
That then I would have sworn he meant to die.

Burbage was Shakespeare's most famous interpreter during the author's lifetime and, if the old rumours are to be believed, his love rival too. The famous anecdote tells of a female fan who, after falling for Burbage when she saw him play Richard III, begged him to come to her chambers that night under the name of King Richard. But Shakespeare overheard the proposition and left the theatre early to take Burbage's place. Shakespeare was 'at his game ere Burbage came'. Then, the message being brought that Richard III was at the door, Shakespeare retorted that 'William the Conqueror came before Richard III'.

The biggest character in this book is really the Globe itself, the theatre which was constructed from the remains of James Burbage's old Theatre in Shoreditch. It was carried across the river to build a new theatre among the bear gardens and brothels of Bankside. The Globe became the glory of the Bankside, the most successful theatre in London, until the terrible day when the thatched roof caught fire during *Henry VIII* and the theatre was burned to the ground within two hours. Like many other writers, I feel that Shakespeare never entirely recovered from this catastrophe, although nobody died and the only moment of jeopardy came when a man's breeches caught fire. Tragedy was averted when the resourceful individual tipped beer over himself and extinguished the flames. While Shakespeare continued to work in the rebuilt Globe, he wrote less, and operated more as a script doctor, spending increasing periods of time back in Stratford-upon-Avon, where he died in 1616.

As with so many other aspects of Shakespeare's life, we do not have an exact explanation as to the cause of death, but it seems as though he went out for birthday drinks with Ben Jonson and Michael Drayton, drank too much, developed pneumonia and died. As diffident in death as in life, Shakespeare was not buried in Westminster Abbey, but interred at his parish church, Holy Trinity. Although admired by other writers during his lifetime, it was not until after his death that Shakespeare developed the reputation he enjoys today as England's national poet, thanks to Jonson's commemorating him as the Swan of Avon and the efforts of generations of actors, readers, writers and historians.

The final chapter of my book brings the story up to date as we learn how, 300 years after the second Globe was demolished, Shakespeare's Globe opened once more upon the Bankside in 1997, rising like a phoenix from the flames thanks to the tireless efforts of American actor Sam Wanamaker and his supporters. And now, in the first month of 2014, the long-awaited Sam Wanamaker Playhouse has opened at last with an acclaimed production of Webster's *Duchess of Malfi.* The book concludes with an interview with the current artistic director of Shakespeare's Globe, Dominic Dromgoole, as we speculate about how Shakespeare would react to the twenty-first-century Globe.

My task in this book was to create a portrait of Shakespeare and his London from Shakespeare's own plays and contemporary sources, combining a novelist's eye for detail with a historian's grasp of Shakespeare's unique contribution to the development of the English theatre. However, the problem with writing about Shakespeare the man is that we know so little about him. Trying to focus on Shakespeare is haphazard and frustrating, like sitting up in the gods of an old London theatre and trying to focus on the stage with a pair of opera glasses. At one moment there he is, we see him, with a prismatic rainbow blur about the edges, and then he is gone, and there is nothing there apart from a pillar or the black space of the orchestra pit. It is almost as if he wanted it that way: 'cursed be him that disturbs my bones'. Shakespeare was not interested in posterity and seemed less concerned with being an *auteur* than a businessman and, to quote from *Hamlet*, 'a great buyer of land', returning to Stratford to consort with the men he had been to school with, the traders, the civic dignitaries and the local doctor, who married Shakespeare's daughter Susanna. Across the centuries, many scholars and critics have struggled to give us their Shakespeare, but in the end we are left baffled as the writer disappears once more. In response, we are all tempted to create our own Shakespeare, in our own image.

Which is perhaps one explanation for the extraordinary efforts, by many writers and academics, to strip Shakespeare himself of the authorship of his works and attribute them to someone – anyone? – else. Is this the reason for the frequently touted theories that Shakespeare was Irish, French, even German? Or that he was not the author of his own plays, a distinction which must instead be awarded to the Earl of Oxford, Sir Francis Bacon, to anyone it seems apart from William Shakespeare himself. There are over 5,000 books on this subject alone. My own feeling is that these theories originate from literary snobbery, from a mind-set that cannot endure the thought of such talent pouring forth from the son of a provincial glove-maker who never attended university. This is in spite of the fact that, at his grammar school, Shakespeare would have received an excellent education in Latin, Greek and classical rhetoric.

If we all create our own Shakespeare – and that process of projection is inescapable – my Shakespeare was a hard-working provincial in London, who could never quite believe his luck. An early adopter, eternally interested in the next big thing and all-consumingly fascinated by human nature and the mysteries of the human heart. My own interest in Shakespeare developed at birth, and was unavoidable. In the beginning was the word, and the words were there from the day I was born. Shakespeare was the nearest thing to Holy Writ in our house, and the faded orange volume of the Shakespeare Head Press *Collected Works* the equivalent of the family Bible, with my mother's name inked on the flyleaf from Cambridge. I grew up hearing, reading, reciting, inhaling Shakespeare. My father, who had grown up deep in the Warwickshire countryside, honoured no other writer as greatly as Shakespeare. Time moved slowly in pre-war Warwickshire, and he found comfort in the language and the obscure references to a forgotten rural life. As a schoolboy, my father cycled to Stratford to watch productions at the Royal Shakespeare Theatre and trailed around after the actors. Years later, he brought Shakespeare to life for generations of students in our dusty book-lined sitting room. I will never forget how he explained the plot of *King Lear* to one bemused female student in terms of Cinderella and the two ugly sisters, and it worked too. An actor and musician turned academic, my father rejoiced in reciting, declaiming, performing and even parodying Shakespeare as only an old ham can. Throughout the writing of this book, turning the pages of his old volumes, I have been conscious of his benign presence, like an 'affable familiar ghost'. As I grew older, I was by no means an uncritical admirer of Shakespeare. At twelve, convinced of Richard III's innocence after reading Josephine Tey's *The Daughter of Time,* I saw Shakespeare's take on Richard for what it was: a successful work of Tudor propaganda.

We were a theatre-loving family, and from the age of five I was swept off to Nottingham Playhouse in the glory days of John Neville and Richard Eyre, and to the Theatre Royal to see every touring show that came to town, from farces to thrillers. On my first visit to Stratford, I was hypnotised by Richard Pasco's 'mirror' scene in *Richard II* and entranced by Feste's singing in *Twelfth Night* (Act 2 Scene 3). When he sang:

> Trip no further, pretty sweeting;
> Journeys end in lovers meeting

the combination of the poignant lyrics and the music made me feel as if I was on the threshold of some great understanding, as if some deep mystery was being gradually revealed.

When I aspired to the stage, my father deterred me, telling me I had a narrow range and was fit only for tragedy, or perhaps a little Ibsen and Chekhov. But he listened to my lines for the school play and encouraged me to 'Project, child, project!' Sadly, my father never lived to visit me at university. In the hot summer before I went to Cambridge, he died suddenly, and I threw fresh flowers into his grave with a card bearing the lines from *Cymbeline* (Act 4 Scene 2):

> Fear no more the heat of the sun
> Nor the furious winter's rages
> Thou thy worldly task has done,
> Home art gone and ta'en thy wages
> Golden lads and girls all must,
> As chimney-sweepers, come to dust.

In my first term at Cambridge I boldly auditioned for the *Duchess of Malfi*. After losing out to a young woman called Tilda Swinton I thought my father had probably been right and turned instead to reviewing drama for the university newspaper. Too sympathetic to make an objective critic, I did at least see a different show every night, and what shows they were, starring a generation of student actors who swiftly became household names, including Hugh Laurie and Emma Thompson. Watching live drama night after night taught me that plays were living entities and that Shakespeare, above all, needs to be performed to be appreciated. While I spent mornings in lectures and afternoons in the University Library puzzling over Shakespeare's language like a dog sucking marrow out of a bone, it was in the evenings that Shakespeare came to life, along with Marlowe and Webster. Stephen Fry, now better known as a comic actor, was an astonishing Dr Faustus in a candlelit college chapel.

Later in life, Shakespeare saved my soul. On endless chilly afternoons, as I wheeled my daughters through dreary parks, I recited Shakespeare's soliloquies to them, *Withnail* style, from Hamlet to Macbeth. From this unlikely introduction, my daughters caught the Shakespeare bug, which is how it should be. Even though our lives seem so different, five centuries on, Shakespeare speaks for us all, gay, straight, black, white, male, female, *not for an age, but for all time.*

Acknowledgements

I would like to thank the staff of Cambridge University Library and the Hallward Library, University of Nottingham, for their assistance, and Dr Frank Carney for his insightful comments on the manuscript. Credit is due once again to my agent, Charlie Viney, my editor Kerri Sharp, my long-suffering family and last but no means least William Shakespeare himself, without whom we would all be lost for words.

LONDON, THE FLOWER OF CITIES ALL

And one man in his time plays many parts . . .
As You Like It, Act 2 Scene 7

When did Shakespeare first visit London, and what was the great city like when he arrived? This journey has been the source of enormous conjecture over the centuries, with writers as diverse as John Aubrey and Samuel Johnson speculating over Shakespeare's first steps in the city which was to be the making of him. John Aubrey, the old gossip, circulated the myth that Shakespeare was on the run from Stratford-upon-Avon after poaching Sir Thomas Lucy's deer; Johnson perpetuated the theory that Shakespeare's first employment was tending the horses outside the Theatre, the Elizabethan equivalent of valet parking. Those murky 'lost years' between 1588 and 1592 have inspired as many theories as there are blackberries, of an early career in the law, as a tutor, as a soldier, or travelling overseas.

While it is impossible to establish exactly when Shakespeare arrived in London, we do know what London was like when he reached it, by drawing upon other writers of the day. Let us suppose that, for reasons that will become evident, Shakespeare's first experience of London was not permanent exile from Stratford but a brief excursion. This mission left a lingering impression of the great city and all that could be achieved in it, the sense of infinite possibility which has drawn millions to London over the centuries. Once having tasted London, Shakespeare had to go back.

Imagine a fine May morning in 1586 and young Will Shakespeare riding into London on a borrowed cob, his for the journey. As a courier, his mission was to deliver a sealed letter, the contents of which he neither knew nor cared about, consumed as he was with the spirit of adventure and the prospect of a day in London.

In an age where social class was strictly defined by dress, Will's appearance would have marked him out as a countryman, a 'hempen homespun'[1] in a russet jacket faced with red worsted, blue 'camlet' or goats' hair sleeves and a dozen pewter buttons. In his grey hose and stockings, large sloppy breeches and the floppy hat that was all the rage in Stratford but *passé* in town, Will could not pass for anything but a rustic.[2] But this would have been of little consequence to a young man newly arrived in London. Leaving his horse at an inn in Holborn which had been recommended to him, he ventured forth to deliver his letter. Like every visitor to London, he was filled with wonder. To all the Queen's subjects, London *was* the city. London stood alone, unique, and any Elizabethan who did not live in London lived in the country. London was the magnet, 'which draweth unto it all the other parts of the land, and above the rest is most usually frequented with her Majesty's most royal presence'.[3] London was the seat of government, the home of 'Gloriana', the most excellent Queen Elizabeth, a city famed for the beauty of its buildings, its infinite riches and such a variety of goods that it was considered the storehouse and market of Europe. Craning his head back to look, glancing around him, awestruck, Will was put in mind of old Dunbar's salutation, 'O town of townes, London, thou art the flower of Cities all'.[4]

By eight o'clock in the morning the streets were already crowded and noisy and the day growing warm. Hammers beat, tubs were hooped, pots clinked, tankards overflowed, and the air was full of street cries, a chorus of men and women whetting the appetite and stirring the blood with calls of 'Hot pies, hot! Apple pies and mutton pies! Live periwinkles! Hot oatcakes, fresh herrings, hot potatoes!' An orange girl pranced by offering 'fine Seville oranges! Fine lemons!' while another buxom lass proffered 'Ripe, hearty-chokes ripe! Medlars fine!' Should one surfeit on this excess of riches, a quack in a shabby black doctor's gown, green with age, promised salvation in the form of patent medicines and remedies 'for any of ye that have corns on your feet or on your toes!' A chimney sweep, grimy from head to foot, walked by, the whites of his eyes glittering against his coal-black skin. The sweep introduced himself to the mistress of a house with a proposal to 'Sweep chimney, sweep, mistress, from the bottom to the top, Then shall no soot fall into your porridge pot!'[5] Will watched the lady conduct the sweep inside before elbowing his way down the thronging street. As often happens, the scenes struck a chord in his heart. A fragment of poetry darted into his mind, like a sparrow flying through a window into a great hall and out the other side. *Like chimney sweepers, come to dust* . . . He resolved to remember it for later, when he had time alone to write.

Meanwhile, London was already open for business. The apprentices were busy taking down the shutters and opening the shops, setting up their stalls and preparing for the day's trading. Passing an open doorway, Will spotted a small boy with a satchel in his hand racing down the stairs, as the boy's father, standing in the shop, demanded, 'Are you ready yet? It is eight of the clock! You shall be whipped!' Then he waved the lad off to school, after telling him to invite the schoolmaster to supper, an invitation which would probably save the boy from a beating for his late arrival.

Walking on down Cheapside, Will watched the schoolboy shamble along. Soon the boy was joined by a companion, another schoolboy, and as an old woman rounded the corner crying, 'Cherry ripe! Cherry ripe!' both boys started begging her for fruit. The older lad took his chances and seized a bunch of cherries from her basket, whereupon the old woman leaped forward and boxed his ears. The boys dashed away and vanished into a churchyard, and the school that stood within the mighty bulk of St Paul's. For a penny, Will climbed to the top of St Paul's steeple, as far as he could go, for the old wooden spire had gone, incinerated by lightning in 1561. But the steeple provided a magnificent panorama of London, the parks and palaces, the mansions of the merchants and the stinking slums. There were young men hawking in Liverpool Street and the River Thames glittered in the sunlight, white with swans and crammed with innumerable boats and vessels from every corner of the known world, and some unknown realms, too. Across the river on Bankside were the distinctive round shapes of the cockpits and the bear gardens, and in the distance was London Bridge, one of the wonders of the world for its length, strength, beauty and height. Twenty magnificent arches spanned the river, with houses built upon it as high as those on the ground and so close that the gables touched. More like a small town than a thoroughfare, London Bridge carried two hundred businesses jostling for attention above a narrow street choked with horses and carts. And on the southern end of London

Bridge, too far away for close scrutiny, Will recalled that the skulls of more than thirty executed traitors were displayed on iron spikes, the heads of noblemen who had been beheaded for treason. The descendants of those men boasted of this strange honour, pointing out their ancestors' heads and believing that they would be esteemed the more because their antecedents were of such high birth that they could covet the crown, even if they were too weak to attain it and ended up being executed as rebels. An intriguing prospect, that such people could make an honour of a fate which was intended to be a disgrace and set an example.[6]

View of London Bridge by Cornelius Visscher. Note the traitors' heads stuck on pikes over the south entrance.

The steeple of St Paul's contained more names than a parish register. Pausing for a moment, for he was a law-abiding young man, Will added to their number, drawing out his own knife and carving his name upon the leads in what had already become a distinctive signature:

At the bottom of the winding stairs lay St Paul's Walk, otherwise known as the Mediterranean. Within a minute, Will had been carried along by the bustling crowd, nervous perhaps, as even he would have heard of this den of iniquity. Despite the fact that it was located in the middle of a cathedral, St Paul's Walk was filled with lowlife exhibiting every aspect of bad behaviour, from jostling and jeering to swearing confrontations and raised fists. Elbow to elbow and toe to toe stood a living tarot of Elizabethan stereotypes, all playing their parts like actors in an endless masquerade. Here were The Knight, The Naïve Gull, The Gallant, The Upstart, The Gentleman, The Clown, The Captain, The Lawyer, The Usurer, The Citizen, The Bankrupt, The Scholar, The Beggar, The Doctor, The Fool, The Ruffian, The Cheater, The Cut-Throat, The Cut-Purse and The Puritan.[7] In its noise and spectacle, St Paul's Walk resembled a map of the world, turning in perfect motion, populated with a vast index of characters, a fascinating place for any writer. A lawyer chattered with his client, merchants discussed their affairs, gallants traded saucy anecdotes and flung back their cloaks to reveal new finery. And all surrounded by potential robbers, cut-purses and conmen. If they had seized Will's precious letter, they had as good as stabbed him. He had been ordered to guard this document with his life, which was as good as over if his mission failed. Faint with hunger, he elbowed his way out of the crowd in search of dinner.

Outside St Paul's, the scene was even busier than before. Carts and coaches rattled past, and the streets were thronged

with shoals of people, laughing, gossiping, quarrelling, so
many men, women and children that it was a wonder the
very houses had not been jostled aside under the sheer
weight of humanity. As Will stood in a doorway wondering
which way to turn, three apprentices in the shop behind
him began to sing:

> O the month of May, the merry month of May,
> So frolic, so gay, and so green, so green . . .[8]

From next door came the sound of the viola da gamba as
some good citizen's daughter took her music lesson. In every
doorway, an apprentice called out his master's wares, every
conceivable need from scarves to cabinets, from a rich girdle
to a coat hanger. A tradeswoman enticed a grand lady into
her shop with promises of 'fine cobweb lawn, madam, good
cambric, fine bone lace', and two lads approached Will with
fine silk stocks and a French hat as he fingered his own rustic
hat self-consciously. He held up his hands and backed away
as they called after him in unison.

The veritable cornucopia of items to buy was only rivalled
by the astonishing variety of sights which surrounded him.
On Goldsmiths' Row, every conceivable character came past
and he studied them all, enthralled. Porters staggered under
heavy trunks; sober merchants strode past self-importantly
in their robes and gold chains; a noisy group of young
gallants, resplendent in silk breeches that cost the price of
a farm, peacocked along with a cursory 'by your leave' as
they almost knocked Will into the path of a passing coach.
A large crowd gathered by the conduit at the far end of
Cheapside, as the Lord Mayor and his aldermen and masters
from the twelve livery companies inspected the conduit,
upon which the city's water supply depended. They were

mounted on horses and followed by packs of hounds in preparation for a ceremonial hunt which would conclude with the killing of a hare and a fox near St Giles, with 'a great cry at the death and blowing of horns'.[9]

But something else had caught Will's attention by now, something much closer to his heart, for he had seen the brightly coloured signs of the booksellers of St Paul's swinging from every house. The booksellers' signs were a library in themselves: the Bible, the Angel, the Holy Ghost, the Bishop's Head and the Holy Lamb, the Parrot and the Black Boy, the Mermaid and the Ship, Keys and Crowns, the Gun and the Rose and the Blazing Star. Around the churchyard was a menagerie of Green Dragons, Black Bears, White Horses, Pied Bulls, Greyhounds, Foxes and Brazen Serpents. Outside the shops stood trestle tables covered with the booksellers' wares: volumes fresh from the printer alongside old favourites and the neglected volumes which had never caught on. Booksellers stood in their doorways with their thumbs under their girdles, attempting to catch the eye of a potential buyer with a 'What lack ye, sir? Come see this new book, lately come forth.'

When one bookseller approached him, Will asked if he had anything by the celebrated author Robert Greene. Invited to step inside, Will hesitated and then shook his head, remembering that he still had to deliver the letter to an address on Fish Street Hill, near London Bridge. This mission was what brought him to London and he could not allow himself to be distracted by the sight of more books than he had ever seen in his life.

When Will eventually found the house on Fish Street Hill, it was to be told that the recipient, Sir Toby Gathercole, was not yet home but was expected soon, for dinner. Gathercole's apprentice invited Will in to wait, and Will soon fell into conversation with the lively youth who was minding the wine merchant's premises in his master's absence. Will had heard tell of the London apprentices; intimidating young men who bellowed and roared, rioted at Whitsuntide, stoned foreigners and handed out a beating to anyone who aggravated them. But this lad, Andrew by name, was approachable, ready to talk about learning his trade but equally ready to moan that his master worked him too hard and he never had a minute to himself. There was no time to go a-Maying, no time for fencing lessons, or dancing classes, or a game of football in the street. Andrew was at his master's beck and call at every hour of the day and night. Just as Andrew was lamenting the fact that his master did not give him leave to go out into the street to watch a fight yesterday, Sir Toby Gathercole himself returned home, sweating profusely in a flurry of red velvet, remarking on the unseasonable weather and mopping his brow with a silken handkerchief. Will stepped forward nervously, explained his errand and handed over his parchment document with its embossed waxen seal. Gathercole bestowed upon him one penetrating glance from slate-grey eyes, snatched the letter without so much as a word of thanks and disappeared into an inner room. When he emerged some minutes later he was in high good humour, clasped Will upon the shoulder like an old comrade and slyly dropped ten shillings into his palm, before inviting him to join them at their table.

At that point, Mistress Gathercole appeared, flushed and angry, her ample bosom heaving as she rebuked her husband. 'Fie! Why have you tarried so long at the Exchange? The meat is marred!'

'Have patience, Maria!' her husband replied. 'We have company. Look to the children.'

Will, who had been expecting a 'shilling ordinary' or a meagre tavern dinner of bread and cheese, was only too happy to accept Gathercole's offer, whether the meat was burned or not. The merchant's four children emerged, their hands and faces freshly scrubbed, and were seated at the board. As soon as Sir Toby had said grace in Latin, the servants laid the dishes before them. Will was impressed: this was good, satisfying fare. At home in the country, meals were simple and meat was scarce, but here it was evident that Sir Toby was a good trencherman. A dish of roast capons was set upon the table, along with a game pie, its pastry topping yellow with spices. Will was offered a glass of charneco, a sweet red wine, and a foaming tankard of ale; there were sweetmeats and quince jellies, a salad of lettuce leaves, and a marchpane or marzipan tart. To round off dinner a dish of *gellif,* a fruit ice pudding, was borne in to cries of excitement from the children.

Over dinner, talk turned to the Royal Exchange, and the value of the merchants having a building where they could meet, sheltered from the wind and rain. Sir Toby Gathercole extolled the virtues of Sir Thomas Gresham, who founded the Royal Exchange in 1565, telling Will he had been to Venice, and the Rialto was a 'mere bauble' compared with the Exchange. Gresham had done much to adorn the City of London and Gathercole felt assured his fame would long outlive him.

When Will expressed an interest in seeing the Royal Exchange, Gathercole offered to take him there that afternoon. As the merchant led Will up Fish Street, he pointed out other places of interest as they passed. Gathercole conducted Will up Gracechurch Street, and at the corner of Cornhill and Leadenhall called his attention to the fine views of houses and gardens as they looked up Bishopsgate. To

the left was Gresham's own house, where Gresham entertained Queen Elizabeth herself at a notable banquet. And
there, almost opposite, was Crosby Hall, a splendid mansion
built by the wool merchant Sir John Crosby in 1466 'and
once,' Sir Toby added with a frisson of intrigue, 'the seat of
old King Richard Crookback, that vile murderer, where
crouchback Richard wooed poor Lady Anne, while her
husband lay dead in his coffin. The funeral baked meats
were scarcely cold.'

By this time, Will was overwhelmed by the combination
of the noonday sun, the capons lying heavy upon his belly,
wine during the day and the ceaseless noise. Constantly,
continually, coaches and carts rattled past and thundered
through the narrow lanes. For the rest of his life, Will would
remember that distinctive sound of the London streets, the
continual ringing of church bells, the rumble of cartwheels
and the thunder of horses' hooves, the counterpoint of street
cries playing over the bass of grumbling porters, an old bawd
scolding her whores and a couple of 'carmen' or coach drivers
quarrelling about the right of way. The citizens cursed the
coaches, flattening themselves against the walls to stop the
wheels going over their toes. Coaches jammed the streets,
left standing empty as their rich owners bargained over a
pair of earrings or a dog's collar. According to the regulations,
coaches were not to be driven through the City of London
at all. The driver was supposed to dismount and lead his
horse at the city gates; but the regulations were routinely
flouted, and drivers merely sat atop their chariots, lashing
their animals and ignoring those who went upon their feet.
The traffic of carts and coaches was so heavy that several
times Will and Sir Toby ducked into doorways as the vehicles
rumbled past, ferrying their burden of fine ladies to Gresham's
Royal Exchange, splashing them with mud.

The ground floor of the Royal Exchange resembled pictures Will had seen of an Italian square or an Oxford college. It consisted of a quadrangle surrounded by cloisters, lined with shops. Unlike a college, the Exchange was horribly crowded and extremely noisy, while swarms of small boys made matters worse by darting in and out of the throng and getting in everybody's way. Most of the shops on the ground floor were gloomy and damp, and used only for storage, and the better shops were to be found on the first floor or the 'Upper Pawn'. Resolving to investigate this for himself, Will took his leave of his host, and headed for the steps.

On the Upper Pawn, apprentices and servant girls stood in the doorways, calling out lists of their wares to attract customers. For Will, the son of a glove-maker, many of these luxury items were familiar: 'purses, gloves and points, cutworks, partlets, suits of lawn, gorgets, sleeves and rugs, linings for gowns and cauls, coifs, crippins, cornets, billaments, musk boxes and sweet balls: pincases, pick-tooths, beard-brushes, combs, needles and glasses'.[10]

A seamstress's apprentice, selling her wares, tried to catch the attention of the fine ladies as they strolled past. 'Would ye have any fair linen cloth? Mistress, see what I have and I will show you the fairest linen cloth in London; if you do not like it you may leave it; you shall bestow nothing but the looking on, the pain shall be ours to show them you.' A young gallant, clearly attracted, suggested to his lady friends that they should enter the shop. The ladies, who admitted that the young seamstress was reasonably pretty, agreed and in they went. Watching through the window, Will observed them examining hollands and cambrics. While the young girl maintained that she would accept nothing less than twenty shillings an ell (an English ell was about 45 inches, or 1.15 metres), her customers refused to offer more than fifteen. A compromise was eventually reached with the customers offering sixteen shillings as the young girl protested that she was giving her goods away.[11]

Will enjoyed the spectacle and the endless parade of fancy men and women; it reminded him of his wife, Anne, and her endless appetite for shopping. It was a pastime which he did not share, and soon he longed for peace and quiet. Will walked back down to the river, discovering that the streets were less crowded than they had been in the morning. The gallants had all gone off to the theatre, while the ladies were at the Exchange, the schoolboys back in the classroom and the merchants and stallholders sleeping off their dinner. After visiting the Palace of Whitehall, Will entered the Abbey, paid his penny to the verger, and was permitted to gaze upon the tombs and monuments of the dead kings and queens of England. Here was history: the gilded, the stories, the legends and the myths. Here lay Edward the Confessor and the shooting star, fallen to earth, Richard II; and here lay England's greatest king, Henry V. Displayed alongside his tomb were his heraldic crest, decorated with a leopard, the saddle which the heroic prince used at Agincourt and even his shield. The verger, trying to sell Will a guidebook, plucked at his sleeve in vain; Will was lost in silent contemplation of the tombs, and their contents, overwhelmed by the sheer volume of events contained within this narrow space, the sacred space of kingship.

By the time Will emerged from the Abbey he was hungry again, and tired, but it was too early to repair to his lodging in Holborn. Instead, having gained some feel for London's geography, he headed back to sup at a tavern in Fleet Street. As he walked east from Charing Cross, there was no shortage of potential taverns. The Bear and Ragged Staff, with the arms of Warwick, his native county, caught his eye, but then there was the Angel, which promised a well-kept pint, the King Harry Head with its image of Henry V, whose very tomb Will had just visited, and the Golden Bull, a splendid beast straight out of the Ovid he studied at school. But none of these hostelries really appealed to him. As Will reached Temple Bar, a ballad singer began to perform. Slowly, a small crowd gathered: first a porter stopped, and then a fishwife with her basket on her arm halted, stilled her cries and stood to listen. A cat-eyed gypsy woman, with raven-black hair, ceased quarrelling with her handsome soldier and fell silent; then along came a cut-purse, ready with a knife but enthralled by the song and indifferent to his potential target, a country cousin standing near him. A constable of the watch approached, and a whore, all drawn by the sweet singing:

> It was a lover and his lass
> With a hey, and a ho, and a hey nonino,
> In springtime, in springtime, the only pretty ring time,
> Sweet lovers love the spring.[12]

Will listened for a moment, and then walked on. He knew the song, he had heard it many times before, but he acknowledged its fleeting beauty as the words floated out across the narrow street, out across London.

By the time he reached Fleet Street, Will had scarcely the energy to notice the play which was about to start, or hear the barker trying to draw a crowd with his mighty lung-power. Will had no time for an interlude concerning the 'City of Nineveh with Jonah and the Whale!' He had already seen so much, and heard so much, within one day that his faculties were numbed; and he was desperate to eat.

In the distance, two street vendors were strolling up and down in opposite directions, selling salt and straw. The noise of London, which had surrounded him all day, was at last dying down. The sun had sunk low in the sky, and most people had retreated indoors. Then Will heard the creaking of a tavern sign swinging overhead, pushed open the door and went inside.

The tavern was packed to the rafters. There appeared to be a party in full swing upstairs, with enthusiastic singing, while downstairs the narrow, low-ceilinged bar was full of men eating and drinking in small groups, as young women bustled to and fro between them with tankards of ale, responding to impatient drinkers with cries of 'Anon, sir! Anon!' In one corner, near the big open fireplace, half a dozen men were listening gravely to a tall man with a long bushy beard who was reading the text of a play aloud in a deep, rich voice. Fascinated, Will dropped quietly into a seat nearby as the men discussed the play. Although a goblet of wine stood before each of them, this was clearly a working supper. The wine went almost untouched as comments were passed on every aspect of the play and each player was assigned a part, in some cases more than one part. From what Will could gather, the play was set in ancient Britain, and the characters had outlandish names such as King Gorboduc, Ferrex and Porrex. The most youthful and slender of the company was to play Gorboduc's wife, Videna. The tall man with the beard, who the others addressed as 'Ned', had already cast himself as Gorboduc. As the talk passed on to the props required, Will was impressed by their sober, businesslike demeanour. Far from being the vagrant travelling players in stolen livery Will had glimpsed in the yards of country inns, they could have been mistaken for prosperous merchants and accepted at Sir Toby Gathercole's table without comment. They would not have looked out of place strolling through the Royal Exchange. When the players had finished, Ned paid the bill, all two shillings of it.[13] Will longed to speak to them, to hear where *Gorboduc* was to be played, to learn their names and all about their company, but was overcome by shyness.

As the players made their exit, two noisy young men entered, crying out for a drink, kissing the serving wench and regaling the company with the dismal sight they had just witnessed. A young girl had fallen into the ditch at Moorfields, apparently out of her wits, and they had seen men drawing her drowned body out of the water as they walked past.[14] Will was intrigued by their narrative, the vivid, drunken descriptions of the full moon, the mad girl dragged under the surface of the water by her clothes, the garland of flowers around her neck. It would haunt him all night until he found a moment to write it down.

Will fell into conversation with the young men, and at closing time they offered to walk him back towards Holborn, guided by the lantern which one had brought along with him. The streets were in darkness now, but for the occasional chink of light gleaming out between closed shutters. From time to time other groups of people passed them, also hurrying home with flaming torches or lanterns. Suddenly one of the young men stepped aside and drew Will into a doorway with him. For a moment Will feared the worst; had he been decoyed into this dark alley so they could rob him and cut his throat? But then came the sound of heavy footsteps, and the constables of the watch appeared armed with lanterns and staffs. They were older men, comically grizzled and bowed, but not without an air of authority. As Will and his companions watched from their hiding place, two drunken young men inadvertently walked straight into the constables' arms.

'Who goes there!' demanded the lead constable, and held up his lantern to get a better view of the young man. 'Where have you been, out so late?'

'I was at supper, forsooth, with my uncle, and he is showing me home!' said the younger man. After further questions, the constables of the watch were satisfied, and the two men were released. As soon as the coast was clear, Will and his new friends slipped out of their alleyway and hurried home. They parted from him at Cheapside and directed him to Holborn. When Will eventually got back to his lodgings, after knocking on the door for an eternity he was eventually admitted with grumbling admonitions, given a candle and sent to bed. Soon Will was tucked up under the covers, listening to the city churches chiming the hour and the voice of the watchman floating up through his window: 'Twelve o'clock, look well to your lock, your fire and your light, and so good night.' He was exhausted, but he could not sleep for all the sights he had seen and the words going round and round in his head. Seizing parchment and a quill from his pack, he pulled the candle close to his bed, and began to write . . .

2

A FELLOWSHIP OF PLAYERS

LORD: *How now? Who is it?*
SERVINGMAN: *An't please your honour, players*
That offer service to your lordship.
LORD: *Bid them come near.*
Enter PLAYERS
Now, fellows, you are welcome.

The Taming of the Shrew, Induction

This extract, from the prologue or 'induction' of *The Taming of the Shrew,* shows us the treatment a company of travelling players might expect when touring the countryside. Here they are, tired and footsore, knocking on the door of a remote manor house. Weary from travelling, the company is eager for a hot supper and warm bed in return for which they will offer live entertainment.

Fortunately, the good lord is in the mood for a spot of drama. He too is tired, after a hard day's hunting. It has been a long day in the saddle, pursuing the subtle fox over the Downs, or the sharp-fanged boar perhaps, or else the twisting

hare. The actors have called by on the chance that the lord
will hire them for the night, as he has done before. They are
obviously regulars; although he has forgotten the principal
player's name, the lord has not forgotten his performance,
the time when 'he play'd a farmer's eldest son . . . that part
Was aptly fitted and naturally perform'd,'[1] and the company
is offered supper and a bed for the night.

> Go, sirrah, take them to the buttery [pantry],
> And give them friendly welcome every one,
> Let them want nothing that my house affords.[2]

In addition to amusing the lord and his retinue that night, the
players have a secondary task. Christopher Sly, a local drunk,
has passed out in the kitchen, and the lord has decided to play
a practical joke on him. When he awakes, Sly will be greeted
as a gentleman and any protests to the contrary will be met
with nods and winks to the effect that he has lost his wits.
According to the players, they are there on doctors' orders:

> 'For so your doctors hold it very meet, Seeing too much
> sadness hath congeal'd your blood, And melancholy is the
> nurse of frenzy. Therefore they thought it good you hear
> a play And frame your mind to mirth and merriment,
> Which bars a thousand harms and lengthens life.'[3]

And the nature of this particular 'mirth and merriment'? Sly
asks with a drunken slur whether the players are going to give
'a comonty' a 'Christmas gambold or a tumbling-trick?'[4]

This repertoire sounded familiar to Shakespeare's playgoers: a
comonty (comedy), a gambol (dancing) or tumbling (acrobatics).
But the players have another genre up their sleeves, and one which
always met with a roar of approval from Tudor audiences.

> PAGE: No, my good lord, it is more pleasing stuff . . . It
> is a kind of history.[5]

That history is, of course, the strange tale of the taming of
a shrew, a standard theme of the day which continues to
divide audiences over four centuries later. What a show it
must have been that night, in the smoky great hall of the
remote country house, as the travelling players strutted across
the rush-strewn flagstones, their moth-eaten velvet robes and
faded silk doublets transformed by the flickering candlelight
into the rich costumes of medieval Italy. The rafters echoed
as the lord and his retinue cheered on the bullying Petruchio,
while the lady of the manor and her female servants catcalled
and whistled boisterous support for Katherina, the spirited
'shrew' of the title, impersonated by a reedy youth with a
wobbling voice, in a classic battle of the sexes. And afterwards,
a jug of ale, flagons of mead, pies and sweetmeats and a bed
for the night on good clean straw, lit by the glow of the
embers in the last of the heat from the fireplace. Not a bad
life for a young man, that of the travelling player.

This was the life young James Burbage signed up to when
he joined a travelling company in the troubled England of
the 1550s. Looking back across the centuries, one wonders
what motivated him to throw his lot in with the 'strutters'.
Was he captivated by the prospect of life on the road? Did
he succumb, as so many have, to the simple love of changing
one's clothes, and pretending to be somebody else? Acting is
a natural human instinct, beginning early in life. Or had
Burbage already grasped that theatre was about to emerge
as the dominant art form of the coming decades? If so, he
joined his company of players at a critical juncture, with the
theatre boom just around the corner – although one could
be forgiven for thinking otherwise when Burbage first trod

the boards. Conditions were grim for England's travelling players, a strange underclass emerging from the radical social and economic changes of the Reformation. Just as stray dogs will form themselves into packs, so this motley crew of masterless men, vagabonds, runaway slaves, defrocked priests, homeless monks, younger sons, penniless scholars, gypsies, tramps and thieves banded together into theatrical mercenary armies for their own survival, offering drama and entertainment in return for food and shelter.

And all brought to this eccentric enterprise their own talents and experience. Among the ranks of strutters roaming the lanes of England were numbers of helpless monks with no source of support, but who had once performed mystery plays, religious allegories derived from the Bible, in their monasteries, and who could still be eloquent, and knew how to dress and advise. Rich ecclesiastical vestments, worked with embroidery and trimmed with lace, doubled for the robes of gentlemen, while a communion cup, saved from the Reformation vandals, served as a chalice. Traipsing alongside were the many younger sons of the minor gentry, whose family estates had been seized for recusancy – refusing to abandon their Roman Catholicism for the new-fangled Anglican faith. Destitute, but educated at Oxford and Cambridge, where they had performed the Roman plays of Seneca, Terence and Plautus in Latin, these young men could translate an Italian romance or devise the outline of a plot from classical sources. Alongside them were the old soldiers, braggart *miles glorioses* and battle-scarred veterans, ready to teach fencing or display their skills with the sword in martial roles. Ancient minstrels, who still knew how to draw a tune from an unlikely instrument, provided the additional attraction of music to a play. Tagging along, losing themselves in this crowd, like hunted hares hiding themselves in a flock of sheep, were the cheats and tricksters, the thieves and highwaymen on the run who faced the gallows if they were caught, for human life was considered of less value than the means of supporting it.

From all these elements developed the travelling companies who created England's own national drama. They were inspired by a heady mix of old legends, stories and traditions such as Robin Hood and his merry men, and medieval morality plays like *Everyman,* where the protagonist, summoned by Death, has to account for his good and bad deeds before God. Then came the increasing popularity of the 'Tudor interludes', plays performed at Court and in town guilds, history plays such as *King John* by John Bale (1495–1563) and the earliest and crudest English comedies like *Ralph Roister Doister,* *c.* 1553, penned by the schoolmaster Nicholas Udall (1504–56), who was gaoled for buggery while teaching at Eton. The players brought all these narratives to life by acting in great halls or outside windswept inns, in the shelter of abandoned churches or on shaky scaffolds outside bustling taverns. From the limbo of forgotten skeleton plots, comedies and tragedies were reborn once more by the players' art, the actors' wit.

A romantic view of travelling players performing outside an inn.

There were, sadly, no women players. Life on the road was considered inappropriate for women and they were forbidden to perform on stage, or in the male bastions of the church, or the guild halls. In Italy, women appeared in the *commedia dell'arte* or popular drama, but in England the professional stage would remain out of bounds to women until the Restoration.

Women's roles were played by young boys or apprentices, as in *A Midsummer Night's Dream* when the 'rude mechanicals' or tradesmen prepare to perform the tragedy of Pyramus and Thisbe and young Francis Flute the bellows-mender is cast as Thisbe, even though he complains that he is too old for the role: 'I have a beard coming!'[6]

Touring companies of players were always met with suspicion when they rolled into town, regarded by the mayor and his aldermen as a threat to public order and the virtue of the womenfolk. For what woman, daily surrounded by horny-handed hayseeds and smug, fat burgesses in fur robes could possibly resist these swaggering, handsome professional charmers, roaring the night away in the tavern after a good performance, before vanishing with the morning dew and leaving town in a trail of dust?

There was another reason why travelling players were regarded with particular suspicion in Elizabethan times. It was feared that within their ranks the players concealed Roman Catholic spies plotting to assassinate the Queen and place a rival monarch on the throne. The only hope for a company to acquire any sort of respectability was by the patronage of a benevolent nobleman who would allow the actors to slip his livery on over their clothing. As official members of the noble's household, the players were immune from prosecution for vagrancy. Among the earliest companies to be created by this means were the Earl of Worcester's Men, the Earl of Warwick's Men and Lord Strange's Men, all in 1559. The same year, James Burbage and his players became the Earl of Leicester's Men.

Despite the best efforts of the mayors and aldermen to have travelling players arrested as 'sturdy beggars' and 'masterless men', players always found a ready audience. Elizabethans of all classes had an inherent love of spectacle and an uninhibited appetite for life which has seldom been equalled. Every social occasion became a party, from birth to death. Elizabethans danced at weddings, and feasted upon baked meats at funerals. Any distraction from the daily grind provided welcome, from London's Bartholomew Fair, held every August upon the smooth fields of Smithfield, with its gingerbread, roast suckling pigs and balladeers, to the glittering spectacle of the Lord Mayor's Show in November. Up and down the country, the old medieval calendar of Catholic saints' days merged with half-forgotten pagan rituals to create an almanac of continuous entertainment, from pancake-flipping in the streets on Shrove Tuesday to the rites of May Day, when celebrants, who had spent the previous night in the woods, returned with branches and garlands to adorn their homes, and the great maypole itself, a fertility symbol incarnate decked with flowers and herbs and covered in multicoloured ribbons, was dragged to the village green by oxen, their horns decorated with flowers, followed by hundreds of men, women and children. Whitsuntide or Pentecost, the seventh Sunday after Easter, was an excuse for dancing on the village green, greyhound racing and wrestling contests, plus traditional folk-plays. 'Methinks I play as I have seen them do In Whitsun pastorals,' says Perdita in *The Winter's Tale*,[7] and in an earlier play, *The Two Gentlemen of Verona*, Julia, disguised as a boy, recalls being asked to take on a female role at a Whitsun celebration:

At Pentecost,
When all our pageants of delight were played,
Our youth got me to play the woman's part,
And I was trimmed in Madam Julia's gown . . .[8]

The Twelve Days of Christmas crowned the year, presenting
an uproarious opportunity for good-humoured social anarchy,
presided over by the bacchanalian Lord of Misrule, 'a grand
captain of mischief', with his troupe of thirty or forty men
in brightly coloured liveries, bedecked with scarves, ribbons,
laces and jewels. With rings on their fingers and bells around
their knees, these ancestors of today's morris men performed
the devil's dance with hobbyhorses and bagpipes. For the
Puritan commentator Philip Stubbes (1555–1610, not to be
confused with the unfortunate John Stubbe we met in the
Introduction) this was all too much: 'then these heathen
companies march towards the church and churchyard, their
pipers piping, their drummers thundering, their stumps
dancing, their bells jingling, their handkerchiefs swinging
about their heads like mad-men, their hobby-horses and other
monsters skirmishing amongst the route.'[9] Naysayers aside,
theatrical spectacles such as this fed the Elizabethan appetite
for romance and wonder. With new stories arriving every
year from Renaissance Italy, 'Englysshed' by the bright young
pups of Oxford and Cambridge, audiences were ready for
fresh tales of humanity in all its aspects. All these factors
influenced the development of England's most distinctive art,
the drama.

   This was the world James Burbage chose to enter. But
Burbage could not have known, when he first set foot upon
a shaky scaffold in the courtyard of a noisy inn, that he would
play a pivotal role in the development of the English stage.
Ten years before the birth of Shakespeare, James Burbage

had no idea that his son, Richard, would become the greatest tragedian of his generation or that his lines would be penned by a fellow Warwickshire man later hailed as the greatest poet of all time. But Burbage was a shrewd, ambitious young man and in an era when becoming an actor was a trade rather than an artistic vocation, he must have been keenly aware of the benefits of his new career.

James Burbage was born around 1535, possibly in Warwickshire, although some scholars favour Kent as his place of origin. Little is known of his early life but a John Burbage was Bailiff of Stratford-upon-Avon in 1555. In the way of small-town life, Burbage's father (if it were indeed the same family) would have been acquainted with Shakespeare's father, John Shakespeare, a glove-maker and sometime alderman, before financial disgrace saw him go down in the world. William Shakespeare gravitated to the Burbage family when he came to London, most likely because of the existing connection. Before he became an actor, James Burbage was apprenticed to a joiner, in the process of which he acquired the practical skills and business knowledge which would prove so valuable when he built the first theatre in London.

The first record of Burbage's employment as a player comes in 1559, when he signed up as chief of the Earl of Leicester's Men. In a letter to the Earl of Shrewsbury in June 1559, the Earl of Leicester, Sir Robert Dudley (1532–88), described his players as 'honest men, and shall play none other matters than such as are tolerable and convenient'.[10] Sir Robert had a reputation for being both magnificent and discerning and would not have accepted anything less than the best 'servants'. From this we may deduce that James Burbage possessed the attributes of a handsome appearance, charming manners, tact and wit that his master

required. Robert Dudley had long been a patron of the
drama in its courtly form, enjoying the erudite Latin plays
performed at Oxford and the Inns of Court, where he was
the Governor of the Inner Temple. Being signed up by
Dudley offered Burbage the immunity from prosecution
he and his men needed to pursue their calling and assured
their position. Noble patronage brought Burbage other
benefits too. The Earl of Leicester's men frequently played
at Court for the entertainment of the Queen and were
known in other great cities. The Gloucester Records
1569–70 show payment of thirteen shillings and four pence
'In rewarde to the Erle of Leysester's players playing before
Mr Mayor'.[11]

James Burbage was to learn early in his career that the
government, both local and national, disapproved of plays
and players. This prejudice, composed of a bitter blend of
Puritanism, prejudice and social control, was to blight his
life and that of many other men of the theatre. The running
battle between the players and the authorities will be a recur-
ring theme of this book, as the actors sought to continue
playing against numerous bureaucratic and political obstacles,
and the Lord Mayor and his henchmen – vain men, dressed
in a little brief authority – threatened to tear their theatres
down on the grounds of public health, public safety and the
defence of the realm. The first onslaught arrived on 3 January
1571 when a proclamation was issued against noblemen such
as the Earl of Leicester ordaining that lords should not 'retain'
more men than they actually used as servants, domestic or
otherwise, and those who did so after this notice beyond
20 February 1571 would incur the displeasure of the Queen.[12]
This proclamation was specifically directed against players,
and has its origins in the Queen's anxieties about her courtiers
plotting against her and raising private armies. Retainers,

little more than 'gallowglasses', mercenaries disguised as actors, posed a real threat to a monarch who was forever insecure upon her throne.

It is during this early crisis in the origins of the profession that James Burbage comes clearly into view for the first time. Faced with the prospect of his company being disbanded, Burbage wrote to the Earl of Leicester, appealing for support. Addressed to 'The Rt Hon Earle of Leicester, their good Lord and Master', the letter is signed by all 'your players', giving the names of his troupe to posterity: James Burbage, John Perkin, John Laneham, William Johnson, Robert Wilson and Thomas Clarke. This eloquent letter begins with an appeal to the Earl of Leicester to keep the men on, despite the proclamation:

> May it please your honour to understand that forasmuch as there is a certaine Proclamation out for the reviving of a Statute as touching Retainers, as your Lordship knoweth better than we can informe you thereof, We therefore, your humble servants and daily orators, your players . . . are bold to trouble your Lordship with their our suite, humblie desiring your honour that (as you have always been our good Lord and Master) you will now vouchsafe to retaine us at this present as your household servants and daily waiters.[13]

In the course of the letter, Burbage makes it clear that he is not asking for more money from Sir Robert, and that he is very grateful that his men can wear the Earl of Leicester's livery and tour the country, 'when we shall have occasion to travel amongst our frendes, as we do usually once a year, and as other noblemen's players do, and have done in tyme past'.

Burbage concludes with a few lines of flattering poetry, designed to sway Sir Robert's judgement:

> Long may your Lordship live in peace
> A peer of noblest peers
> In health wealth and prosperitie
> Redoubling Nestor's years.[14]

Nestor, a heroic king from Greek mythology, was already over 110 years old when the Trojan War began. This carefully calculated appeal to the Earl of Leicester's better nature was successful, for on 7 May 1571 a Royal Patent addressed to 'all mayors, bailiffs and officials as well within our city of London and the Liberties of the same, as also within the liberties and freedoms of any other cityes, towns, boroughs, etc., whatsoever throughout our realm of England', advised them to permit the actors 'to use, exercise and occupy the art and facultie of playing Comedies, Tragedies, Interludes, Stage Plaies and such other . . . for the recreation of our loving subjects as for our solace and pleasure when we shall think good to see them . . . provided that the same be allowed by our Master of the Revels and that they be not shewen in the time of Common Prayer, or in the time of great and common plague in our said City of London.'[15] The Master of the Revels, who had been a minor household functionary during the reign of Henry VII, had become increasingly important under Henry VIII. By the rule of Elizabeth he was a powerful figure who could make the reputation of a company by inviting them to perform before the Queen. In the years to come, the Master of the Revels would add the role of censor to his duties, and crack down on any hint of sedition.

Later in the year, the authorities decided that issuing a Royal Patent allowing the Earl of Leicester's Men and other companies to tour the country was too generous. This time, a proclamation was issued to the effect that players must have a licence to perform at any public venue such as an inn, tavern, fairground or village green. The penalties for defying this order included arrest, incarceration and branding. Burbage was swift to obey, for what else could he do to protect himself and his company? A document dated 6 December 1571 records Burbage obtaining a licence from the Lord Mayor of London: 'to play within this Cittie such matters as are allowed of to be played, at convenient howers and tymes, so that it be not at the time of Devyne Service'.[16]

By 1575, James Burbage was a married man, living in Holywell Street, Shoreditch, with his family. The Burbages had two sons, Cuthbert, born 1565, and his younger brother Richard, born two years later. Shoreditch, with its mixture of modest cottages and grand timber-framed merchants' houses, was already something of a bohemian enclave. Many other players and musicians lived there, including the Queen's musicians, the distinguished Bassano brothers, and in the years to come many of the great names of the Elizabethan stage, including Christopher Marlowe and Thomas Kyd, would be Burbage's neighbours. Burbage's wife, Ellen Brayne, was connected with the world of the London stage through her brother, John Brayne. Although John Brayne was nominally a grocer, his interests extended beyond mere shopkeeping. Brayne dabbled in theatricals at his inn, the Red Lion, Whitechapel, the first purpose-built theatrical venue in London, designed specifically to accommodate troupes of travelling players. This connection clearly provided Burbage with the ideal opportunity to showcase the Earl of Leicester's Men when they played in London.

Married and clearly thriving, this should have been the
time when Burbage was surging ahead with his career.
Favoured by the Queen, protected by the Earl of Leicester
and, subsequently, by Edward Manners, the Earl of Rutland
(1549–87), licensed to perform by the Lord Mayor of London,
Burbage should have been the uncrowned king of the London
stage. Unfortunately for Burbage, the time was out of joint.
He had emerged at a point where the authorities were waging
war against the stage in all its manifestations and he, along
with many other performers, was cast in the role of victim.
To appreciate just what Burbage and his fellow performers
were up against, one has only to look at the existing conditions of the London stage.

The most obvious feature of performing in London in
1575 was that there were no purpose-built theatres as such.
The closest thing to theatres, on the south bank of the
Thames, were the specialised buildings devoted to
animal-baiting.

Bear-baiting. Bear gardens, with their circular structures, were the
origins of playhouses.

Georg Hoefnagel's pre-Elizabethan map shows two 'rings' with open roofs and roofed seating for spectators.[17] They stand in yards or gardens lined with dog kennels. One is named 'the Bull Bayting' and the other is 'The Beare Bayting'. These buildings testify to acts of animal cruelty which today we would regard as barbaric. Bull-baiting was practised all over England up to the middle of the nineteenth century, although it was officially outlawed by statute in 1835, and is commemorated in place names up and down the country to this day. There was a belief that bull beef had a better flavour if the animals had been baited before slaughter, and butchers in some parts of the country were liable to prosecution if they sold unbaited beef. The original bull ring in London was in Cheapside, and relocated to the South Bank where there was more space. The dogs involved were mastiffs, and the experience of bull-baiting was considered good training for a guard dog.

Bears, not regarded as edible, remained part of life's entertainment, and many bears became familiar figures, regarded affectionately by the regular patrons. Famous bears included Harry Hunks and Sackerson, with the latter gaining immortality through a mention in *The Merry Wives of Windsor*:

> Slender: I love the sport well; but I shall as soon quarrel at it as any man in England. You are afraid, if you see the bear loose, are you not?
> Anne: Ay, indeed, sir.
> Slender: That's meat and drink to me, now: I have seen Sackerson loose twenty times, and have taken him by the chain; but, I warrant you, the women have so cried and shrieked at it, that it passed: but women, indeed, cannot abide 'em; they are very ill-favoured rough things.[18]

Another reference is to be found in *Macbeth,* when the embattled Macbeth declares: 'They have tied me to a stake; I cannot fly, But, bear-like, I must fight the course.'[19]

Occasionally a blind bear was brought into the ring and attacked by men with whips. Having lost its sight in combat, it was still retained to play a crude blind-man's buff with the men as a comic interlude between the regular displays of bear-baiting, but it could still stand up for itself and occasionally broke loose from its tethers to create uproar among the audience. Bear-baiting was very unpopular with Puritans because it took place on Sundays. When the seats at Paris Garden collapsed and eight people were killed during a bear-baiting in 1583, Philip Stubbes observed that it was 'a freendlie warning to such as more delight themselves in the crueltie of beasts . . . than in the works of mercie, which ought to be the Sabbath daies exercise'.[20]

One writer, visiting the bear garden in 1584, described 'a round building three storeys high, in which are kept about a hundred large English dogs, with separate wooden kennels for each of them. These dogs were made to fight singly with three bears, the second being larger than the first and the third larger than the second. After this a horse was brought in and chased by the dogs, and at last a bull, who defended himself bravely.[21]

Thomas Platter, a young Swiss doctor who visited London in 1599, described visiting a bear garden:

a large bear on a long rope was bound to a stake, then a number of great English mastiffs were brought in and shown first to the bear, which they afterwards baited one after another: now the excellence and fine temper of such mastiffs was evinced, for although they were much struck and mauled by the bear, they did not give in, but had to be pulled off by sheer force . . .[22]

At Shoe Lane, near Fleet Street, there was a cock-pit consisting of a circular table in the centre covered with straw and with ledges round it, where the cocks were teased and provoked into flying at one another. Men with bets on the poor creatures sat closest, but spectators who were merely there because they had paid their penny entrance money sat around higher up, watching with eager pleasure the fierce and angry fight between the cocks, doing each other to death with spurs and beaks. Since the men whose cock surrendered or died lost the wager, stakes on a cock often amounted to thousands of crowns, especially if the owner had reared the cock themselves. The 'entertainment' usually lasted four or five hours, as the master of the cock-pit kept many birds of his own, segregated in separate cages and trained for the sport. The master maintained that if he discovered that one of the visiting cocks had its beak coated with garlic, to deter rivals, he was fully entitled to kill it. Cocks were often dosed with brandy before a fight, to render them more aggressive and add to the pleasure of the spectators.[23]

The appeal of bear-baiting and the other displays of animal cruelty such as cock-fighting, dog-fights and hunting is lost on the modern reader, but such barbaric forms of entertainment found a ready audience among Elizabethan Londoners and illustrates an important aspect of their character. Elizabethans, particularly Londoners, loved a spectacle. Their cruelty to animals was on a par with their cruelty to each other and they did not appear to be sensitive to suffering, either their own or other people's.

This attitude is reflected in the knockabout world of Elizabethan sport. Football, for instance, played up and down the streets of London, was dismissed irritably by Stubbes as 'a friendly kind of fight, a bloody and murdering practice',[24] particularly when it was played on Sundays, the day of rest.

Football as played in London was obviously very different from the elaborate and well-organised Italian game described by the Florentine author Giovanni Bardi in his treatise of 1580. According to Stubbes the English game consisted of every player lying in wait for his adversary, 'seeking to over-throw him, and pitch him on the nose, though it be upon hard stones, in ditch or dale, in valley or hill, he careth not, so he have him down'. This resulted in severe injuries – 'sometimes the nose gush with blood, sometimes their eyes start out'[25] – including broken necks, backs, legs and arms. Fouls on the pitch included being 'dashed against the heart' by rival players' elbows, being hit on the ribs with fists and being kneed in the hip. No wonder football was banned at the University of Oxford. Associated by the historian John Stow with 'people of meaner sort', Kent in *King Lear* is probably the first football hooligan in English drama when he refers to Oswald the steward as a 'base football-player' while kicking his legs out from under him.[26] Apparently such bad behaviour was a regular accompaniment to the game.

Other violent delights in Elizabethan London included cudgel-play, fencing matches and wrestling. The objective of cudgel-play was to draw your opponent's blood with a sharp blow to the head. A streak of blood coursing down his face indicated that you had won a palpable hit. Wrestling, often the cause of cracked ribs and even a broken neck, was consid-ered an unsuitable spectacle for women, as Touchstone would observe in *As You Like It*. 'It is the first time that ever I heard breaking of ribs was sport for ladies.'[27] Unfit for ladies, but any man worthy of the name would master the necessary throws and holds. All men, regardless of background, were expected to be proficient fighters, whether on the battlefield or in the back alleys of London. The arts of war served as both a method of survival and an entertainment.

Bear-baiting was just one form of entertainment on offer at the Bankside. Once this was concluded, the performance turned into a combination of a circus act and a comic sketch:

> The next was that a number of men and women came forward from a separate compartment, dancing, conversing and fighting with each other: also a man who threw some white bread among the crowd, that scrambled for it. Right over the middle of the place a rose was fixed, this rose being set on fire by a rocket; suddenly lots of apples and pears fell out of it down upon the people standing below. Whilst the people were scrambling for the apples, some rockets were made to fall down upon them out of the rose, which caused a great fright but amused the spectators.[28]

Despite the lack of actual theatres, performances went on all over London, as they had done for many centuries. The earliest site was Clerkenwell Pump, where mystery plays had been performed from medieval times by the clergy and schoolboys attached to religious foundations, for the delight and edification of the common people. The majority of performances took place at the 'players' inns', specific public houses which offered the strutters somewhere to perform in exchange for a share of the takings after the hat had been passed round. The first recorded performances were at the Saracen's Head, Islington, and the Boar's Head, Aldgate, in 1557, but inn-yard performances had been attracting crowds long before this date.

There were obvious advantages to performing at players' inns such as the Cross Keys in Gracechurch Street, the Bull in Bishopsgate Street and the Bell Savage on Ludgate Hill. A big inn-yard provided sufficient space for a makeshift stage, room enough for the crowd to stand, and leeway for the essential traffic of horses and coaches. Seating, and a better view, was to be obtained in the galleries which ran around the yard and connected the upper rooms. There were plenty of rooms to provide a 'tiring house' or dressing room for the players, and a good supply of alcohol kept the spectators happy and guaranteed an income for the innkeeper. Many innkeepers went to great lengths to carry out structural alterations to convert their establishments into little less than permanent theatres, but these were not always successful. In July 1567, the stage at John Brayne's Red Lion in Whitechapel collapsed during a performance, resulting in a lawsuit between Brayne, James Burbage's future brother-in-law, and the carpenter, William Sylvester, who was obliged to patch up his faulty workmanship before Brayne would pay his bill of £8.10s. Following this work, the play, *The Story of Sampson*, was to be performed.[29]

The Bell Savage on Ludgate Hill was a favourite with players who performed there up until 1577. This inn possessed a less than savoury reputation, after the wife of the host was 'carted as a bawd and whore' on 12 June 1560. Despite – or perhaps because of – this, the Bell Savage remained popular. Entertainment was not restricted to plays alone. Players' inns profited from other amusements, such as fencing matches with a generous purse for the winner and novelties such as 'Banks's performing horse' which went on display at the Cross Keys Inn in 1588. Over in Bishopsgate Street, the Bull Inn enjoyed an enduringly lurid reputation. As late as April 1594, Anthony Bacon, brother of Sir Francis, settled in Bishopsgate, much to the anxiety of his mother, 'on account of its neighbourhood to the Bull-inn, where plays and interludes were continually acted, and would, she imagined, corrupt his servants.'[30]

These inn-yard shows were less than popular with the Lord Mayor of London, who made regular and unsuccessful attempts to ban them. A proclamation in April 1559 officially prohibited plays in hostels and taverns, but these rulings were gleefully ignored by the innkeepers as the players carried on regardless. Innkeepers regularly flouted the injunctions, since plays were not wholly forbidden on Sundays and Holy Days. How could they be, when the traditional mystery plays were performed as an extension of the liturgy and had been for generations? The demographics were in the players' favour. London at this period enjoyed an almost unprecedented population of young people. Around 80,000 people, 40 per cent of London's population, were under the age of fifteen, due to the large numbers cramming into the city in search of work as apprentices and servants. Boisterous, irreverent, these youngsters had money in their pockets and refused to be told what to do by the authorities. Enthusiastic crowds flocked to the inn-yards, the gates already open while the bells were still ringing for divine service in empty churches.

In 1574 the Lord Mayor of London, James Hawes, made another attempt to control the players' inns. He issued a proclamation against the 'Sundry great disorders and Inconveniences' which had ensued due to the 'inordinate haunting of great multitudes of people, specially youth, to plays, enterludes and shows'. In a bravura display of puritanical finger-wagging, Hawes objected to play-going on the grounds that such entertainments constituted a waste of money, distracted citizens from divine service and posed a threat to law and order, providing an opportunity for 'sondry robberies by picking and cutting of purses, and many other corruptions of youth' as there were 'evil practices in Great Innes, having chambers and secret places', where chaste maids and good citizen's children might be corrupted. Warming to his theme, Hawes condemned inn-yard shows as a threat to public safety, declaring: 'sondry slaughters and maimings of the Queenes subjects have happened by ruins of Skaffolds frames and stages, and by engines weapons and powder used in plays'. He even blamed the performances for triggering epidemics: 'In tymes of Godes visitation by the plague such assembles of the people in throng and press have been very dangerous for the spreading of Infection.'[31]

It must be admitted that, regarding his last item, the Lord Mayor did have a point. Inn-yard performances were certainly not the safest entertainment in London and any such event did pose actual risk to life and limb. Where there was a crowd, there could be a quarrel, and a fight could escalate into a full-blown riot, requiring intervention by the constables of the watch. This would result in injuries, even deaths, and create a bad impression of the ward of the city where the trouble broke out, as riots had to be referred to the Star Chamber. The most pressing physical danger associated with crowds was infectious disease. An outbreak of plague meant strict quarantine had to be imposed, resulting in the closure of premises, disruption of the business upon which the city depended and personal and financial distress. Any entertainment which attracted a random crowd of artisans, apprentices, ostlers, tavern-loafers and the like, jammed shoulder to shoulder with more respectable citizens, was to be suspected and if possible avoided as a potential spreader of disease.

The fear of plague was understandable. Plague, or bubonic plague to give it its full name, was a particularly ghastly way to die. First the bubo arrived, the telltale swelling of the lymph nodes in armpit and groin, swiftly followed by sweating and vomiting, blood in the lungs and the intense desire to lie down and sleep which, if indulged, ensured that death swiftly followed. Death came in days, sometimes hours, once the patient had acquired the disease, and very few survived. For there was no cure for plague, although wise-women and physicians offered desperate remedies, from burning rosemary, lavender and rue to drinking vinegar.

Bonfires smouldered in a futile attempt to fumigate the 'visitation'. Through clouds of smoke emerged the nightmare figures of the bird-headed doctors in their plague masks, their beaks stuffed with bergamot to combat the infection. Whole families were mewed up, prisoners in their own homes, forbidden by the watchmen to venture forth, a yellow cross splashed on the door and the desperate prayer 'Lord Have Mercy Upon Us'. The very young and the very old, and all who were already weakened by hunger and disease, succumbed quickly. Their bodies were flung into the street to await the lumbering dead cart, while the gutters over-flowed with excrement and carrion kites wheeled overhead, swooping down to peck the eyes of the unburied. To para-phrase Defoe, the chronicler of London's most infamous plague, the victims died in heaps and were buried in heaps.[32]

The other physical risk was fire, used on stage to create a wide range of effects from candles and tapers in a night-time scene to small cannons, 'chambers shot off within', to create sensational effects such as explosions or thunder and light-ning. Fire was dangerous anywhere in London with its thou-sands of wooden dwellings rammed in side by side, but it was particularly hazardous in a wooden-framed inn-yard, with buildings roofed with thatch, and bales of hay stored nearby. An outbreak of fire, in a yard crammed with an overexcited crowd, and surrounded by other tinder-dry houses, spelled an immense risk to life and property. Fire-fighting consisted of leather buckets from the parish council being lowered into the nearest well with long-handled iron hooks and then passed along the line, which was hardly effective for coping with an inn-yard full of frightened people and terrified horses. A whole street, indeed an entire ward, could go up in flames, and the authorities who had given permission for the play to take place would get the blame.

On these grounds, in 1574 the Lord Mayor and his aldermen, together with the members of the common council, banned public performances in London and ordained that from henceforth: 'Therefore be it ordered that all such Interludes in publique places, and the resort to the same, shall wholly be prohibited as ungodly, and humble suit be made to the Lords that lyke prohibition be in places near unto the Cittie.'[33]

Given this draconian legislation, it looked as though the players, and the inns where they performed, were doomed. The Lord Mayor had banned plays and players from the city. James Burbage, with so much to offer, had been cut down in his prime. With the Red Lion officially closed, there was nowhere else to go, at least nowhere else in London. Apparently resigned to his fate, Burbage did the only thing an actor-manager could do. He took his company away on tour.

In the summer of 1575, James Burbage and the Earl of Leicester's Men performed at the Earl's country seat, Kenilworth Castle in Warwickshire. The Earl had built this magnificent castle to impress Queen Elizabeth, and the Queen was entertained with an array of glorious activities, designed to make her the centre of attention, which culminated in a masque entitled 'The Lady in the Lake'. Crowds streamed in from far and near to catch a glimpse of Gloriana and to witness the spectacular show. It takes no great stretch of the imagination to picture the eleven-year-old Will Shakespeare at this extraordinary event, sitting on his father's shoulders to get a better view over the heads of the crowd. This masque, which surely inspired scenes in *A Midsummer Night's Dream*, was later

described by John Laneham, one of the Earl of Leicester's men.
Laneham recalled Arion on the dolphin's back and the delectable music 'in the evening of the day resounding from the
calm waters . . . the whole harmony conveyed in tyme, tune
and temper thus incomparably melodious . . . with what lively
delight this might pierce into the hearer's harts, I pray ye
imagine . . . '[34] Compare this with Oberon's words:

> Once I sat upon a promontory,
> And heard a mermaid on a dolphin's back
> Uttering such dulcet and harmonious breath
> That the rude sea grew civil at her song
> And certain stars shot madly from their sphere,
> To hear the sea-maid's music.[35]

The masque clearly impressed Queen Elizabeth, as the Earl
of Leicester's Men were invited to perform again before the
Queen at Court on Innocents' Day, 28 December 1575, and
again on the Sunday before Shrove Tuesday 1576. For the
first time, Burbage's troupe is described in the Warrants for
Payment as 'Burbage and his company, Servants to the Earl
of Leicester'.[36]

To be invited to perform before the Queen herself was a
great honour. To be invited to perform 'a Christmas gambol'
far surpassed this. At Christmas, the only official holiday in
the Elizabethan year, work was suspended for the best part
of a fortnight and everyone, in town and country, from prince
to peasant, gave themselves over to pleasure:

> When Christmastide comes in like a Bride
> With holly and ivy clad;
> Twelve days i' the year much mirth and cheer
> In every household is had.[37]

The fashion was for noblemen and courtiers to celebrate Christmas in London, although some said the best Christmas of all was to be had in the country:

> And yet by report, from City to Court,
> The Country gets the day;
> More liquor is spent, and better content
> To drive the cold winter away.[38]

Christmas offered old and young alike a glowing, life-affirming combination of Christian festival and pagan celebration, providing welcome relief from the hardship of winter:

> When icicles hang by the wall,
> And Dick the shepherd blows his nail,
> And Tom bears logs into the hall,
> And milk comes frozen home in pail . . .[39]

Every house was filled with merrymaking and feasting: 'now capons and hens, besides turkeys, geese and ducks, besides beef and mutton, must all die for the great feast,' as Nicholas Breton noted.[40] Life at Court was one long sequence of banquets, plays and masques. The Master of the Revels spent weeks in preparations, auditioning different acting companies and selecting plays and players to appear before the Queen. It was a delicate task, which called for tact and diplomacy, with any offensive material edited out. Indeed, by 1578, such were the anxieties about seditious material that the Master of the Revels, Sir Edmund Tilney (1536– 1610), would add the position of official censor to his other roles. Endless rehearsals ensured a smooth-running performance, with the Master of the Revels as stage manager. Enormous candelabra, with dozens of candles, had to be hoisted into place. Props and clothes had to be organised and the Office of Works had the task of building a platform upon which the players could perform. The Earl of Leicester's Men were just one item on a lavish bill of entertainment, alongside a masque, a spectacular mixture of singing and dancing, during which guests mingled freely with the disguised performers while the flickering candlelight gleamed on their beautiful clothes, the silks and satins, the jewels and the feathers, the cloth of gold and the glowing colours that beggared all description.

Out in the country, entertainments were cruder and earthier, the distant ancestors of our modern pantomimes:

> To mask and mum kind neighbours will come
> With wassails of nut brown ale;
> To drink and carouse to all in this house
> As merry as bucks in the pale; [41]

And the payment was correspondingly more basic:

> Where cake, bread and cheese is brought for your fees
> To make you the longer stay.[42]

The festivities at Court culminated with Twelfth Night, the twelfth day of Christmas, a spectacular night of anarchy or 'what you will', which was to provide Shakespeare with inspiration for his greatest comedy.

Although James Burbage and the Earl of Leicester's Men had the distinction of being singled out to play before the Queen at Christmas 1575 and then again on Shrove Tuesday the following year, they could not rely on being asked to perform at such events on a regular basis, or even live on the proceeds of two or three shows a year. By 1576, James Burbage needed a more consistent source of income, and somewhere permanent for his company to perform. Londoners would pay good money to watch plays, so the obvious answer was to create something which Londoners had never seen before: a purpose-built playhouse.

3

THE FIRST THEATRE IN LONDON

We few, we happy few, we band of brothers . . .
Henry V, Act 4 Scene 3

The Earl of Leicester's Men needed a new home, but the Lord Mayor had forbidden players to perform in the city, at the players' inns, and he had also forbidden them to play in open spaces. There could be only one solution. While appearing to obey every letter of the law, and avoiding all performances in the city itself, Burbage decided to open a purpose-built theatre beyond the jurisdiction of the Lord Mayor, in the liberty (precincts) of Shoreditch. As soon as this decision had been reached, Burbage was faced with another dilemma. He wanted to build a theatre but he lacked one vital ingredient: money. The only way he could obtain money would be to borrow at a high rate of interest, and it is likely that he borrowed from John Hyde, a wealthy Londoner who later became a business partner. Burbage may also have discussed his plans with his brother-in-law, John Brayne, but there is no evidence that Brayne came in on the venture at this point.

On 13 April 1576, about a month after the birth of his daughter Alice, Burbage signed the lease for an extensive tract of land which was formerly part of the old Holywell Priory, lying between a stretch of land owned by the Earl of Rutland and the brick wall which bounded Finsbury Fields, not far from the current site of Liverpool Street station.[1] These fields were part of a common, where children played, lovers courted and maidservants spread their linen sheets across the hedges to dry. Nearby, on the other side of London Wall, stood the houses of merchants, inhabited by the new middle class, people of different tastes and interests from the artisans and apprentices who crammed into the inn-yards to watch the strolling players.

And there were rival attractions, too, competing for business with any purpose-built playhouse. Wrestling matches took place on the common, and the twelve-score archery range was still popular, a legacy from the times when every man was expected to be proficient with a bow, in case of invasion. The practice of archery was so commonplace that most of Shakespeare's audience would have recognised this scenario:

> In my schooldays, when I had lost one shaft,
> I shot his fellow of the self-same flight
> The self-same way with more advisèd watch,
> To find the other forth; and by adventuring both,
> I oft found both.[2]

Archery was also the cause of several fatal accidents. As a child, Dame Alice Owen got an arrow in her hat while playing in the fields and founded a famous school in Islington to commemorate her escape. Ralph, the comical apprentice in *The Knight of the Burning Pestle* by Beaumont and Fletcher, enters with a forked arrow through his head, and explains that he has been shot while walking through Moorfields.³ Would such a lethal pastime deter playgoers from making their way over the fields to a new theatre?

Firearms, which were coming to replace the longbow as weapon of choice, were even more dangerous. The Artillery Yard near Spitalfields was a walled enclosure where London's citizens could practise their marksmanship by shooting at butts built from earth or turf with a target fastened to them. According to John Stow, in his *Survey of London*, every Thursday cannons from the Tower of London were brought up for artillery practice. The Artillery Yard ran right past the gun-foundry in Houndsditch, making it the ideal place to test new ordnance.

Irregular musketry, outside the walled confines of the Artillery Yard, was particularly dangerous. In July 1579 a young man named Thomas Appletree was a passenger in a boat on the Thames between Deptford and Greenwich, along with a couple of friends and two or three choirboys from the Chapel Royal. Thomas had a loaded gun in the boat with him and, slightly drunk and in high spirits, he fired the gun three or four times, 'shooting at random very rashly'.⁴ Carelessly discharging a loaded weapon is a dangerous activity at any time, but it was even more rash on this occasion. One of Thomas's random shots reached the Royal Barge, upon which no lesser person than Queen Elizabeth herself was taking the air, along with the French Ambassador and several distinguished courtiers. There was consternation when a shot came out of nowhere and hit the waterman, who was rowing the vessel less than six feet away from the Queen. Struck in both arms, the waterman collapsed on the floor of the barge, convinced he was dying. Queen Elizabeth's reaction was to throw him a scarf and tell him to be of good cheer, the bullet had clearly not been meant for him. She did not add that if there was to be a second shot, it would be for her. Fortunately, there was no second shot; following an investigation Thomas Appletree was arrested, charged with treason and led out to be hanged on the river bank, close to the spot where he had apparently tried to shoot the Queen. In keeping with tradition, young Thomas was allowed to make a farewell speech on the gallows, declaring that he had not intended to kill the Queen but that he deserved to die for endangering her life. At the last moment, as the hangman placed the noose around Thomas's neck, word reached the executioner that Thomas had been pardoned. Perhaps that last-minute reprieve, delayed until Thomas was on the brink of death, was the Queen's revenge for those terrifying moments she had suffered on the barge.[5]

The ground of the old Holywell Priory belonged to Master Giles Alleyn, who signed the other half of the lease knowing perfectly well that the land would be used to build a theatre and that the Corporation of London would object to this. But Alleyn also knew that Burbage was a favoured servant of the Earl of Rutland, whom it was not prudent to offend. The agreement seemed perfectly reasonable at the time. The rent was to be £14 a year, with a deposit of £20. The owner, Robert Myles, would not give a longer lease than twenty-one years, but was willing to consider extending the lease after the first ten years for another ten, if both parties were in agreement. The conditions on the landlord's side were that James Burbage before the end of the term of ten years should have expended on the rebuilding or restoration of some tenements on the property at least £200, and that he should pay the legal expenses of drawing up this second agreement.

It is probable that James Burbage was in possession of the property some time before the final indenture was signed, as was the custom then. Indeed, his lease was reckoned from

25 March, a quarter day, and may have begun even earlier. And he had planned what to do with the land before he had secured it. As the lease indicates, the land included cottages, barns, gardens, a well, sewers, a pond and a piece of empty ground. There was also an inn on the estate, the George Inn, perhaps the very inn that Shakespeare refers to when he speaks of 'St George that swinged the Dragon and e'er since, Sits on his horse-back at mine hostess' door'.[6]

At last, here was the opportunity for a playhouse where Burbage's own company could perform. The strolling players had found a home, or perhaps opened a shop.[7]

All James Burbage's hopes and dreams went into building his theatre. He drew on his expertise as a joiner to become his own architect and builder. The old inn-yards where he himself had performed inspired him with their balconies and galleries, but he did not follow these originals to the letter. Instead, he made his building round. The elegant halls where he had appeared before the Queen had shown him the value of attractive decoration. Learning a lesson from the notorious collapsing scaffold at the Red Lion, Burbage ensured that his stages and galleries were all constructed from seasoned timber, solid and soundly built. He created his theatre out of wood, the material which, as a joiner, he knew best, supported by brick foundations. Some ready-prepared boards and pillars were sent up from the country via the river, and the building was thrown up in a very short space of time. At that time, men were not restricted to eight-hour working days, and Burbage was able to do a great deal of the practical work himself as well as overseeing the construction. His players, 'resting' over the early spring, were only too eager to help get the place ready so they could perform, and their labour kept the costs down. The actual building work was completed within a month but, however careful Burbage had been, it was still more expensive than he had anticipated – and more than he had. Fortunately, his own hectic work on the building had inspired his brother-in-law John Brayne to invest in the venture in return for a share of the profits.

Burbage named his building the Theatre, a nod to the classical tradition, as it was derived from the Greek word meaning 'a place for viewing'. And even the name was pioneering, for this particular 'theatre' would become the general name of all its successors. Rising from the play-grounds of Finsbury Fields, the Theatre was its own best advertisement, filling onlookers with curiosity and anticipation. As it grew towards completion, the Theatre could even be seen from Bankside.

Crowds flocked to the Theatre when it opened in April 1576, willing to pay if only to see the interior. Even larger crowds of penniless folk arrived, hoping to slip in unseen, as they had done at the old inn-yards. But these hopefuls were turned away because, for the first time ever, they were stopped at the door by the 'gatherers' with their collecting boxes. No admission to the house without payment! No collection bucket circulating afterwards or hopeful strutter with out-thrust cap. Scenes of turmoil followed, with the poor reluctant to leave and the ticket-payers eager to get through.

As the fortunate playgoers struggled at the entrance, what did they see? They found themselves in an enclosed central space like a bear-pit, without a roof. When they looked up, they saw the sky and faced the elements. When they looked in front, they saw an open stage crossing one end of the circle, with doors and curtains at the back. Above the stage was a Player's House, which could represent a balcony, a tower, a steeple, a bridge, a prison or any location which required a higher level than the stage. If they looked around, they would see galleries, as they would have in inn-yards, but draped with magnificent fabrics. The galleries also had seats of varying degrees of comfort, from the ordinary gallery to the luxurious Lords' Rooms. And over all the galleries, as over the stage, was a thatched roof with projecting eaves. If the first playgoers spotted a drop of rain, they might have dashed to the galleries, only to discover that they were expected to pay again, another penny or two, depending on the class of the gallery. If they could not afford to pay more, they would have stayed where they were, out in the open, in the wind and the rain, among the crowds who surged forward, the good-humoured ones cracking nuts, the bad-tempered picking fights. It must have seemed such a long wait, until the drum beat, and the beautifully dressed actors appeared, when a sudden stillness fell and the crowd became silent, eager to hear.

As to the play with which Burbage chose to open the Theatre, one can only speculate. Was it an old favourite, worn smooth by rehearsal and touring, some reliable fool-proof classic that had been perfected and honed at Bristol, Gloucester, Leicester and all the other cities the Earl of Leicester's Men had toured? Was it a play specially commissioned for this great occasion, or one of the familiar dramas based on old Italian romances, such as *Chariclea,* or *Philemon and Philecia*? The play could have been *The History of the Collier*, the 'collier' of the title being not, as one might expect a miner, but a charcoal-encrusted demon prowling about the village of Croydon and seeking whom he might devour. Other possibilities for that first night spring to mind. Did Burbage favour *Gorboduc,* a Senecan offering dating from 1561, written by the law students Thomas Sackville and Thomas Norton and first performed at the Inner Temple of the Inns of Court? As the first English play written in blank verse, this would have had real appeal. Or *Damon and Pythias* (translated by Richard Edwards, 1564) or *Horestes* (translated by John Pickering in 1567). Any of these plays, with their classical five-act structure, heady mix of sensational plotlines, ghosts and bombastic rhetoric, would have proved a big draw. Alternatively, Burbage might have hedged his bets and selected a comedy, such as Udall's *Ralph Roister Doister* (1553) or *Gammer Gurton's Needle,* a bawdy romp in the style of Terence thought for a long time to have been penned by John Still, one-time Bishop of Bath and Wells, but now attributed to William Stevenson. That the plot concludes with the eponymous missing needle discovered stuck in someone's bottom tells you everything you need to know about this farce, but it was astonishingly popular.

The truth is that Burbage and the Earl of Leicester's Men would have had all these productions in their repertoire, and more. Unlike twentieth-century repertory companies which offered three or four different plays per season, Elizabethan actors had to be word-perfect in up to thirty-six productions, and prepared to switch from one play to another at a moment's notice. If a hail of apples, nuts and tankards indicated that a Senecan tragedy was dying on its feet, a nod from the leading actor was all that was required to make a swift transition from doom and gloom to a raunchy comedy. If this meant that scenes were muddled and lines mangled, any protests from the authors would have met with a dismissive wave. Writers had little significance in this period. While the players relied upon authors such as Udall and Stevenson to provide a storyline and speeches, these men were not professional writers in the modern sense. Udall had been a schoolmaster, before being sacked from Eton and gaoled for buggery. Classical plays, such as the plays of Seneca and Plautus, were translated by university wits, more than happy to sell their 'Englysshed' versions in return for a crust.

New plays were not being published, and companies cannily kept any material to themselves, rather than risk pirate editions circulating among their rivals. In 1576, the achievements of the first wave of English playwrights such as John Lyly (1553–1606), Thomas Nashe (1567–1601) and George Peele (1556–96) were still in the future. William Shakespeare was at grammar school in Stratford, wondering how to avoid his destiny as a glove-maker. Christopher Marlowe (1564–93) was at King's School Canterbury, and Robert Greene (1558–92) was preparing to enter the University of Cambridge. As for other writers such as George Chapman (1559–1634), Henry Chettle (1564–1606) and Thomas Lodge (1558–1625), they too were still in their green and salad days. The watershed of London's greatest playwriting years was yet to come.

Whatever the choice of play, the Theatre was an immediate success and the first performance only whetted the appetite of the audience and sightseers for more. The Earl of Leicester's Men had a proper theatre at last, the first of its kind in London, where they could perform to their heart's content beyond the reach of the Lord Mayor of London and his beady-eyed enforcers. A playhouse where Burbage could showcase his brilliant and talented company, with audiences flocking to enjoy the spectacle. A theatre which would take its place in the history books as *the* Theatre, immortalised by Stow in 1598 as 'a public house for the acting and shewing of comedies tragedies and histories'[8] and earning an enviably notorious reputation thanks to the sanctimonious Puritan John Stockwood (*c*.1550–1610), who dismissed it in a sermon on 24 August 1578 as 'the gorgeous playing place erected in the Fields . . . called a Theatre, that is, even after the manner of the old Theatre at Rome, a shew place of all beastlie and filthy matters'.[9] Far from deterring audiences, Stockwood's admonishment must have had the Theatre packing them in.

One can almost imagine the wily James Burbage propping up a board outside the Theatre proclaiming it to be 'a shew place of all beastlie and filthy matters!'

But the life of an actor-manager was never an easy one and success quickly brought trouble in its wake. The Theatre soon aroused jealousy against Burbage from less successful operators who schemed against it and Burbage became weighed down with the familiar problems of debt and interference from the authorities, combined with the additional responsibility of running a playhouse. Later the same year, a second playhouse opened at the archery ground at Newington Butts. Fortunately for Burbage, this establishment never really thrived, not even when Shakespeare's own company, the Chamberlain's Men, performed *The Taming of the Shrew* and *Titus Andronicus* there in the 1590s. Newington Butts Playhouse never matched the success of the Theatre, owing to 'the tediousness of the way' across St George's Fields, and by 1599 it was 'nothing but a memory'.[10]

The Theatre inevitably attracted attacks from the Mayor of London, who condemned it as a threat to civic order and public safety, and drew fire from fundamentalist preachers. Running costs and constant litigation made it unlikely Burbage would ever pay off his debts, but first and most pressing of all his concerns was the opening of another rival theatre in the form of the Curtain in the autumn of 1576. As authors knew to their cost, there was no such thing as intellectual copyright in Elizabethan London and this freedom extended from drama and song to bricks and mortar. In an age of imitation, it was inevitable that another aspiring impresario would soon produce a pirated version of Burbage's pioneering structure.

The Curtain popped up like a mushroom alongside the Theatre, impudently slap-bang in the same liberty, in the same parish, in another part of the same old Holywell Priory as the Theatre itself. Erected on the site of the former prioress's wing, the Curtain was built on land which had belonged to a draper called Maurice Long, who bought it for £60 and then sold it for £200 on 23 August 1571 to Sir William Alleyn, then Lord Mayor of London. The land was known as 'the curtain', after the old curtain wall of the city fortifications, and this became the name of the theatre, with a sign hanging outside depicting a curtain.[11]

The diarist John Aubrey later described the Curtain as 'a kind of nursery or obscure playhouse, somewhere in the suburbs' and recalled that Ben Jonson 'acted and wrote, but both ill, at the Green Curtain'.[12] Despite Aubrey's comments, the Curtain later proved to be one of the most successful theatres in London, resisting all efforts to close it, but at its inception it represented a real threat to Burbage. Centuries later, its name lingers on in Curtain Road, between Old Street and Great Eastern Street.

These two very different theatres had two things in common: namely the continuing antipathy of the Lord Mayor and the damage to their incomes when forced to close due to outbreaks of plague, or the threat of plague. This was another familiar obstacle to Burbage's ambitions. The Corporation of London had already used the fear of plague as a method of shutting down the players' inns in the city and driving the players out of town. Now the same proclamations were being issued to refrain from playing further afield. The clerics, meanwhile, straining for another excuse to have the theatres closed, resorted to holy writ for evidence that theatres actually *caused* plague. In a sermon at St Paul's Cross on 3 November 1577, one preacher declared that the . . .

. . . sins of the people had brought down God's wrath
upon them in the Plague . . .

Look but upon the Common Playes in London and see
the multitude that flocketh to them, and followeth them;
beholde the sumptuous Theatre houses a continual monument of London's prodigalitie and folly . . . the cause of
the plague is sinne, and the cause of sinne are plays; therefore the cause of plagues are playes.[13]

The preacher made no reference to the fact that large crowds
were considered to contribute to the spread of plague. If
this was the case, the same would have been true of the
gathering at St Paul's Cross! But nobody seemed particularly
concerned about the consequences of a crowd gathering to
listen to a sermon.

Burbage's fortunes took another dive in 1578 when he fell
out with his brother-in-law, John Brayne, after Brayne
refused to contribute to the expenses of the Theatre, although
he still expected a share of the profits. The whole of his
original share had been spent in the building, but Burbage
still required Brayne's contribution of working expenses to
remain in operation. The dispute between the two became
so bitter that they went to court and the friction between the
partners led to violent disputes. On one occasion, after a
heated exchange in a scrivener's shop, Burbage punched
Brayne and they 'went together by the ears' so fiercely that
a bystander could hardly prise them apart.[14] Eventually, the
law found in favour of Burbage, and caused Brayne to be
bound to him in a bond of £200, that he would pay his share
of the expenses or forfeit the bond. But this was only the
first in a series of bitter legal battles between Burbage and
Brayne which would drag on until 1591, five years after
Brayne's death.

On 17 September 1579 Burbage mortgaged the Theatre to John Hyde, probably because the heavy interest rate on property was a drain on his resources, particularly after closures caused by outbreaks of plague and the withdrawal of Brayne's contributions to expenses. Burbage remained owner and manager, and fought to keep the Theatre going in the face of debt and interference from the Lord Mayor and the London Corporation. The end of the latest plague outbreak gave him new courage as greater crowds than ever hastened across the fields to Holywell, but they inevitably brought noise and nuisance in their wake. So popular did the Theatre become that Burbage and Brayne found themselves summoned to the Middlesex Assizes on 21 February 1579. The pair were charged with 'bringing together *unlawful* assemblies to hear and to see certain playes or interludes at a certain place called the Theatre at Holywell in the county of Middlesex, by reason of which great affrays, assaults, tumults, and quasi-insurrections and divers other enormities were perpetrated to the danger of the lives of divers good subjects against the form of the Statute.'[15]

It is interesting that Brayne is mentioned first, but as a businessman with an interest in the Theatre it seems that he took precedence over Burbage, a mere manager. The wording also implies that Brayne was not only responsible for but involved in the productions, in a capacity as a performer. Sadly there is no record of the decision after this summons, but it is likely that Brayne and Burbage were bound over to keep the peace and presumably the cost of the summons was met by funds from the Theatre or their own pockets.

When London was hit by an earthquake on 6 April 1580, the authorities were quick to seize on this natural calamity as an act of divine retribution. 'At the play-houses, the people

ran forth surprised with great astonishment,' wrote one
eyewitness. 'Many were sore crushed and bruised' during a
dash for the exit.[16] Meanwhile a balladeer admonished good
people to:

> Come from the Play
> The House will fall so people say
> The earth quakes, let us haste awaye![17]

According to the preacher Abraham Fleming (1552–1607), 'the
great earthquake threw down chimneys in Shoreditch', while
another writer claimed that it 'shaked not only the scenical
Theatre, but the great stage and theatre of the whole land.'[18]

The Lord Mayor of London took the opportunity to tell
the Privy Council that the earthquake was all Burbage's fault.
On 12 April 1580, he declared that: 'the players of plays which
are used at the Theatre and other such places are a *very super-
fluous sort of men* . . . and their exercise of those plays is a great
hindrance of the service of God, who hath with His mightie
hande so lately admonished us of our earnest repentance.'[19]

Fortunately, the damage sustained by the Theatre was
little more than a crack in the façade. Burbage the joiner
had done an excellent job building his theatre and not a
stage or galley fell, not even a chimneypot in Burbage's
house on Holywell Street, though many chimneys fell in
other parts of London. Another disaster, two years later,
lent further credibility to the Puritan theory that God was
showing his displeasure. On 13 January 1582, the stage at
Paris Garden collapsed during a bear-baiting, killing several
people and injuring many. This disaster was taken as
another divine judgement against pleasure-seekers and
sightseers and increased the murmurings against the players
in the liberties.[20]

The Theatre may have escaped damage during the earthquake, but damage of another sort arrived with a particularly virulent outbreak of plague the following month. On
13 May 1580, an order of the Privy Council banned all plays
in and around the city until the following Michaelmas
(29 September), by which time it was believed that 'the
sickness' would have ceased.

Poor James Burbage faced the prospect of five months'
unemployment but still had to pay rent and the interest on his
loans. His creditors were clamouring at the door while his
actors were asking for advances, and Ellen Burbage demanded
to know how exactly she was expected to feed her family. All
this, in the knowledge that if only he could be left in peace to
get on with rehearsing and performing new plays, all would
be well. Left to his own devices, Burbage could supply the
eager demands of his audiences and gain an income sufficient
to pay off his debts and make him a free man. But fighting
regular minor battles against familiar foes was one thing; being
up against the Privy Council quite another. A Privy Council
interdict and the threat of plague were too much even for a
man of Burbage's calibre. The only solution was once again
to take the Earl of Leicester's Men out on tour. And there was
consolation to be found in the fact that he and his company
did at least perform at Court that Christmas, on Boxing Day.

A more cheerful development saw Burbage's son, Richard,
follow him onto the stage. In 1583, both profession and actor
were still young, but over the course of the next thirty-five
years Richard Burbage would elevate his craft, and English
drama, to the highest level. As a man of the theatre, taking
pride in his son's obvious talent must have been both a
pleasure and a consolation for James Burbage. Richard probably began his training as a chorister, one of the Children of
the Chapel selected to sing for the Queen, and may well have

been a child actor before joining his father's company, the Earl of Leicester's Men. Handsome, charming and talented, Richard was the apple of his father's eye, and Burbage coached him with his expertise and skill.

James had given both his sons the best education possible, and his eldest son, Cuthbert, became a lawyer. Cuthbert does not appear on any records as an actor, so perhaps the stage did not suit him, but it is likely that he stood in as an understudy and an extra when required. In a sense, the two sons represented both sides of James's character: Cuthbert the sensible and responsible businessman, and Richard the handsome, charming performer. In times to come, the Burbage sons would make a formidable team.

Meanwhile, Burbage had to brace himself for another onslaught by the authorities. In 1583, the Corporation made another of its periodic attempts to expel the players from London and to pull down all the playhouses and dicing-houses in the liberties. A jeremiad from Philip Stubbes is a typical example of the Puritan attack on theatre. In the *Anatomie of Abuses* (*1583*) Stubbes describes plays as 'invented by the Devil, practised by the Heathen Gentiles, and dedicated to their false gods', on the grounds that the subject matter of both tragedy and comedy is sin. 'Theatres and Curtains are Venus Palaces. I beseech all players and founders of plays and interludes to leave off that cursed kind of life, and give themselves to honest exercise.'[21]

On 3 May 1583 the Lord Mayor of London, Sir Edward Osborne, wrote to Sir Francis Walsingham (1532–90), principal secretary to the Queen, requesting powers to destroy the theatres. In a desperate attempt to see the theatres closed, the Lord Mayor even claimed that the Theatre represented a threat to public safety because it had become 'so weak a building' after the earthquake.[22]

As it turned out, the Lord Mayor had appealed to the wrong man. Far from instructing the Privy Council to destroy the theatres, Sir Francis Walsingham had a completely different approach. As the Queen's private secretary and self-appointed head of the secret service, Walsingham was an expert in exploiting statecraft to promote his own agenda, and the fate of the players was to be no exception. Sir Francis suggested to the Queen that, instead of summoning players to perform for her when she pleased, the time had come to form her own royal company. The Queen already had the right to choose child choristers to sing in her chapels and she was entitled to hire any workman or craftsman she needed. Now, on Walsingham's recommendation, the Queen decided to select twelve men from the existing acting companies. They were to be known as the Queen's Men and would be the Queen's own servants and grooms of the Royal Chamber and wear a red livery. Sir Francis Walsingham plucked the most talented performers in London for the new troupe, including Earl of Leicester's Man Robert Wilson, 'for a quicke, delicate, refined, extemporal wit', and Richard Tarlton the clown, since 'for a wondrous plentiful pleasant extemporal wit, he was the wonder of his time'.[23] Once again, James Burbage, a former joiner, saw his actors rescued by patronage from the highest in the land. James Burbage himself was not selected for the Queen's Men, perhaps because he was ageing, and was no longer the 'glass of fashion and the mould of form'[24] or because he was best suited to his existing role, managing the Theatre so that the Queen's Men might make it their official headquarters.

During the spring of 1583, the Queen's Men took off on an extensive tour of the country, performing in Bristol, Shrewsbury, Gloucester, Leicester, Nottingham and Aldeburgh. The Queen's Men did not always cover themselves in glory while on tour, as the following anecdote reveals. While the Queen's Men were playing the Red Lion in Norwich on 15 June 1583, a dispute over payment arose between the servant of a Mr Wynsdon and the player John Singer, who, wearing a black doublet and a fake beard, was taking the money on the door. Tarlton and another actor, John Bentley, who was playing a duke, jumped off the stage and Bentley broke the offender's head with the hilt of his sword. The man fled, pursued by Singer with a broadsword which he grabbed off the stage, and by Henry Browne, a servant of Sir William Paston. Both of them struck Wynsdon's servant, and one of the blows – it was not certain whose – proved mortal.[25]

Despite this incident, the Queen's Men blazed a trail across England before making their triumphant return to London and continuing to play the liberties. But their Royal Appointment did not render them immune from attacks by the Lord Mayor. Over the following year, the Lord Mayor pressed ahead with his plans 'for the suppressing and pulling down of the Theatre and the Curtain',[26] justifying his efforts on the grounds of a threat to public order. Evidence came from sources such as the *Report of Sundry Broiles in Whitsontide 8th June 1584* by the Recorder of London, William Fleetwood. 'At the time of the plays there lay a prentice sleeping upon the grass and one Charles alias Grostock did turn the toe upon the belly of the same prentice; whereupon the apprentice start up, and after words they fell to plain blows.' Two days later, on 10 June 1584, 'one Browne, a serving man in a blue coat, a shifting fellow, having a perilous wit of his own, intending a spoil if he could have brought it to pass, did at Theatre door quarrel with certain poor boys, handicraft prentices, and struck some of them; and lastly he with his sword wounded and

maimed one of the boys upon the left hand.'[27] Events swiftly
spiralled out of control and developed into a full-blown riot
involving over one hundred apprentices.

Although Burbage could not be held responsible for what
went on beyond the stage door, as the perceived ringleader
he was duly summoned to appear before the Lord Mayor.
When he refused, the Lord Mayor promptly had Burbage
arrested, referring to him as 'a stubborn fellow'.[28] Burbage
did himself no favours in court, losing his temper and
threatening to assault the Lord Mayor, only composing
himself after the Lord Mayor warned him that he faced
gaol for contempt.

The conclusion to this case is unknown but it must have
been a terrifying experience for Burbage. Although he had
seen a number of his players elevated to the rank of Queen's
Men, he was once again faced with the prospect of losing his
beloved Theatre. Financial ruin could not be far behind. And
yet, somehow, the Theatre survived, and the actors were not
banished. What could have happened to have given the
Theatre a stay of execution?

A desperate plea to the Lord Mayor from the players
themselves may provide a clue. Dating from the autumn of
1584, this letter is signed by 'her Majesty's Poor Players' and
consists of an appeal to give some 'tender consideration' to
their plea to perform in London, the 'season of the year being
past' when they could earn money by performing at any of
the grand country houses outside London. Concluding with
the promise 'whereby we shall cease the continual troubling
of your lordships' if their request is granted, they sign off
graciously praying 'for your lordships honor health and
happiness long to continue'.[29]

This letter must have made something of an impact, for,
after turning down the petition immediately, the Lord

Mayor and Privy Council eventually agreed to let the players perform in London if they observed the following conditions:

> That they hold them content with playing in private houses, at weddings, etc., without public assemblie . . .
>
> That they play not openly till the whole death in London [from plague] have been by 20 days under 50 a weeke, nor longer than it shall so continue. That no playes on the Sabbath.
>
> That no playing be in the dark, nor continue any such time but as any of the audience may return to their dwellings in London before sunset or at least before it be dark.
>
> That the Queen's players only be tolerated and of them their number and certain names to be notified in your Lordships letters to the Lord Mayor and to the Justices of Middlesex and Surrey.[30]

These rulings, and the Queen's decision to have her own troupe of actors, meant that a very different list of performances before the Queen was drawn up that Christmas. None of the Earl of Leicester's Men were chosen, unless they were appearing as individuals. It is tempting to suspect the hand of Sir Francis Walsingham in all this. What better way to regulate the emerging theatrical profession than to select players by Royal Appointment? The Earl of Leicester, Sir Robert Dudley, had once been the Queen's favourite, but his star was already waning following his second marriage, against the Queen's wishes, to Lady Lettice Knollys. What better way to humiliate the Earl of Leicester than by breaking up his troupe of players?

Leicester's loss would prove to be the making of the Queen's Men. Between the years 1583 and 1588 the Queen's

Men toured extensively, making a memorable appearance at Stratford-upon-Avon in 1586, when they played the Bear and received twenty shillings, the largest reward players had ever received in the town, from the bailiff, Thomas Barber. In a night full of incident a bench was broken and the city fathers had to lay out sixteen shillings to get it repaired.[31] Perhaps they were giving a particularly vigorous performance of *The Famous Victories of Henry V,* designed to whip up patriotic sentiments in the advent of a Spanish invasion. Was the young William Shakespeare in the crowd at the Bear, watching the play? Did this performance, the best travelling show he had ever seen, harden his resolve to shake the dust of Stratford off his feet and head for the bright lights of London? By all accounts the Queen's Men were a stunning company, remembered with awe by the next generation of actors such as Thomas Heywood, who looked back at the likes of William Knell, John Bentley, Toby Mills, Robert Wilson and John Laneham as giants of the past.

Meanwhile, back in London, the Theatre was proving so successful that in 1585 James Burbage decided to extend the lease. The new lease, for another twenty-one years, was drawn up in April and among the conditions was a free seat in the gallery for landlord Giles Alleyn, whenever he wanted to visit. However, not only was Alleyn unmoved by this offer, but he was distinctly unimpressed with the state of the Theatre itself. Refusing to accept that Burbage had spent £200 improving the property, Alleyn wanted another lease with different conditions more favourable to himself, including a share of the profits and raising the rent from £14 to £24 a year.[32] Alleyn also stipulated that if he did add ten years to the lease, then the use of the Theatre for playing purposes should be restricted to five more years. Burbage might retain the lease for the last five years and use it for any other purpose but *not as a theatre*. It is difficult to understand what the motive might have been for this extraordinary demand. Burbage was being presented with an impossible lease which involved paying a higher rent, giving Giles Alleyn a share of the profits and finally, insultingly, not being able to use the Theatre for the purpose for which it had been intended for the final five years. Understandably, Burbage refused to agree to Alleyn's conditions. This situation drifted on, unresolved and would eventually lead to a *grand finale* of bitter litigation in 1598.

A year later, in 1586, Burbage's brother-in-law John Brayne died. Brayne had no children and, despite his legal disputes with his partner, had always treated Burbage's children as if they were his own. On his deathbed, Brayne had promised that Burbage's children were the heirs to his estate. However, after Brayne's death it emerged that his affairs were in turmoil and he had bequeathed all his effects to three business associates. Nothing had been mentioned of these three men during Brayne's lifetime, but the funeral baked meats were scarcely cold before his creditors were petitioning for their share of the estate. Worse was to come: part of this share of the estate was the Theatre. Poor Margaret Brayne, newly widowed, had to take legal action against James Burbage to ensure that she received some part of her husband's estate. The case eventually saw Burbage going to court against his own sister-in-law and dragged on in Chancery until 1591. The case left Burbage experiencing the wear and tear of legal proceedings, with the time, money, effort and anxiety of litigation all taking their toll on his health and strength. The proceedings also resulted in some unedifying scenes such as the following incident from the winter of 1590.

One evening in November, Mrs Brayne appeared at the Theatre with a group of her supporters and demanded her share of the money. James Burbage retorted that Mrs Brayne was a 'murdering whore' and would get no money here. Then his son, Richard Burbage, emerged armed with a broomstick and started laying into Mrs Brayne's supporters. They might have come for a moiety of the takings, said Richard, but he'd shown a moiety of wit by sending them packing.[33] This incident does not reflect well upon James Burbage, and may be one of the reasons why he fell out with his leading actor, 'Ned' Alleyn, who took Mrs Brayne's side in the dispute and later deserted the Queen's Men for a new company. It certainly provides some idea of the rough and tumble of the Elizabethan stage, a tough trade with little room for compassion, as the following developments will indicate.

Fearing that he would lose the Theatre, Burbage had already approached Henry Lanman, owner of the Curtain, in 1585 and asked his rival to enter into a reciprocal arrangement, so that the Queen's Men could perform at the Curtain if Burbage and Lanman pooled the profits. Lanman agreed and thus the Curtain, once a feared rival, became a sanctuary for Burbage's company. Lanman benefited too, as audiences flocked to watch the Queen's Men, the most successful company in London, play at his Curtain. Within months, however, another threat emerged, in the form of serious competition from yet another new theatre, known as the Rose. The opening of the Rose Theatre on Bankside in the autumn of 1587 added a further burden to James Burbage's portfolio of woes.

The original 'Rose' was a tavern,[34] 'built upon a veritable rose garden lying between the King's highway next the water of Thames on the north, against a tenement called the Rose on the other side, and a tenement sometimes the Lady Stratford's on the west side and against Maiden Lane

on the south'.[35] The Rose Tavern also possessed a less salu-
brious reputation, as it was not only a tavern but a brothel,
one of many operating in the traditional red-light district
of Bankside. This tradition was maintained when the new
proprietors opened a bawdy-house next door to the theatre.

The Rose was the brainchild of Philip Henslowe, a
tradesman, and John Cholmley, a grocer. In their contract,
Henslowe undertook to have 'the said playhouse with all
furniture thereunto belonging set up with as much expedi-
ency as may be' by John Griggs, carpenter, while Cholmley
undertook to bear any further costs in maintaining the premises and to pay Henslowe the sum of £816 in quarterly instal-
ments. In return for this, Cholmley would take half the
profits arising from 'any play or playes that shall be showen
or played there or otherwise howsoever' and had the right
to sell victuals to playgoers from the small house where he
lived close by, in Maiden Lane.[36]

The practical tone of this contract indicates Henslowe's
pragmatic, businesslike character. Far from being a man
of the theatre, Philip Henslowe was a dyer by trade, with
a sideline in pawnbrolling and prostitution. Before
opening the Rose, his theatrical experience consisted of
running the bear-baiting at Paris Garden, and his greatest
ambition was to become the Queen's bear warden. A
comical figure, to be seen bustling about Bankside with
his account book tucked under his arm, Henslowe was
really London's first impresario. The Rose was built as
an investment, and it was with a similar approach that
Henslowe put money into producing plays. A hard-
headed businessman with a good eye for detail, Henslowe's
greatest legacy is his ledger or 'diary', begun in 1592,
when the Rose was extended to accommodate the Lord
Admiral's Men. In this diary, Henslowe recorded the

minutiae of his financial transactions and the day-to-day management of the Rose. It is thanks to Henslowe that the world knows that Edward Alleyn's Tamburlaine strode across the boards in crimson velvet breeches and a coat trimmed with copper lace, and that if an actor showed up drunk for a performance, he had ten shillings docked from his wages.[37] A peep at Henslowe's extensive list of props makes entertaining reading, with props to cover every eventuality including: 'i rocke, i cage, i tombe, i Hell mouth, i bedstead, i heifer for the play of Phaeton, i golden fleece; i wooden hatchet; i leather hatchet, i lionskin; i bearskin; Neptune fork and garland; Cupids bow, & quiver; the clothe of the Sun & Moone, i boar's head & Cerberus iii heads, ii moss banks, & i snake, ii coffins; i lion; i great horse; i wheel and frame in the Siege of London; i Pope's mitre; iii imperial crowns; i black dog; i cauldron for the Jew.[38] The 'Jew' in this case is a reference to Barabas, eponymous protagonist of *The Jew of Malta,* who accidentally trips and falls into his own cauldron and is boiled alive.

Fortunately, despite Burbage's misgivings, relations between the Theatre and the Rose were cordial enough, although they might have been very different if Burbage, seeking a replacement for the Theatre, had chosen to build a new one alongside the Rose. As it was, by the following year, 1588, James Burbage was a worried man, in danger of losing everything he had worked so hard to achieve. His beloved Theatre was mortgaged to the hilt and he was involved in a debilitating legal battle with his sister-in-law, the widow Brayne. In failing health, it seemed only a matter of time before he succumbed to destitution and death. Had it not been for the support of his sons, the stoical Cuthbert with his sharp legal brain and the talented actor Richard, James Burbage would have had nothing to live for.

But then, from out of nowhere, Burbage's saviour appeared in the form of that rare individual, an actor who could write and a writer who could act. A young man of some twenty-four years, both handsome and intelligent, armed with a formidable work ethic, a man who would profit from the theatre boom and make English drama the envy of the world. Like Burbage, this youngster came from Warwickshire and was the son of a tradesman. Like Burbage, he was not a university man, although he had been equipped with a first-class classical education courtesy of the local grammar school. Unlike Burbage, he already possessed a fascination with human behaviour that enabled him to entertain the most ribald of audiences while penetrating the mysteries of the human heart. This was Burbage's secret weapon. This was William Shakespeare.

THE UPSTART CROW

With his Tiger's heart wrapt in a player's hide . . .
Robert Greene, *A Groatsworth of Wit*

On a hot August night in Southwark in the dog days of 1592, a dying man dragged himself over to the table in his stinking garret and tried to write. Considered handsome in his youth, still with a distinctive long, red beard, he had long since lost his looks to drink. Dripping with cold sweat, shivering with ague and labouring under a colossal hangover after an afternoon bingeing on Rhenish wine (a sweet German white), he tried to string together the words which had come so easily before. This was the only way he knew to get money for more drink. He was lonely and isolated, as almost everyone he knew had left London to avoid a particularly virulent outbreak of plague. Incubated by a hot, dry summer, this epidemic had closed the theatres and seen the cancellation of his latest play, bringing more hardship. But at least his publisher and his eager readership awaited his latest efforts, if he could only write something, and he had never disappointed them before.

Romances such as his big hit, *Pandosto*, sensational true-crime stories of cut-purses and coney-catchers and other London lowlifes, even dramas, despite his hatred of actors, had always sprung freely from his pen. Until now, when the letters squirmed meaninglessly as his forgotten Greek beneath the quill. He had degrees from both universities, a bachelor's from Cambridge and a master's from Oxford, but now he could scarcely write his own name. And yet this name had been a good one in its time: Robert Greene, Master of Arts, a man who could truly claim to be the first professional writer in London. 'The King of the Paper Stage' according to his publisher, Henry Chettle. *Look at me now*. Crippled with oedema which puffed up his ankles, hallucinating with pain, Greene tossed aside his latest manuscript, a pamphlet about the London underworld, and suddenly, from the depths of despair, inspiration struck. None of this was his fault, he reasoned, with the vicious logic of the alcoholic. This illness, this failure, was all down to one man, and thanks to him he, the great Robert Greene, was about to die destitute. As if dipping his pen in vitriol, Greene decided that his famous last words would be a warning to his few remaining friends. A caveat to Thomas Nashe, with whom he had shared that over-convivial lunch of pickled herrings and Rhenish wine, for which his kidneys would never forgive him. A caution to his writing partner, Thomas Lodge, and Christopher Marlowe, the presiding genius of the London stage, to watch their backs. Warming to his theme, Greene set about his work and his hangover, his mortal illness, his sweats and his bloated fingers were forgotten as the magic returned, the words poured forth, and he prepared to destroy the reputation of the presumptuous young newcomer who had brought him to this sorry state. This impudent young dog had filled Henslowe's Rose theatre in the weeks before it was closed by plague. Every seat in the galleries to the last inch of standing room packed to capacity and for why? To watch, not Greene's *Friar Bacon and Friar Bungay*, or even his *Orlando Furioso,* but an indifferent history, a tedious historical epic entitled *Harey the Sixth*! What if this new play had broken Henslowe's box-office records by increasing takings to £3.16s.8d for fifteen performances? It was rude, crude fare, a farrago of scraps cobbled together in the style of Marlowe and Kyd, the work of a pretentious young actor from the provinces.

A caricature of Robert Greene in his shroud, vilifying Shakespeare as an 'upstart crow', with a 'Tiger's heart wrapt in a player's hide'.

Greene's pen scratched away with a will. His greatest work, he now realised, had been that in-depth reportage of London's criminal underworld exposing the tricks and cheats of rogues and thieves. Now he had a last chance to expose

the corrupt workings of the London stage, and warn his
fellow authors before it was too late. And there was an
underlying motive, too, to settle scores.

He would warn them all, all three of them: Nashe, 'that
young Juvenal, that biting satirist'; Marlowe, 'that famous gracer
of tragedians'; and Lodge, another writer living hand-to-
mouth. By his own misery, he would warn them of the evils
of actors, 'those puppets that speak from our mouths, those
antics [fools] garnished in our colours – trust them not!'[1]

And then he went on the attack.

For there is an upstart crow, beautified with our feathers,
that with his 'Tiger's heart wrapt in a player's hide'
supposes he is as well able to bombast out a blank verse
as the best of you; and being an absolute *Johannes factotum,*
is in his own conceit the only Shake-scene in a country.
O that I might intreat your rare wits to be employed in
more profitable courses, and let those apes imitate your
past excellence, and never more acquaint them with your
admired inventions . . . seek you better masters, for it is
pity men of such rare writs should be subject to the pleasure
of such rude grooms.[2]

Greene died on 3 September, and his bitter character assassination of the 'upstart crow' was included in a posthumous
collection entitled *A Groatsworth of Wit bought with a million
of Repentaunce* [*sic*], a deathbed confession for his wicked
ways. Accused of writing it themselves, and eager to maintain
their working relationships with William Shakespeare, the
subject of this attack, Nashe and Marlowe were keen to
distance themselves from such allegations. In the fullness of
time, this letter would have little impact on the career of
England's greatest dramatist. If it reveals anything at all apart

from the ramblings of a bitter and twisted dying man, the letter demonstrates the impact that the 'upstart crow' made upon the English stage. Who was this 'Shake-scene' who Greene credited with destroying his own career and stealing everyone's ideas? Where did that striking description of a tiger's heart wrapped in a player's hide originate? The quotation 'O tiger's heart wrapt in a woman's hide!' is a line from a history play entitled *Harey the Sixth,* now better known as the *Henry VI* series. As to the identity of its author, step forward William Shakespeare . . .

Greene's reference to the 'upstart crow' is the first documented mention of Shakespeare as part of the London theatrical world, clearly referring to him both as an actor, with his 'player's hide', and as a writer, a predatory 'tiger', stealing other men's ideas. But there is plenty of evidence to suggest that Shakespeare had been in London for at least four years by this time, learning his trade and honing his skills. In an age where copyright was unknown, the reference to apelike imitation is unsurprising. Shakespeare was truly the first example of Eliot's remark that while immature poets imitate, mature poets steal, and good poets make it into something better, or at least something different.[3]

Given the family links with Stratford-upon-Avon, and Shakespeare's obvious interest in the theatre, it would not be surprising if young Shakespeare made James Burbage his first port of call when he came to London. Most scholars agree that Shakespeare arrived in London at some point around 1588. Although Greene's splenetic attack dates from 1592, many factors suggest that he was already in London and working with James Burbage and the Queen's Men four years earlier. These arguments are based on the content of the dramas performed by the Queen's Men, written evidence in the form of documents and records and a variety of theories about what brought Shakespeare to London in the first place. The most obvious explanation was that Shakespeare joined the Queen's Men, or one of the rival companies such as Lord Strange's Men, and served an apprenticeship as a touring player before being promoted to the Queen's Men once his rare combination of gifts had been recognised.

The theory that Shakespeare came to London as a player, intending to further his stage career, is the most persuasive, although over the centuries many others have emerged. Shakespeare's extensive legal vocabulary, 'his quiddits . . . his quillets, his cases . . . his recognizances',[4] suggest that he may have been employed as a lawyer's clerk, or supported John Shakespeare in the complex lawsuit he was pursuing at that time. Given his education and literacy, it is more than possible that Shakespeare had been a schoolmaster, or private tutor to a noble family. There is also the enduring myth, propagated by Shakespeare's first editor Nicholas Rowe and by the antiquarian Anthony à Wood, that Shakespeare was on the run from the Stratford beadles after poaching deer from Charlecote Park, home of Sir Thomas Lucy, and then penning a ballad poking fun at Sir Thomas.[5] While this is a persuasive story, it has little basis in reality as deer were not kept on the Charlecote Estate until the eighteenth century.

John Aubrey, that loveable old gossip, conjectured that Shakespeare's first employment in London was 'in a very mean Rank' and that he was 'there received into the playhouse'[6] as a servant. Samuel Johnson believed that Shakespeare 'owed his rise in life and his introduction to the theatre, to his accidentally holding the horse of a gentleman at the door of the theatre on his first arriving in London; his appearance led to enquiry and subsequent patronage'.[7] Johnson's theory was that Shakespeare was such a good groom he made a name for himself looking after people's horses while they watched the play. Since riding across the fields to Shoreditch was the easiest way to get to the Theatre, this theory is an appealing one. Edmond Malone, one of the earlier Shakespeare scholars, suggested that the young actor's first job was that of call-boy (telling the actors how soon they would be required on stage) and prompt.[8] These are all good theories, appealing as they do to the old theatrical myth of the boy from nowhere who goes from understudy to leading man overnight, but with one failing. If Shakespeare possessed demonstrable acting skills, and had already toured with companies of players, what on earth would he be doing as a groom or a call-boy? Young Shakespeare left a wife and three children behind in Stratford, so it seems unlikely that he arrived in London upon a whim. Someone, or something, was waiting for him. The most likely candidate is a job in the theatre. Or rather, at the Theatre. Like the majority of actors and writers, then and now, the young William Shakespeare knew that London was the only place to be. The work was there. The theatres were there. While theatrical agents in the modern sense did not exist, there were many rich and influential benefactors, and that most influential of all patrons, Her Majesty Queen Elizabeth. The most likely explanation is that Shakespeare encountered an established troupe of players on tour in Stratford, recognised his vocation, and fell in with them. He may have served a few weeks as a groom or a call-boy, but it is far more likely that such a company immediately recognised his talents and were only too happy to offer him a place.

What did the youthful Shakespeare look like? John Aubrey, born too late to have met Shakespeare himself but relying on anecdote, tells us he 'possessed a very readie and pleasant smooth Witt' and was 'a handsome well shap't man',[9] characteristics which would be of great value in a young actor. Young Will Shakespeare was also congenial and popular, and could mix with all classes, an essential skill for a writer. His attractive combination of youthful good looks, acting talent, genial nature and work ethic made him an asset to any company he might wish to join. Sadly, these very qualities would also provoke jealousy from his contemporaries, particularly the bitter and twisted Robert Greene.

John Aubrey tells us that Shakespeare lived in Shoreditch. If Shakespeare's family had known the Burbages in Stratford, then it is understandable that he lived near them in Holywell Street, close to the Theatre and the Curtain. Tradesmen habitually lived near their place of work and Holywell Street was the actors' street, and the street of the authors who wrote for them. The most famous resident of Holywell Street was Richard Tarlton, jester, tumbler, fencing master, and one of the founder members of the Queen's Men. The story goes that Tarlton was spotted herding swine in a field in Shropshire by one of the Earl of Leicester's Men. This player was so taken with Tarlton's 'happy unhappy remarks'[10] that he brought him to London, and Tarlton rejected his trade of swine-keeping to become the most famous jester at Queen Elizabeth's Court. This account of Tarlton's humble origins seems somewhat romanticised, as he was enough of a gentleman to be a master swordsman and the owner of a pub, but it enhanced his appeal. When the Queen was down in the dumps, it was Tarlton who could 'undumpish her at his pleasure' and some courtiers would even go to Tarlton to discern the Queen's mood before approaching her. 'In a word, he told the Queen more of her faults than most of her Chaplains, and cured her melancholy better than most of her physicians.'[11] With his distinctive features, his squint and his flat nose, Tarlton's appearance was so comical that he had only to stick his head out from the tiring-house curtains for the audience to fall about. When he teamed up with fellow player Robert Wilson, a more scholarly wit, the overall effect must have been that of a Tudor Morecambe and Wise. Like Yorick, for whom Tarlton was the original, he lit up every room. He was 'a fellow of infinite jest, of most excellent fancy'. When Hamlet speaks of 'your flashes of merriment, that were wont to set the table on a roar', it sounds like a personal tribute to the funniest man in London.[12]

Another actor, Gabriel or 'Gab' Spenser, lived near Tarlton in Hog Lane, blissfully unaware of the terrible fate which awaited him, while a little further away, in the tiny liberty of Norton Folgate, dwelled the playwright Christopher Marlowe. 'Kit' Marlowe was also destined for tragedy. Occasionally sharing Marlowe's chambers and quite possibly his bed was the dramatist Thomas Kyd, author of *The Spanish Tragedy* or *Hieronimo is Mad Again* (1582). Not far from Marlowe and Kyd, also in Norton Folgate, lived Robert Greene, one of the first generation of university men attempting to live by the pen. Greene considered actors beneath contempt, but when his Falstaffian tavern bills and perpetual hangovers began to nudge out his talent, he turned to the theatre himself and had plays produced at the Rose. In the course of time, these three writers would have a massive influence upon Shakespeare's own work, and each in different ways – Kyd for structure and narrative, Marlowe for tragedy and his 'mighty line', and Greene, despite his later hostility towards Shakespeare, for humour. Near Greene lived Thomas Watson, a poet now remembered only for his friendship with Christopher Marlowe and his influence upon other writers. Watson's translations from Seneca inspired many plays but none of his own have survived.

The reputation of Shoreditch had not improved significantly since James Burbage first moved there in the 1570s and remained lurid even by the rumbustious standards of

Elizabethan London. This was an early version of 'Bohemia', although it would be four centuries before 'bohemian' would be used to describe the artists' lifestyle. According to the university wit Thomas Nashe, Shoreditch, with its beery alleyways and dung-filled overflowing ditches, was a neighbourhood where actors and writers rubbed shoulders with 'poore Scholers and soldiers, pox-ridden prostitutes, fortune tellers, cobblers and stocking menders'.[13] Shoreditch provided Shakespeare with a rich seam of authentic lowlife which he mined for years to come. His tavern scenes ring with authenticity for he had seen it all at first hand, 'gaming . . . drinking, fencing, swearing, quarrelling, drabbing [whoring]'.[14] Taverns reeking of stale ale, furnished with but the bare necessities of drinking – a table, a stool, a piss pot – were the places where men came to meet friends, to quarrel, to while away the afternoon and murder a rainy day. The tavern was the busy man's recreation, the idle man's business, the melancholy man's sanctuary, the stranger's welcome, the Inns-of-Court man's entertainment and the scholar's diversion. It was an institution devoted to the study of sparkling wits, and the book was a cup of Canary wine, which filled the brain with 'nimble, fiery and delectable shapes', inspired 'excellent wit' and warmed the blood. Why else would Falstaff vow that 'if I had a thousand [sons], the first humane principle I would teach them should be to forswear thin potations and to addict themselves to sack'.[15]

Taverns were masculine preserves, but not entirely devoid of female company. The doxies, hussies and harlots who hung about the drinkers provided inspiration for warm-hearted Mistress Quickly and bawdy Doll Tearsheet. A place to see life and watch the world unfold, taverns provided Shakespeare with a lifetime of material and some remarkable specimens of human nature.

Of course, not every Londoner viewed the effects of alcohol in the same fashion. The killjoy Philip Stubbes in his *Anatomie of Abuses* condemned drunkenness as 'a horrible vice, and too much used in England. You shall see them all sitting at the wine and good-ale all the day long, yea, all the night long too, so long as any money is left; swilling, filling and carousing from one to another, till never a one can speak a ready word . . . how they stut and stammer, stagger and reel to and fro like madmen.'[16]

For all his lively depictions of tavern life, Shakespeare was no hell-raiser. Aubrey noted that, while he was sociable, Shakespeare was not the type to be found in his cups every night. 'He wouldn't be debauched,' said Aubrey, 'and if invited to, writ he was in pain.'[17] (Debauchery, in this context, referred to carousing rather than whoring.) After a swift half-goblet, the young dramatist was away, hastening back to his lodgings to write the next act. This was a time when plays were written, and rewritten, at great speed the night before a performance. Topical references would be inserted and roles enlarged, shrunk or even deleted to reflect an actor's availability. Writing for the stage had yet to become respectable employment, if indeed it ever has, and playwrights were regarded as artisans, producing scripts as quickly as possible. This was no time to be oversensitive or precious. Shakespeare's loyalty to his craft meant less time in the tavern and more time at his table, scribbling by candlelight while drunken revellers stumbled home through the streets below accompanied by their screeching whores. Unlike Greene, he had no need to write to pay the reckoning.

Shakespeare's relatively abstemious character ensured his professional standing and longevity and enabled him to hold his own against rivals such as Ben Jonson, who would become his most serious rival for technical skill and literary ability.

Thomas Fuller (1608-1661), born too late to have met Shakespeare, enhanced Shakespeare's sober reputation when he related this battle of wits between Shakespeare and Jonson at the Mermaid Tavern in Cheapside. Sadly, the scene is an imaginary one as Shakespeare did not frequent the Mermaid (although Ben Jonson and Beaumont and Fletcher were regulars), but the myth endures:

> Which two I behold like a Spanish great galleon and an English man-of-war. Master Jonson (like the former) was built far higher in learning; solid, but slow, in his performances. Shakespeare, with the English man-of-war, lesser in bulk, but lighter in sailing, could turn with all tides, tack about, and take advantage of all winds, by the quickness of his wit and invention.[18]

Shakespeare arrived in London as English drama was undergoing a glittering transformation, thanks to his neighbours Marlowe, Kyd and even Greene, whose personal attack on him would, ironically, guarantee the jaundiced author's own posterity. Shakespeare himself was already writing and he had clearly developed a tremendous facility with the English language before he arrived in London. This very language, mercurial and flexible, was already changing and so were its themes and subjects.

English drama had been dominated in the 1570s and early 1580s by the two existing strands of public drama and the court masque. While law students at the Inns of Court performed the artificial confections of John Lyly, stuffed with puns and wordplay, the populace enjoyed crude interludes populated by stock characters such as Vice, the Seven Deadly Sins and the Nine Worthies. Capering Tarlton, the clown of the Queen's Men, had developed his own brand of knockabout comedy. But by 1588, as the political scene began to cloud, playgoers were tiring of comedy. England was at war with Spain and the Spanish Armada loomed on the horizon, ready to invade. Sir Philip Sidney, the aristocratic soldier poet, had been slain in battle in the Netherlands, and Mary Stuart, 'the Queen of Scots' who posed a real threat to Queen Elizabeth's monarchy, had been executed. Against this backdrop of bloody and most violent deeds, playgoers were demanding stronger fare, and the actors were only too happy to provide it. The revenge tragedy, based on translations from Seneca by authors such as Thomas Watson, was a compelling new genre which offered plenty of action and a high body count. Given the opportunity to sup their fill of horrors, audiences could not get enough. The most influential example of the genre appeared over a year before Shakespeare arrived in London, courtesy of Thomas Kyd. Although Kyd may not have written the very first Elizabethan tragedy, he penned the most significant one. This is not only because of Kyd's dramatic expertise, but his facility with the English language. Kyd had the good fortune to have been educated by Richard Mulcaster, headmaster of Merchant Taylors' grammar school and a man determined to raise 'our English tongue' to the same level of esteem as Latin as a fit language for poetry and prose:

> Our own tongue bearing the joyful tide of our liberty and freedom, the Latin tongue remembering us of our thraldom and bondage. I love Rome, but London better; I favour Italy, but England more; I honour the Latin but I worship the English . . . why may not the English wits, if they will bend their wills, either for matter or for method in their own tongue, be in time as well sought to by foreign students?[19]

Kyd, whose fellow students included Thomas Lodge and Edmund Spenser, clearly bent his will to writing in the English language and became an important playwright. The author Francis Meres (1565–1647) placed Kyd among 'our best for tragedy', Thomas Heywood referred to him as 'Famous Kyd', and Ben Jonson mentioned him in the same breath as Christopher Marlowe and John Lyly in the Shakespeare First Folio.[20]

To the tune of *Queene Dido*.

The Spanish Tragedy *by Thomas Kyd sparked a craze for blood-soaked revenge drama.*

The Spanish Tragedy first appeared in 1586 and was an immediate success. Its full title, in the style of the time so extensive as almost to make watching the play redundant, was *The Spanish Tragedie, Containing the lamentable end of Don Horatio, and Bel-imperia: with the pitifull death of olde Hieronimo.* For ease of reference, the play was usually known either as

The Spanish Tragedy or *Hieronimo,* after its protagonist, a role which the supremely talented young actor Edward 'Ned' Alleyn was swift to make his own. In his early twenties, tall with a commanding stage presence, Alleyn was the outstanding actor of his day. Thomas Nashe described him as 'so acting to the life that he made any part to become him', while Thomas Heywood later described Alleyn as 'inimitable, the best of actors, Proteus for shapes and Roscius for a tongue'.[21]

The role of Hieronimo was certainly a demanding one. This speech, from Act II, indicates the sheer level of histrionics required as Hieronimo is roused from his bed by the sound of screaming:

HIERONIMO: What outcries pluck me from my naked bed
And chill my throbbing heart with trembling fear,
Which never danger yet could daunt before?
Who calls Hieronimo? . . .
But stay, what murd'rous spectacle is this?
A man hanged up and all the murderers gone:
And in my bower, to lay the guilt on me.
This place was made for pleasure, not for death.[22]

At this point, Hieronimo makes his dreadful discovery: cutting down the body, he recognises the corpse's garments and then: 'Alas, it is Horatio, my sweet son. Oh no, but he that whilom was my son.'[23]

The sensational subject matter and Edward Alleyn's towering performances made *The Spanish Tragedy* the most popular play of the day and provided a template for many others in the same vein, crammed with classical influences, romantic Christian names and convoluted plot revolving around revenge, murder and suicide, a genre best described by Nashe and Marlowe in these lines from *Dido, Queen of Carthage:*

Young infants swimming in their parents blood,
Headless carcasses piled up in heaps,
Virgins half dead dragged by their golden hair,
And maine force flung on a ring of pikes,
Old men with swords thrust through their aged sides,
Kneeling for mercy to a Greekish lad,
Who with steel pole-axes dashed out their brains.[24]

'The bloody deed, the tardy revelation, the obstacles to vengeance, revenge achieved,'[25] are all here for the delectation of the willing audience. So popular was it that *The Spanish Tragedy* would continue to play to packed houses until the theatres were closed by the Commonwealth in the 1640s. Kyd's influence on Shakespeare was inevitable. It was not a matter of if Shakespeare would create a tragic drama, but when. Shakespeare's own revenge tragedies, such as *Titus Andronicus*, with its abject depictions of rape, mutilation and infants served up to their own parents in a pie, would out-Kyd Kyd for blood and guts. An early version of Shakespeare's greatest revenge drama was also already circulating in the late 1580s. Teasing references abound in footnotes and in chronicles, to some early performances of the 'Ur-*Hamlet*'. In 1589, in the preface to Robert Greene's *Menaphon*, Thomas Nashe lampooned the young men he called 'noverints' or scriveners, scribes whose task it was to provide fair copies of manuscripts. Nashe was full of contempt for these clerks, who had turned to writing drama although they were so uneducated they could scarcely translate their own neck-verse into Latin if they needed to. 'Yet English Seneca read by Candlelight yields many good sentences, as "Blood is a beggar," and so forth; and if you entreat him faire in a frosty morning, he will afford you whole Hamlets, I should say handfuls of Tragical speeches.' Thomas Lodge, in 1596, alludes to a character who 'walks for the most part in black under cover of gravity, and looks as pale as the vizard [mask] of the ghost who cried so miserably at the Theatre like an oyster-wife, "Hamlet, revenge!"' This was long before William Shakespeare officially emerged from the 'hell' under the stage as Hamlet's father's ghost.[26]

The impact of *The Spanish Tragedy* was only matched, two years later, by the spectacular ascent of Christopher Marlowe. While Shakespeare was freelancing between the Queen's Men, Lord Strange's Men and the Earl of Pembroke's Men, and devoting the hours of darkness to perfecting his craft as a writer, Marlowe had come down from Cambridge to take London by storm. He succeeded immediately with his first play *Tamburlaine*, a work of 'giantly presumption'[27] equal in ambition to that of Tamburlaine himself. Setting the scene for this epic, the prologue alerts the audience to the massive scale of his theatrical ambitions. In his characteristic bombastic blank verse, he promises that:

> We'll lead you to the stately tent of war,
> Where you shall hear the Scythian Tamburlaine
> Threatening the world with high astounding terms,
> And scourging kingdoms with his conquering sword.[28]

Like his alter-ego Tamburlaine, a shepherd boy turned warlord, Marlowe sprang from modest origins as the son of a shoe-maker. And like Tamburlaine, it sometimes appeared that 'his looks do menace heaven and accuse the gods'.

> . . . he was never sprung of human race,
> Since with the spirit of his fearful pride,
> He dares so doubtlessly resolve of rule,
> And by profession be ambitious.[29]

Born in Canterbury, Marlowe attended King's School before going up to Corpus Christi College, Cambridge, on a scholarship in 1581. After taking his BA in 1584, Marlowe stayed on at Corpus, ostensibly to read for holy orders. However, three years later, when the time came for the university to grant Marlowe his MA, a mere formality in most cases, Cambridge refused on the grounds that Marlowe had spent much of those three years out of the country. The most obvious explanation for this absence was that Marlowe, like many students, had developed Roman Catholic sympathies and travelled to the English Catholic Seminary at Rheims, a known centre of anti-English sedition. Marlowe would not have been unusual in this respect. To nurture Catholic sensibilities in the cold heart of the Anglican fens had become a popular form of student rebellion. Charles Nicholl, in his excellent book *The Reckoning: The Murder of Christopher Marlowe,* draws persuasive parallels between Marlowe's possible Catholic sympathies in the Cambridge of the 1580s and the popularity of the Communist Party with idealistic undergraduates in the Cambridge of the 1930s. Had Marlowe simply been a disaffected MA student, unable to receive his award, perhaps no more would have been heard of this aspect of his academic career. As it is, the story takes another twist. On 29 June 1587, the University of Cambridge received a stiff letter from the Privy Council, commanding it to award Marlowe's MA at once. This letter revealed that, during his time overseas, Marlowe had 'behaved himself orderly and discreetly, whereby he had done her Majesty good service and deserved to be rewarded for his faithful dealing'. The letter concluded: 'it was not her Majesty's pleasure that any one employed as he had been in matters touching the benefit of his country should be defamed by those who are ignorant in the affairs he went about.'[30] In other words, Christopher Marlowe was a spy.

Exactly what kind of spy Marlowe was is another matter. At a time when the government feared a Catholic insurgency from the North, seeking to put King James VI of Scotland on the English throne, Sir Francis Walsingham had already founded a secret intelligence service and recruited agents or 'intelligencers' to infiltrate the ranks of the Catholic sympathisers. Far from being a student protestor, studying abroad to keep faith with his co-religionists, Marlowe appears to have been a government agent, spying on his fellow students. If such actions make Marlowe less sympathetic to modern readers, it is worth bearing in mind that he was an extremely ambitious young man living in the shadow of a police state. And one for whom, perhaps, the undercover life had a certain romantic attraction. Writers have always made good spies, not only for their skills of observation and memory, but because of their cold-blooded ability to lie through their teeth when necessary. Marlowe, like Graham Greene four centuries later, had the requisite cold splinter of ice in his heart necessary for the successful writer – and the successful spy.

But Marlowe's first loyalty was to his muse, and his career flourished. He saw his first play produced at the Rose in 1587, the same year that he came down from Cambridge. *Tamburlaine the Great, who from a Scythian shepherd, by his rare and wonderful conquests became a most puissant and mighty monarch, and for his tyranny and terror in war, was termed 'the Scourge of God'*[31] was a rhetorical broadside fired like a warning shot across the bows of his fellow dramatists. While Robert Greene would include a life-threatening reference to 'that atheist Marlowe'[32] as a vindictive passing shot from his deathbed, the ever-pragmatic Shakespeare swiftly snapped up his technique and appropriated his sweeping historical perspective and verbal heroics. Although *Tamburlaine* was not the first use of blank verse upon the stage, it was the most notable. In some respects, *Tamburlaine* was not a play at all; it was an epic poem, with long speeches to be recited by different characters. But Marlowe's language was astonishing, as was that of his next play, *The Jew of Malta* (1589), which featured another anti-hero, Barabas, a Jewish usurer who is understandably resentful given the treatment of his people. Marlowe was able to give full rein to his poetic skills in lines such as:

> Bags of fiery opals, sapphires, amethysts,
> Jacinths, hard topaz, grass-green emeralds,
> Beauteous rubies, sparkling diamonds,
> And seld-seen costly stones of so great price . . .
> May serve to ransom great kings from captivity . . .
> Infinite riches in a little room.[33]

Both plays proved to be the ideal vehicle for 'Ned' Alleyn, since the ambitious young actor had already perfected an impressive line in villainy and could represent a character many years older than himself with sheer technique and the application of a few painted-on wrinkles.

The immediate impact of Kyd and Marlowe was to raise the bar for dramatic writing and to change the subject matter of English drama itself, which was undergoing a profound shift. By 1588, Death had twice laid its icy fingers upon the London stage. First came the sudden death of Lord Dudley, the Earl of Leicester, the noble patron who had offered James Burbage's men the chance to wear his livery and perform as part of his household. Leicester had already fallen out of favour with the Queen and a disastrous sortie into the war in the Netherlands had not enhanced his reputation. With his death, the Earl of Leicester's Men were disbanded. A second bitter blow followed, with the death from plague of Tarlton. As well as being a great loss for his many friends, Tarlton's death effectively split up the company. Tarlton was buried in St Leonard's, Shoreditch, the actors' church, and fondly remembered by his admirers. 'He was so beloved that men use his picture for their signs.'[34] The death of two such significant figures, the handsome Leicester and Tarlton the clown, seemed emblematic. Drama itself was undergoing a sea change, from comedy to tragedy. The larger-than-life comic spirit of the early days fled, chased away by darker shadows. Tragedians were needed now, not clowns. Ultimately, this would be to Shakespeare's advantage, allowing him to create complex, conflicted tragic heroes and villains, convincingly brought to life by Edward Alleyn and then by Richard Burbage. The old comedies of the early 1580s were being replaced by violent blockbusters where the very language constituted an assault on the audience's senses. With *Edward II*, Marlowe would respond to the new fashion for history plays, a genre which Shakespeare subsequently made his own.

Unlike Shakespeare, Marlowe possessed a pronounced self-destructive streak. While Shakespeare, in common with most men, carried a sword and a dagger, he was unlikely to have had recourse to the sword except on stage. The dagger occasionally came in handy for eating. Marlowe, by contrast, was a man of violence, and was also regarded with suspicion in some quarters for his friendship with Sir Walter Raleigh, a notorious malcontent. Raleigh himself had come under scrutiny for founding a learned society, where the great minds of the day met to discuss philosophy, religion and science, inspired by Renaissance humanism. Later dubbed 'the School of Night' by academics in a reference to 'black is the badge of hell, The hue of dungeons and the school of night,'[35] this civilised activity was enough to earn Raleigh accusations of atheism and running a secret society in the paranoid political climate of the 1580s. Taking into account Marlowe's previous experience with the secret service, one can only speculate as to whether his involvement with Raleigh was based on friendship, intellectual curiosity or some labyrinthine and complex undercover mission the nature of which was known only to himself.

That Marlowe was no effete poet but a street fighter when the occasion demanded is clearly revealed in the following anecdote. In 1589, Marlowe's friend, the poet Thomas Watson, quarrelled with another man, one William Bradley. Bradley had become so frightened of Watson that he feared for his life and had tried to take out an injunction against him. On the afternoon of 18 September 1589, Bradley encountered Marlowe in Hog Lane, Shoreditch. Swords and daggers were drawn and the two men started fighting. Then Watson appeared, and as soon as Bradley saw Watson, he cried out: 'Art thou now come? Then I will have a bout with thee!'[36] Bradley turned away from Marlowe and attacked Watson with his dagger in one hand and his sword in the other, driving Watson towards the edge of a ditch. In great danger, Watson fought back desperately. He thrust his dagger at Bradley and ran him through, giving him a fatal wound to the chest. Marlowe and Watson were arrested and taken to Newgate Gaol. Next day, the coroner's jury decided that Watson had killed Bradley in self-defence, but both he and Marlowe were remanded at Newgate awaiting pardon. Marlowe remained at Newgate until 1 October 1589 when he was able to raise £40 bail and Watson was pardoned the following year, on 10 February 1590. Such a shocking incident was not unusual at a time when many young men met a violent death, as events in the life of Ben Jonson will later indicate, but it is a stark reminder of the dangerous quality of Elizabethan life.

By 1592, when Shakespeare had been in London for four years and begun to make his mark on the London theatre world, James Burbage still remained in control of the London stage. Although the Earl of Leicester's Men were defunct, the Queen's Men remained popular at the Theatre, as did the Lord Admiral's Men, thanks to their leading player, Edward Alleyn. Lord Strange's Men played the Curtain, and Burbage presided over both venues, while the young Shakespeare moved seamlessly between the two, his writing duties steadily taking precedence over his role as a performer. And then, for reasons that remain unclear, James Burbage and Ned Alleyn fell out. Given Burbage's volatile reputation it is tempting to speculate that he was the cause of the disagreement. After all, Burbage had a history of disputes, ranging from his quarrel with his brother-in-law to the ongoing legal battle with John Brayne's widow. Alleyn may also have taken Mrs Brayne's side in the running legal battle between Burbage and his former sister-in-law, feeling that she had been badly treated. A spat over pay does not seem uncharacteristic for Alleyn or Burbage. Whatever the cause of the argument, James Burbage soon regretted it when Alleyn took himself and the Admiral's Men off to the Rose on the opposite bank of the Thames and teamed up with the rival theatre's owner, Philip Henslowe. This was a significant time for the Rose and for its proprietors, as the combination of Henslowe and Alleyn would be a propitious one. Alleyn made an enormous difference to the running of the Rose. By marrying Joan Woodward, Henslowe's daughter, Alleyn consolidated his influence and became part of the family.

Not only did Alleyn walk out on Burbage, but he took a significant number of players with him from the Admiral's Men and Lord Strange's Men, as well as costumes and, even more significantly, plays. Henslowe actually had to enlarge the Rose Theatre, from a spherical shape to one that resembled an egg, in order to make room for Alleyn's costumes and props.

Those who stayed with Burbage were his own son Richard, and the actors John Sinclair or 'Sinklo', Henry Condell, Nicholas Tooley and Christopher Beeston. With the exception of Tooley, these players would later come under the patronage of the Earl of Pembroke and become Pembroke's Men. Shakespeare, too, remained with the Burbages, perhaps from some residual sense of loyalty to the man who had originally taken him in when he arrived in London, or because he now became the principal writer with a company at his disposal to perform his new plays. And what plays these were: *Titus Andronicus*, *The Taming of the Shrew*, and two embryonic history plays, *The First Part of the Contention of the Two Famous Houses of York and Lancaster* and *The True Tragedy of Richard Duke of York*, the prototypes of the second and third parts of *Henry VI*. Scholars have argued, for generations, as to the amount Shakespeare contributed to these early plays. Given that the playwriting of the period was a collaborative activity, such reservations are understandable. What these plays do indicate is that Shakespeare, always swift to latch on to the newest theatrical fashion, had grasped the fact that history plays were the latest craze and audiences, both rich and poor, were fascinated by true-life tales of royalty and the struggle for supremacy.

This state of affairs, with two rival playhouses both alike in dignity slugging it out for audiences, might have continued unopposed for several years. But 1592 proved to be a turbulent year for London's theatres, and indeed for the city itself. At first, when an outbreak of plague closed the theatres in February 1592, Burbage and Henslowe shrugged it off as bad luck and opened for business once more as soon as the authorities permitted. Over at Henslowe's Rose takings were reasonable. Robert Greene, he who had loathed actors and the theatre, had turned for money to writing plays of his own. *Friar Bacon and Friar Bungay,* the first pastoral comedy, and *Orlando Furioso*, a vehicle for Ned Alleyn which allowed him to portray the poet, the lover and the madman and be furious in all three (simultaneously), proved moderately successful. But not as successful as Shakespeare's new history play, *Harey the Sixth,* which saw the Rose packed to capacity during the spring and early summer.

Sensing the popular mood, and anticipating yet another visitation of plague, Greene wrote *A Looking Glass for London* with Thomas Lodge, the son of a wealthy merchant who had risen to become Lord Mayor of London before going bankrupt. In this morality play, Greene showed London as a city filled with adultery, corruption, whoredom, drunkenness and pride:

> London, awake, for fear the Lord do frown;
> I set a looking glass before thine eyes.
> O turn, O turn, with weeping to the Lord,
> And think the prayers and virtues of thy Queen
> Defers the plague which otherwise would fall . . . [37]

But at this point, another disaster struck. Although plague was a constant threat, the proprietor of the Rose could not have predicted the next calamity. On 11 June 1592, the Knight Marshal's men, responsible for maintaining order within the Court of Marshalsea, arrested the servant of a felt-maker and threw him into the Marshalsea gaol. That afternoon, a new play premiered at the Rose theatre. *A Knack to Know a Knave* was a comedy by William Kemp, the comic actor who had taken on the mantle of the late Tarlton, becoming London's most popular clown. The Rose was full of apprentices and, fired up when the show was over, the young men promptly marched over to the Marshalsea and demanded that their incarcerated brother be handed over. With this, the Marshal's men arrived, set about the apprentices with cudgels and daggers, and then drew their swords. When the apprentices retaliated, the Marshal's men had to be rescued from the angry mob by the arrival of the Lord Mayor and *his* men. A menacing atmosphere lay over the city for three days after these riots, with the apprentices threatening more trouble on Midsummer's Eve, a traditional night of disorder. The authorities put on an extra watch and householders were instructed to keep their servants indoors for fear that they might join forces with the apprentices. As a final precaution, it was announced that no more plays were to be performed in London until Michaelmas. Considering themselves to be innocent victims of the apprentices' riot, the players petitioned the authorities for a change of heart. They found allies among the watermen, who made a handsome living ferrying playgoers from one side of the Thames to the other, and who soon issued their own special plea. Not only was their livelihood at stake, they begged in a letter to the Council, but the lives of 'our poor wives and children!' Both appeals proved successful and the authorities relented. Performances would recommence at the Rose, 'so long as it shall be free from infection of sickness' and the watermen were free to take up their oars once more.[38] But it was too late to reopen the theatres. Following a hot dry fortnight at the beginning of June, an epidemic of plague had broken out.

Realising that there was no more money to be earned in the city, the players did what had become traditional in these circumstances, and went on tour. From Bristol, Edward Alleyn wrote home to his wife Joan with the following instructions for defending her household from plague:

My Good Sweet Mouse . . . hoping in God though the sickness be round about you yet, by His Mercy, it may escape your house, which, by the grace of God, it shall. Therefore use this course; keep your house fair and clean, which I know you will, and every evening throw water before your door and your back door and have in your windows good store of rue and herb of grace, and with all the grace of God, which must be obtained by prayers; and in so doing, no doubt but the Lord will mercifully defend you.[39]

Henslowe and Joan wrote back to Alleyn, telling him that 'we have been flitted [afflicted] with fear of the sickness, but thanks be unto God we are all this time in good health in our house; but round us it hath been almost in every house about us and whole households died.'[40]

Thomas Nashe, in his masque *Summer's Last Will and Testament*, also reflected upon this particular outbreak with *A Litany in Time of Plague.*

Rich men, trust not in wealth,
Gold cannot buy you health;
Physic himself must fade.
All things to end are made,
The plague full swift goes by;
I am sick, I must die.
Lord, have mercy on us!

Beauty is but a flower
Which wrinkles will devour;
Brightness falls from the air;
Queens have died young and fair;
Dust hath closed Helen's eye.
I am sick, I must die.
Lord, have mercy on us!
Haste, therefore, each degree,
To welcome destiny;
Heaven is our heritage,
Earth but a player's stage;
Mount we unto the sky.
I am sick, I must die.
Lord, have mercy on us![41]

In August, the Court left London for its customary royal progress, visiting the royal palaces and stately homes of the nobility. Shakespeare, with his customary skill of self-preservation, weathered this difficult season by turning his attention to poetry. When it was eventually published, in 1594, the erotic verse sequence of *Venus and Adonis* earned him a glittering reputation and the patronage of the young nobleman to whom it was dedicated, the Earl of Southampton.

For Robert Greene, however, there would be no handsome courtiers hanging on his every word. He would not be summoned by the Master of the Revels to appear before the Queen, or drop sweet conceits into the ears of admiring ladies. Not for Greene the aristocratic patronage and the drooling envy of fellow authors. Instead, an old man by the age of 34, Greene was destitute. His wife had deserted him, taking their son Fortunatus (seldom has a name been more inappropriate). True, his mistress, Em Ball, remained at his side, but he had been forced to pawn his cloak and sword. Greene would have died in the street had it not been for soft-hearted Mistress Isam, who offered him a room in her house for his final days. Greene owed money all over London and had driven away many of his friends with his offensive, drunken behaviour. Only Thomas Nashe, a fellow reprobate, took pity on him and invited him to lunch in the stinking dog days of late August, with his friend, one Will Monnox. The menu, Rhenish wine and pickled herrings, was scarcely suitable for a man on the verge of kidney failure, but Greene accepted Nashe's hospitality, reeling home at twilight before passing out on the bed, only rising again to compose his warning letter to Nashe, Marlowe and Lodge on the evils of actors and the stage.

Greene's final act had been to write a letter to his wife, begging for her forgiveness and asking her to pay his land-lord. 'I owe him ten pounds, and but for him I had perished in the streets. Forget and forgive my wrongs . . . farewell till we meet in heaven, for on earth thou shalt never see me more. Written by thy dying husband, Robert Greene.'[42] A few hours later, Greene was dead. 'The King of the Paper Stage' had played his last part, and gone to join Tarlton. He was buried at the New Churchyard near Bedlam, and the loyal Mistress Isam paid the four shillings for his winding sheet and the burial fees of six shillings and four pence.

Following the posthumous publication of Greene's attack on Shakespeare, his fellow writers were anxious to distance themselves from his letter and many wondered if it was actually genuine or a forgery designed by his publisher, Chettle, to exploit Greene's sudden demise. Nashe dismissed it as a 'lying, trivial pamphlet'[43] while Shakespeare, although he must have been hurt by Greene's attack on him, was charitable enough to smuggle a reference to Greene's wretched demise into *A Midsummer Night's Dream*: 'The thrice three Muses mourning for the death Of Learning, late deceased in beggary.'[44]

Late in the summer which had seen the death of Robert Greene and the terrible visitation of plague, Christopher Marlowe stumbled across an obscure book entitled *The Historie of the damnable life and deserved death of Dr John Faustus,* originally published in German in 1587 and translated by one 'P. F., Gent' in 1592. In Marlowe's hands, this cautionary tale of a scholar willing to sell his soul to the devil in exchange for intellectual prowess translates into an epic battle between good and evil. In another towering role for Edward Alleyn, Marlowe created his most distinctive anti-hero. Faustus is a man willing to endure eternal damnation in exchange for knowledge, the greatest form of power. A tragic hero brought low by his own hubris, Faustus pays the ultimate price twenty-four years later, when the devil arrives to claim his soul. Hoping against hope, Faustus pleads for more time:

> Now hast thou but one bare hour to live,
> And then thou must be damned perpetually;
> Stand still you ever-moving sphere of heaven,
> That time may cease, and midnight never come . . .
> The stars move still, time runs, the clock will strike,
> The devil will come, and Faustus must be damn'd.[45]

After two dozen years of dismissing the power of the Almighty, Faustus appeals to God for mercy:

> O I'll leap up to my God: who pulls me down?
> See where Christ's blood streams in the firmament.
> One drop would save my soul, half a drop, ah my Christ![46]

And finally, in utter desperation, knowing that he is damned forever, as the clock strikes twelve, a violent storm breaks out offstage and the devils enter, Faustus offers to make his final sacrifice: 'Ugly hell, gape not! come not, Lucifer! I'll burn my books!'[47]

THE
HISTORIE
OF
THE DAMNABLE
LIFE, AND DESERVED
DEATH OF DOCTOR
IOHN FAVSTVS.

Newly printed, and in conuenient places, imperfect
matter amended : according to the true Copie printed
at *Frankfort* ; and translated into English,
By *P. R. Gent.*

*Raising Hell. Audiences claimed real devils appeared on stage during
productions of* Dr Faustus.

Marlowe's description of Faustus's dying moments, his remorse and despair, are the equal of Shakespeare's tragic speeches. On the page, Faustus's doom is impressive; on the stage of the Rose, with the devils dragging him away to the hellmouth, it must have been an extraordinary sight. A writer at the height of his powers and an actor able to embody his tragic creation. Indeed, so persuasive was this vision that many spoke of seeing real devils on the stage, and rumours flew around London that it was Marlowe who had sold his soul to the devil in exchange for such special effects. An apparition at Dulwich proved so terrifying that the actors spent the night praying and fasting, and Ned Alleyn, the actor who had played Faustus, vowed to found a college in that town and name it the College of God's Gift. Whether the famous actor was prompted by the supernatural or not, Dulwich College, founded by Alleyn, stands to this very day.[48]

Dr Faustus was but one production in a good winter season at the Rose when the theatres finally reopened in December 1592. The autumn had been a difficult one, with the Lord Mayor's Feast cancelled and the Michaelmas Law Term postponed due to plague. The public were desperate for entertainment and flocked to watch Lord Strange's Men perform *The Spanish Tragedy, The Jew of Malta, Titus Andronicus, Friar Bacon, Harry the Sixth* and a new play from Marlowe, *The Massacre at Paris.* Before either proprietors or players could take full advantage of this success, however, plague returned in January 1593. On 28 January the Privy Council prohibited 'all plays, baiting of bears, bulls, bowling and other like occasions to assemble any number of people together (preaching and Divine Service excepted).'[49]

Plague was just one aspect of an uneasy spring. Religious tensions were running high in London, with prejudice rampant on all sides. In Parliament, one group proposed a bill to curtail the powers of bishops, while another group proposed a bill against recusants. The authorities experienced a growing conviction that some vast but undefined subversive movement was growing. The 'Martin Marprelate' controversy of 1588–89, in which an anonymous author or authors attacked the governance structure of the Anglican church in a series of tracts, had

already put the government on its guard against propaganda
campaigns. So much so indeed that writers including Robert
Greene and Thomas Nashe had been hired to write pseud-
onymous counter-blasts against the elusive 'Marprelate'. Now,
in 1593, as other subversive material surfaced, extreme Puritan
sects were scrutinised. Barrow, a Puritan preacher, was
arrested in Islington on 9 March and hanged on 6 April, along
with another preacher, Greenwood. Propaganda bills against
the government circulated, while libellous graffito about
foreigners, particularly the Dutch, appeared on London walls,
warning them to leave England before July or 'take what
follows!' in the form of 2,336 apprentices and journeymen
rising up against 'Flemings and Strangers'.[50] After a particularly malicious piece of graffiti appeared on the wall of the
Dutch church on 11 May the government was granted additional powers to arrest any suspects, search their persons and
their houses and even use torture to extract the truth. One of
the suspects who found himself rounded up and taken to
Bridewell Prison was the author of *The Spanish Tragedy,*
Thomas Kyd. When they searched Kyd's lodgings, the authorities found nothing to suggest that he was involved in a hate
campaign against Dutch immigrants, but instead they found
something far more incriminating. This was a page from a
leaflet denying the divinity of Christ. Asked to explain the
origins of this compromising document, Kyd could only tell
his inquisitors that it had been left behind by Christopher
Marlowe when they roomed together two years earlier. Kyd
was tortured to obtain this 'evidence'; he should not be judged
too harshly by posterity.

On 18 May a warrant was issued for Marlowe's arrest, and
a list of allegations against him of 'vile heretical conceits' was
handed in, collated by one Richard Bains. This charge sheet
was considered so important that a copy was sent to Queen

Elizabeth. Along with contentious statements to the effect that 'Christ was a bastard and His mother dishonest', and 'That St John the Evangelist was bedfellow to Christ and that he used him as the sinners of Sodom', other comments certainly do have the ring of the authentic Marlowe voice, including the professional writer's observation that 'all the New Testament is filthily written' and, most memorable of all, 'That all they that love not tobacco and boys were fools'.[51]

Marlowe duly appeared before the Privy Council on 20 May, where he was bailed. Despite the serious nature of the allegations, it appeared that the authorities were content to allow Marlowe his liberty. Unlike Kyd, he was neither tortured nor confined; indeed, he appears to have been treated more like a witness than a felon. Marlowe was still on bail ten days later, on 30 May 1593, when he accepted an invitation to dine with three men at the home of Mistress Eleanor Bull in Deptford. This was no low-life tavern. Mistress Bull was a respectable widow who allowed her house to be used as a private dining club, and the invitation had been issued by three acquaintances from the secret service, Ingram Frizer, Nicholas Sheres and Robert Poley. Marlowe may have had his doubts about the meeting. No one ever truly leaves the secret world, and he must have wondered, with his trial looming, exactly what these men had in store for him. But Marlowe went to Deptford anyway, and dined with the three men, and after dinner they walked in the garden, and drank wine, and appeared deep in discussion. At around six o'clock in the evening, all four trooped back into the house and ate supper, fish in a pastry coffin prepared for them by Mistress Bull. What happened next has been a matter of conjecture for centuries. At some point there was a violent altercation and Marlowe was stabbed in the head. The blade of the dagger penetrated his eye, and, in the words of the coroner, 'the aforesaid Christopher Marlowe then instantly died'.[52] The coroner went on to record the verdict that Frizer had stabbed Marlowe in self-defence after a quarrel about the bill – 'the reckoning' – a version of events which has been disputed for many years. Given Marlowe's secret service connections and his hitherto charmed life, it seems as if the row about the bill was no more than a cover-up for an aborted operation, a theory advanced by Charles Nicholl in *The Reckoning*. Perhaps the meeting at Mistress Bull's house had included an offer to drop the charges in return for other vital intelligence or the prospect of one last mission. Some have even suggested that Marlowe concocted the entire incident in a successful attempt to fake his own death and escape to Italy. We will never know, but Nicholl's premise that Frizer, drunk and exasperated beyond endurance, lashed out at his key witness and killed him is a highly convincing one.

A day after he died, Christopher Marlowe was buried in the churchyard at Deptford, and the entry in the parish register records 'Christopher Marlow, slaine by ffrancis ffrezer: the I of June'.[53] Although shocking, Marlowe's death was not unexpected. Something in his character had always suggested that he would never make old bones. An echo of Marlowe's fate may be heard in that cryptic reference to 'a great reckoning in a little room' in *As You Like It*.[54] Or perhaps, for Marlowe the tragedian, this quotation from *Romeo and Juliet* is more appropriate: 'Violent delights have violent ends.'[55] Marlowe's genius had flickered and disappeared,

> brief as the lightning in the collied night,
> That in a spleen, unfolds both heaven and earth,
> And, ere a man hath power to say 'Behold!'
> The jaws of darkness do devour it up:
> So quick bright things come to confusion.[56]

Marlowe was that 'quick bright thing' and he did 'come to confusion.'

Marlowe's sudden death left Kyd in a terrible predicament. Only Marlowe could have cleared his name and taken responsibility for the ownership of the anti-clerical pamphlet found in his room. With Marlowe gone, there was nobody left to defend him. Kyd therefore wrote a letter claiming that the material had belonged to Marlowe all along, in a bid to save himself, and that Marlowe and Sir Walter Raleigh were conspiring against the Crown. Kyd was released, as nothing could be proved against him. Unable to write, or return to his old trade of scrivener, his hands mangled by torture, Kyd died the following year.

With the death of Marlowe, Shakespeare's greatest rival was gone. Greene had been dead less than a year, bequeathing Shakespeare the genre of pastoral comedy, which he would make his own. Marlowe had inspired him with his panoramic vision, his charismatic villains and his mighty line, although Shakespeare had wisely chosen not to emulate his radical atheism and hedonistic personal life. Now Kyd, author of the first great revenge tragedy, also lay dead. If Shakespeare had been the Machiavellian anti-hero of some dark tragi-comedy, he could not have done better to eliminate his enemies. The bodies of his three greatest rivals lay dead at his feet. He had no equal now. As London's premier dramatist, he could take centre stage. Poor weak Kyd, drunken Greene and self-destructive Marlowe: Shakespeare had waded through the blood of all three and gained the throne. The upstart crow had stolen the crown. He was the king of theatreland.

5

THE HOLLOW CROWN

Within the hollow crown
That rounds the mortal temples of a king
Keeps Death his court

Richard II, Act 3 Scene 2

There is a poignant moment in *Richard II* when Richard, aware that he is about to be deposed from the throne by Bolingbroke, reflects upon the melancholy fate of kings:

> Let's talk of graves, of worms, and epitaphs . . .
> For God's sake, let us sit upon the ground
> And tell sad stories of the death of kings;
> How some have been deposed; some slain in war,
> Some haunted by the ghosts they have deposed;
> Some poison'd by their wives: some sleeping kill'd;
> All murder'd.[1]

Kingship, Richard tells the audience, bestows not immortality but indignity and pain. To be a king, the lord's anointed, is to be a sacrificial victim. Far from being God's representative here on earth, the unhappy monarch is forever looking over his shoulder and death is hovering near: 'Croak not, black angel.'[2] It is a salutary reminder to those who view Tudor history plays as bombastic exercises in patriotism to realise that Shakespeare was deeply conscious of the melancholy isolation of kingship. In this brief depiction of the fate of kings, Richard fleetingly glimpses his own future and alludes to the destiny of other doomed Shakespearean monarchs, from Henry VI to Hamlet's father. Indeed, within the compass of this little speech may be found the heart of Shakespeare's complex view of kingship. Upon one level the history plays are exciting Senecan revenge tragedies, populated by towering historical figures. On another, these dramas contain compelling characters full of considerable psychological complexity. Shakespeare extolled the glories of the crown but was also aware of its deadly consequences.

Shakespeare had in effect taken on the role of the historian and was beginning, in the words of Sir Walter Raleigh, prefacing his own *History of the World* in 1614, 'to set before the eyes of the living the fall and fortunes of the dead'.[3] Taken in sequence, the history plays form a vivid theatrical history of England over the preceding two hundred years. That this is a partial view, I admit; Shakespeare's task was not to challenge the prevailing view of history, but to present it as his audience demanded. However, smuggled away inside this conventional view of the role of the monarch is a critique of the nature of kingship, and what it means to be a king. This theme runs like a thread throughout the First and Second Tetralogies and lies beneath the glittering theatrical pageant of the history plays like a skull beneath a golden crown. Shakespeare's ambiguous view is both essentially critical of the role of the monarch while at the same time endorsing it.

On 3 March 1592 *Harey the Sixth,* the original of Shakespeare's *Henry VI* three-play sequence, received a record attendance. The play was repeated thirteen times, making it a big earner for Henslowe, and indeed Shakespeare, at the beginning of a difficult year which saw the theatres closed for months by plague. History plays were extraordinarily popular at this period, reflecting the appetite for the bloodthirsty historical blockbusters ushered in by Thomas Kyd and Christopher Marlowe. Shakespeare's *Henry VI* was a shrewd response to popular demand. Prior to 1592 there had been at least thirty-nine history plays including Marlowe's *Tamburlaine* (1587), Thomas Lodge's *The Wounds of Civil War* (1588), *Edmund Ironside* (anonymous, 1588), Robert Greene's attempt at a history play with *Selimus* (1591) and the anonymous *The Troublesome Reign of King John* (1588) and *The True Tragedy of Richard III* (1591), both of which would underpin Shakespeare's versions of these monarchs' lives. What distinguishes Shakespeare's history plays from these other plays and ensures that they have survived while the others, with the exception of *Tamburlaine*, have been largely forgotten, is the high quality of Shakespeare's dramatic writing and the degree of psychological realism he brings to his characters. These are no one-dimensional Player Kings and Queens mumming a dumb show outside an inn, these are believable human beings with beating hearts and tortured souls, the prototypes for the complex personalities which would later populate Shakespeare's tragedies. The characters possess a universal quality which means that their suffering speaks to us across the ages. Here, from *Richard III*, is the dowager Queen Margaret, telling the widow of Edward IV of her losses at the hands of Richard in a terrible roll call of bereavement:

> I had an Edward, till a Richard kill'd him;
> I had a Harry, till a Richard kill'd him;
> Thou hadst an Edward, till a Richard kill'd him;
> Thou hadst a Richard, till a Richard kill'd him.[4]

As Richard II might say: 'All murdered.'

This is not the bluster of a playwright pandering to his militant audience. This is the work of a maturing writer, developing his considerable powers, creating multifaceted characters as enthralling for the players to perform as for the audiences to watch. Much of this power comes from the quality of Shakespeare's language. Ruthlessly stripped from the texts of Tudor historians, the dry as dust lawyers' prose of Edward Hall and Thomas More is alchemised into gold beneath his quill. The language of the history plays is every bit as original and spectacular as that of the tragedies. Consider the opening lines of *Henry VI Part 1*, which begins with the funeral of the warrior hero of Agincourt, the late King Henry V:

> Hung be the heavens with black, yield day to night!
> Comets, importing change of times and states,
> Brandish your crystal tresses in the sky,
> And with them scourge the bad revolting stars
> That have consented unto Henry's death!
> King Henry the Fifth, too famous to live long!
> England ne'er lost a king of so much worth.[5]

Or the gardener's lament on the neglected condition of England under the erratic rule of Richard II:

> our sea-walled garden, the whole land,
> Is full of weeds, her fairest flowers choked up,
> Her fruit-trees all upturned, her hedges ruin'd,

> Her knots disorder'd and her wholesome herbs
> Swarming with caterpillars.[6]

Thanks to this vivid language, compelling characters and the sheer theatrical spectacle, the history plays appealed to audiences of all types, from courtiers and lawyers to boisterous apprentices. While erudite men responded with chin-stroking nods to the description of Richard III with speeches taken wholesale from Sir Thomas More's character assassination, rowdy lads revelled in the swordplay. History plays provided educated playgoers with the opportunity for learned speculation in the tavern after the show, flattered their erudition and brought the works of Tudor historians to a wider audience.

For scholars and law students at the Inns of Court, history was studied as an intellectual pursuit, alongside the classics. Shakespeare's educated spectators had read William Camden's *Preface to Britannia* (1586), John Foxe's *Acts and Monuments* (1563), Francis Bacon on Henry VII and Edward Hall's *The Union of the Two Noble and Illustre Families of Lancastre and Yorke,* commonly called *Hall's Chronicle* (1542). The study of history was regarded as a form of moral philosophy in a view derived from Cicero, who regarded the past as 'a storehouse of moral exampla that lend guidance to human existence'. Holinshed observed that chronicles and histories 'ought cheefelie to be written' for the moral edification of the reader. Puttenham declared that there is 'no one thing in the world with more delectation reviving our spirits than to behold as it were in a glasse the lively image of our deare forefathers'. It fell to Sir Philip Sidney, courtier poet and man of action, to sound a sceptical note, dismissive of the historian 'laden with old mouse-eaten records' and hearsay.[7] But Sidney was speaking for the minority. Dramatists seized eagerly on the potential of history plays to become living monuments, dialogues with the dead. According to Thomas Nashe, *Henry VI* was 'a reproof to these degenerate effeminate days of ours', conferring immortality as Talbot, the First Earl of Shrewsbury, 'the Terror of the French', triumphed once more on stage.[8] Plays have power to 'new-mold the harts of the spectators and fashion them to the shape of any noble and notable attempt'.[9] Here are the heroes of the past, brought to life once more, to instruct us in nobility and courage. Or in the words of Thomas Heywood, 'to see a soldier shap'd like a soldier, walke, speake, act like a soldier!' To put what 'story coldly tells' onto the stage in 'lively colours' and to 'raise our ancient sovereigns from their hearse and to enliven their pale trunks'.[10] The magic of the performative present gives the lively image of our dead forefathers, before your very eyes!

In theatrical terms, the great appeal of the history plays is that they offered the opportunity for display, a reflection both of the pageantry and the cruelty of everyday life. Elizabethan Londoners were surrounded by eye-catching spectacles on a daily basis, from the piercing fanfares and drum rolls of a royal appearance to the ceremonials of the Lord Mayor's procession and the gloomy pomp of a heraldic funeral. Fights were a feature of everyday life, ranging from the ceremonial jousts at Whitehall to the fencing contests held at every inn and tavern. A stroll through the capital also guaranteed many disturbing sights, from convicted prostitutes being 'carted' through the city streets and whipped at the cart's arse to young men stabbed to death in brawls. Public executions drew massive crowds, as heretics and traitors were drawn to Tyburn and Smithfield before being partially hanged then disembowelled, their entrails ripped out and burned before them in a blazing brazier. Even the Theatre itself was used for executions on the grounds that such events would provide 'a good example' to audiences.

Stow's *Annales* (1603) records the hanging of one W. Gunter, 'a priest from beyond the seas at the Theater' [*sic*], on 28 August 1588 and of W. Hartley, another priest, 'nigh the Theater [*sic*], 1 October 1588'.[11] These shows of violence reinforced a climate of fear and the lingering suspicion that hidden forces were at work. At any moment, it seemed, any man might be accused of treason, bundled off to the Tower, executed and his head spiked on Traitors' Gate. Little credence adhered to the notion of blind justice and an even-handed legal system. The concept of justice which Shakespeare's audiences recognised was one of revenge, described by Francis Bacon as 'a kind of wild justice',[12] exemplified by the terrible and bloody death of Richard III. Far from being dull historical reconstructions, the history plays mirror this disturbing environment upon the stage. These are not comforting entertainments celebrating life in Merrie England. Instead, the Tower of London is a 'slaughter-house' and 'miserable England' is a brutal police state where nobody is immune from the death sentence.[13] The plays ring with the clash of steel on steel, fathers murdered by their sons and sons by their fathers, the tears of mothers for their children and widows for their slain husbands.

In some respects the very term 'history plays' is misleading. These are not just history plays, these are war plays. The central theme of the First Tetralogy – *Henry VI Parts 1, 2* and *3* and *Richard III* – is civil war. The Second Tetralogy formed by *Richard II, Henry IV Parts 1* and *2* and finally by *Henry V* begins with the loss of England's lands in France and culminates with the Battle of Agincourt. In both cycles, military conflict is the pre-eminent theme. War and the concept of war lies at the heart of Shakespeare's history plays. The action turns upon the victor and victim, the conqueror and the conquered, failure and success. These plays are all about battles and they are all about winning, creating a magnificent theatrical experience, extensive dramatic action and physical and psychological conflict between the protagonists. Read or viewed in sequence both cycles of history plays provide an astonishing picture of a country at war and the consequences of an extended period of conflict. For a man who had not, as far as one knows, been a serving soldier, Shakespeare reveals an extraordinary ability to bring the battlefield to life and to conjure up not just the pageantry of war but also the sorrow and the pity. All this was filtered through the theatrical medium, so that by watching the plays the audiences had the feel of being in battle conditions. The mood was right for what Andrew Gurr terms this 'militant repertoire', 'for the drums, swordplay and noise which suited the larger stages and natural daylight' of the open playhouses.[14] Shakespeare's audiences were ready to embrace drama which offered 'a fearful battle rend'red you in music'.[15] War was a sensational subject but it spoke to Shakespeare's audiences and suited the uneasy temper of the times. War, past and present, was a continual preoccupation. Since the death of the chronicler Edward Hall in 1547, internecine disputes had returned to haunt the country, with the accession of Queen Mary Tudor, Sir Thomas Wyatt's failed rebellion, and the tragedy of the 'nine-day Queen', Lady Jane Grey. As a result, Queen Elizabeth, Elizabeth Tudor, grand-daughter of Henry Tudor, was celebrated as the great unifying force, reconciling opposing factions and paving the paths to peace.

However, peace came at a price. By 1592 England was still at risk from a second Armada. The Queen wrote to her generals that 'it is not to be doubted but that they intend to invade England and Ireland next summer'. The generals concluded that 'nothing appears to her more necessary than to have her people trained in the discipline of war'. While the nobility, the choice-drawn cavaliers, were kept in a constant state of readiness for war, commoners were conscripted in ever-increasing numbers when required. As some indication, in 1594, 2,800 men were conscripted; but the figure rose sharply by 1598, when the country was considered most under threat, to 9,164.[16]

The war against Spain was also being fought on another front, across the North Sea in the Netherlands. In addition, there were the continuing hostilities in Ireland with the rebellion of the native 'kerns'. Jack Cade, a former war hero turned rebel, is described as fighting 'a troop of kerns' for so long that his legs were full of darts.[17] This bitter dispute would continue for centuries to come.

The Earl of Essex (on the white horse)
encounters the Earl of Tyrone, 1601.

When a fighting force was required, either to defend England at home or to fight abroad, a 'militia' was recruited through a combination of feudal obligation, with the lord of the manor rallying to arms the men on his estate, volunteer soldiers and conscripts. The term 'militia', from the Latin *miles* (soldier), was first used around 1590.[18]

A good example of recruiting practice may be found in *Henry VI Part 2* as Clifford pleads with the 'rabblement' to desert the rebel Jack Cade and come and fight the French instead. By invoking chauvinism and common cause against the old enemy, the French, Clifford successfully recruits Cade's supporters to discard their 'civil broil' and fight for England: 'To France, to France, and get what you have lost! Spare England, for it is your native coast.'[19]

Once they had been recruited, the men were supplied with arms, and munitions were kept in readiness in every town. By the close of the century, the longbow had been entirely superseded by the musket. The navy, such as it was, consisted of a growing number of ships of war, as well as merchant vessels and fishing boats. William Harrison, in *The Description of England* (1587), reckoned with pride that Queen Elizabeth could have afloat as many as 9,000 or 10,000 seamen. And a census held for the purpose a few years before the coming of the Armada reckoned more than 16,000 persons in England (exclusive of Wales) were in some sort accustomed to the sea.[20]

Military and naval exploits were conducted by exceptional individuals, who appealed to dramatists through their daring deeds and exciting reputations. It was an age for men of action such as Sir Walter Raleigh (1554–1618), Sir Francis Drake (1540–1596) and the Earl of Essex (1565–1601). Swashbuckling heroes of the day all, although many of their dealings were questionable if not criminal, and the Earl of Essex would suffer a fall from grace worthy of a Shakespearean tragic hero. In addition to these legendary individuals, London endured a constant influx of discharged soldiers, a legacy of the struggle in the Low Countries. While some sought a respectable life in Elizabethan 'civvy street', others took to crime, their ranks swelled by beggars who claimed that their bogus 'injuries' had been inflicted fighting for their country.

The majority of the men in Shakespeare's audiences would have seen action in one form or another, the noblemen as officers, the commoners as volunteers or conscripts, press-ganged into service in the 'fearful musters' described by Rumour in *Henry IV Part 2*. By the time *Henry IV Part 2* appeared in 1598, conscription had become grimly familiar.

If Falstaff is to be believed, the militia consisted of the dregs of society, with the high constables of the Shires and the petty constables of the parishes drafting into the militia all the disreputable elements they were keen to get rid of. Tasked with recruiting 150 men, Captain Falstaff complains that his company includes 'slaves as ragged as Lazarus . . . and such as indeed were never soldiers but discarded . . . serving men, younger sons . . . revolted tapsters [barmen] and ostlers . . . A mad fellow met me on the way, and told me I had unloaded all the gibbets and preserved the dead bodies. No eye hath seen such scarecrows . . . The villains march wide between the legs as if they had gyves [chains] on, for indeed I had the most of them out of prison.'[21]

When Prince Hal observes that 'I did never see such pitiful rascals', Falstaff retorts that they are nothing more than cannon fodder. 'Good enough to toss, food for powder, they'll fill a pit as well as better.'[22]

Such experience informs Falstaff's sardonic, disillusioned view of warfare and military glory:

Can honour set to a leg? No. Or an arm? No. Or take away the grief of a wound? No. Honour hath no skill in surgery, then? No. What is honour? A word. What is in that word honour? What is that honour? Air. A trim reckoning! Who hath it? He that died a-Wednesday. Doth he feel it? No. Doth he hear it? No. 'Tis insensible, then? Yea, to the dead. But will it not live with the living? No. Why? Detraction

will not suffer it. Therefore I'll none of it. Honour is a mere
scutcheon – and so ends my catechism.[23]

Throughout the 1590s, war cast its long shadow over the
souls of the English. While some of Shakespeare's finest
comedies, including *The Taming of the Shrew, The Merchant
of Venice* and *A Midsummer Night's Dream* date from the early
1590s, London audiences were preoccupied by the threat of
war. The phenomenon described by Jonathan Bate as the
'thrilling theatrical marathon of the history plays'[24] ensured
packed houses at the Rose and the Theatre as audiences
flocked to see their national history played out before them.
According to the philosopher Sir Francis Bacon, these
productions had a didactic function and existed not only to
entertain but to instruct, in keeping with the ancient
Aristotelian principles of purging spectators of pity and fear
by making them watch tragic material:

> The action of the theatre, though modern states esteem it
> but ludicrous, unless it be satirical and biting, was carefully
> watched by the ancients, that it might improve mankind
> in virtue, and indeed many wise men and great philoso-
> phers have thought it to the mind as the bow to the fiddle;
> and certain it is, though a great secret in nature, that the
> minds of men in company are more open to affections and
> impressions than when alone.[25]

While Bacon's sentiments are laudable, audiences were also
compelled to watch these plays by the sheer excitement of
the best drama in London, the Tudor equivalent of an action-
packed Hollywood blockbuster.

The first sequence of history plays consists of *Henry VI
Parts 1, 2* and *3,* and *Richard III. Harey the Sixth* originally

graced the stage around 1591. It may not specifically have
been written as a trilogy, but this is how subsequent editors
have chosen to handle the plays, from the First Folio of 1623
onwards. In terms of length, actors would have found the
task of performing all three plays in one afternoon impossible, and such a task would have been prohibited by the
laws which stipulated that performances should last no longer
than two hours. Instead, it seems likely that once the first
'Harey' had proved successful, the sequels were performed
regularly and in rotation, just as a contemporary theatre
company might do today. While *Henry VI* contains many of
Shakespeare's distinctive hallmarks, in terms of character,
dialogue and language, it was a collaborative work, with
additional writing from Thomas Nashe, Thomas Lodge and
possibly even Robert Greene. Time was of the essence –
Shakespeare was only just beginning to make a name for
himself, and the requirements of performance left no time
to be precious about authorship.

The theme of *Henry VI,* based on Edward Hall's *Chronicle*,
was civil war. Hall's premise was that the Tudor dynasty had
rescued England from political and economic chaos following
the turbulent years of the fifteenth century: 'What misery,
what murder and what execrable plagues this famous region
hath suffered by the division and dissension of the renowned
houses of Lancaster and York, my wit cannot comprehend
nor my tongue declare, neither yet my pen fully set forth.'[26]

The pens of Shakespeare and his collaborators subsequently set forth plenty of misery and murder, beginning
with a scenario that depicts the original cause of the hostilities
in the Temple Garden, as the rival factions pluck roses to
indicate their allegiance, white for York and red for Lancaster.
When Warwick declares: 'This brawl today, Grown to this
faction in the Temple Garden, Shall send between the red

rose and the white A thousand souls to death and deadly night,'[27] it is a scene set about with foreboding, and Warwick's prediction proves true.

The First Tetralogy is a spectacularly violent sequence, with Shakespeare writing in the gory tradition of Kyd and Marlowe. The body count is exceptionally high. Characters are stabbed, beheaded and, in the case of 'La Pucelle' or Joan of Arc, burned at the stake. Women are routinely widowed and bereft of fathers and sons, and poor distraught dowager Queen Margaret carries the head of her protector, the Duke of Somerset, around in a basket. In the concluding play in the series, *Richard III*, the Duke of Clarence is drowned in a barrel of Malmsey wine and, most notoriously of all, the two young princes in the Tower are murdered, although offstage and not, mercifully, as in *Titus Andronicus*, dished up in a pie.

As well as the visceral terror of murder and execution, this sequence of histories plays on another popular fear, that of civil unrest. In *Henry VI Part 2,* King Henry, already shown to be a powerless monarch, is threatened by a popular uprising led by Jack Cade. This apparent peasants' revolt has actually been masterminded by the Duke of York, who has recruited Cade to lead a rebellion against Henry VI. Cade, who becomes increasingly unhinged as the play progresses, prepares to march on Westminster with his 'ragged multitude of . . . peasants'[28] and proclaim himself king. In Shakespeare's hands, this ill-conceived uprising is the stuff of comedy, concealing a deeper threat of mayhem. Cade promises his supporters a Utopia, where Pissing Conduit runs with claret and seven half-penny loaves will be sold for a penny. But soon a more sinister agenda emerges. In a line designed to strike fear into a significant section of the audience, Dick the Butcher suggests that 'the first thing we do, let's kill all the lawyers!'[29] Scholars, courtiers and gentlemen are all regarded as 'false caterpillars'[30] that must be destroyed, while Lord Saye is dragged off after Cade barks: 'Away with him. He speaks Latin!'[31] Grammar schools and printing are regarded as sources of corruption, somewhat anachronistically as the events take place in 1450 and Gutenberg had only developed the printing press ten years earlier.

Striking his staff upon London Stone, the landmark in Candlewick Street, Cade becomes an increasingly disturbing character as he threatens to ransack the city, set London Bridge on fire and burn down the Tower. Cade's men will parade through the streets with the heads of his enemies borne on poles. 'Up Fish Street! Down Saint Magnus' Corner! Kill and knock down! Throw them into Thames!'[32] After this, the rebels will demolish the Savoy Palace and attack the Court and the King. In short, Cade is intent on destroying all that the Londoners in the audience would have held most sacred.

Cade is thwarted when Old Clifford appeals to the rebels' innate chauvinism by offering the rebels immunity from prosecution if they will join up and go and fight the French. Forsaken by his supporters, a mere pawn of the Duke of York, Cade is forced to hide out in an orchard and live on grass for three days before being killed.

By the end of *Henry VI Part 2*, weak, unstable Henry VI, who has brought the country to its knees with his 'bookish rule', and who would have preferred to be a monk, not a monarch, has retained his shaky grip on the throne, but his days are numbered. *Henry VI Part 3* is the bloodiest of a bloody series, as Henry's enemies fight over the crown like hungry dogs over a bone. With four battles – three on stage and one reported – it serves as a reminder of the terrible human cost of civil war. Fighting for opposing factions, a father kills his son and a son kills his father without realising who they are. 'O piteous spectacle! O bloody times!'[33] cries Henry. But the nightmare does not end there. As he clings to life, Henry VI is confronted by Richard, Duke of Gloucester, the future Richard III. Knowing that Richard is about to kill him, Henry swiftly reminds the audience of Richard's infernal credentials:

> The owl shriek'd at thy birth, an evil sign;
> The night-crow cried, aboding luckless time;
> Dogs howl'd, and hideous tempest shook down trees . . .
> Thy mother felt more than a mother's pain,
> And, yet brought forth less than a mother's hope,
> To wit, an indigested and deformed lump . . .
> Teeth hadst thou in thy head when thou wast born,
> To signify thou camest to bite the world:
> And, if the rest be true which I have heard,
> Thou camest— [34]

But the audience never learns what 'the rest' might be, as Henry is permanently interrupted when Richard stabs him. And stabs him again. *Some slain in war.*

Thus far in the First Tetralogy, the leading characters have been portrayed as weak (King Henry), calculating (Margaret, his Queen), or misguided (Jack Cade). But it is only Richard, Duke of Gloucester, the subject of the last play in the sequence, who can truly be described as evil.

In any informal survey of Shakespeare's most famous characters, conducted among the general public, which creation would be in the top three? Writing some years ago, the theatre critic Ivor Brown put the louche but loyal Falstaff in the lead, followed by Hamlet.[35] A contemporary survey would probably put Richard III in third place, burned into the popular imagination by Sir Laurence Olivier's 1958 incarnation of the original wicked uncle. Of course there have been other memorable Richards, such as those of Sher and McKellen, but Olivier's Duke of Gloucester became the personification of evil for generations of viewers. Our collective consciousness of this character has never been the same again.[36]

While modern audiences have learned to regard Shakespeare's depiction of Richard III sceptically as a product of Tudor propaganda, there can be no doubt as to the relish with which Shakespeare fashioned his Richard. If the devil has all the best tunes, Richard has all the best lines and emerges in all his malignant glory as His Satanic Majesty.

Darkly charismatic, Richard is Shakespeare's most compelling creation so far. Before he even becomes the titular subject of his play, Richard springs upon the stage as a fully fledged monster equipped complete with self-knowledge, irony and 'determined to prove a villain. Why, I can smile, and murder whiles I smile . . . and set the murderous Machiavel to school.'[37] Richard confirms his audience's prejudices by embodying the common Tudor misconception of Machiavelli as a role model for devious politicians. He is, in many ways, Marlowe's creature, with the vaunting ambition of Tamburlaine or Faustus, revealing his intent in confiding speeches which increase in impact when addressed to an audience standing so close to the stage.

The readers in Shakespeare's audience would have nodded in recognition as Shakespeare's Richard quoted More's descriptions of himself, almost word for word: 'little of stature, evil featured of limbs, crook backed, the left shoulder much higher than the right, hard-favoured of visage . . . he came into the world the feet forward [sic], as men be borne outward, and as the fame ran, not untoothed.[38]

The young Duke of York, one of Richard's doomed nephews, observes with schoolboy awe that 'they say my uncle [Richard] grew so fast That he could gnaw a crust at two hours old'.[39]

But Richard wears his deformities like a badge of honour:

> I came into the world with my legs forward . . .
> The midwife wonder'd, and the women cried
> 'O Jesu bless us, he is born with teeth!'
> And so I was; which plainly signified
> That I should snarl, and bite, and play the dog.[40]

In a society where physical deformity was associated with witchcraft and ugliness taken to be indicative of moral depravity, Richard's physical disability is made synonymous with evil. He is doomed from childhood to be a monster, and his distorted form read as an indication of his inward ugliness; he is a 'lump of foul deformity', a 'bottled spider', 'that foul bunch-back'd toad', a 'cacodemon' and a 'cockatrice'.[41] Richard is almost supernatural, his most monstrous act being to order the murder of the princes in the Tower. Again, Shakespeare draws heavily from More: 'Now fell there mischiefs thick . . . the most piteous and wicked, I mean the lamentable murder of his innocent nephews, the young King and his tender brother.'[42]

According to More, the princes were killed on the orders of the ambitious courtier, Sir James Tyrell, indirectly responding to instructions from Richard. After being stifled with their feather bed, the boys were buried at the foot of the stairs, 'meetly deep in the ground under a great heap of stones'.[43] When he learned of this, Richard is said to have had the bodies moved, and buried in a more appropriate location befitting their royal birth. *Some sleeping killed.*

At this point in the proceedings, Shakespeare's Richard III should lose the audience's sympathy. An Elizabethan audience could tolerate the deaths of adult characters such as Clarence, Grey, Vaughan, Hastings and Buckingham with equanimity. After all, they are portrayed as scheming traitors, complicit in their own downfall. The audiences could even accept, if not condone, Richard's intention to poison his wife, Anne, so that he could marry his own niece. Child murder was another matter altogether and should have rendered Richard indefensible. But Shakespeare, taking his inspiration from More, allows Richard some redeeming features. First is the remorse the night before the Battle of Bosworth, when Richard is haunted by the ghosts of those he deposed, and second is the physical courage alluded to in *Henry VI Part 3* when Queen Margaret asks, 'And where's that valiant crookback prodigy, Dicky your boy?'[44] More tells his readers that Richard 'finished his time with the best death and the most righteous, that is to wit his own' and that he was 'slain in the field'.[45] Shakespeare dramatises this to powerful effect, summoning up some touch of pity for this monster as he fights for his life, battling away to the end, and grants him the immortal famous last words of 'A horse! A horse! My kingdom for a horse!'[46] Famous last words which inevitably became Richard Burbage's catchphrase and greeted him every time he entered a tavern.

Part bogeyman, part tragic hero, Richard III represented the ideal opportunity for Shakespeare to create a memorable role for Richard Burbage, the talented young actor who was beginning to overshadow Ned Alleyn. Whatever the true history of Richard III, Shakespeare was never one to let facts stand in the way of a good story.

While Henry Tudor's victory over Richard comes as a gesture of revenge for all those who died at Richard's hands, the conclusion is also an act of healing. England is being restored to health after the clash between York and Lancaster has made the country weep in streams of blood. The underlying theme, the need for a strong leader, which runs like a ribbon through the tragic life story of Henry VI, comes to the fore with Shakespeare's second series of history plays, the cycle known as the Second Tetralogy. *Richard II, Henry IV Part 1* and *Henry IV Part 2* all dwell on the power of the crown and the mystical destiny of kingship. To be a king is to be more than head of state, it is to be God's spokesman on earth.

> Not all the water in the rough rude sea
> Can wash the balm off from an anointed king.[47]

But what happens when the King himself is shown to be unfit for this task? Shakespeare examined this dilemma in *Richard II,* travelling further back in time to the life of Richard II (1367–1400). Like Henry VI, Richard is a weak and unpopular king, although his weakness is not piety but, it is implied, homosexuality, and 'reproach and dissolution hangeth over him'.[48] Feminine and frivolous, Richard is 'that sweet lovely rose',[49] ephemeral, a shooting star falling to earth and totally unsuited to government. Henry Bolingbroke later recalls that 'the skipping king, he ambled up and down'.[50] Richard II is not, therefore, fit to be a king, as John of Gaunt, on his deathbed, laments. Under Richard's lack of governance, the land which was once

> This royal throne of kings, this scepter'd isle,
> This earth of majesty, this seat of Mars,
> This other Eden, demi-paradise . . .
> This precious stone set in the silver sea . . .
> This blessed plot, this earth, this realm, this England[51]

... has been torn apart by the spectre of civil war and become a neglected garden, swarming with caterpillars, overrun with spiders and toads. England's decline is accelerated after Gaunt's death when Richard seizes his assets to fund an unpopular war in Ireland, only to find on his return to England that his nemesis, the exiled Henry Bolingbroke, has invaded and is challenging him for the crown. *Richard II* contains many intriguing parallels with contemporary Elizabethan politics and subsequently, a request to perform the play before the Earl of Essex in 1601 would be mired in controversy.

But back in 1595 the most notable features of the play were the melancholy nature of the subject matter, and the musings on the nature of kingship. In some respects, *Richard II* looks ahead to the problem plays such as *Measure for Measure* or the moral dilemma of *Julius Caesar,* of removing an ineffectual or dangerous ruler.

As a historical source Shakespeare drew on Holinshed but added many of his own embellishments. While the historian recorded that Richard II starved to death, Shakespeare has him murdered at Pontefract Castle by Sir Piers Exton, anxious to impress Henry Bolingbroke. Richard II, though an insubstantial creature, is of sufficient historical interest to carry the play. As characterised by Shakespeare, he is a complex figure with his contradictions, his obvious intelligence and his failure to act in his best interests. Weak and indecisive, his personality emerges as he has to deal with rebellion among his knights, followed by a peasants' revolt, and finally has to face his forced abdication and impending death. In many respects, Richard II is a prototype for Hamlet. Despite his unpopularity and his tarnished reputation, Richard has some of Shakespeare's best speeches. What he lacks in alpha-male leadership he gains in beautiful poetic language such as his elegiac reflection on the death of kings, a speech given in the full knowledge that he too will soon be dead. The play can have brought little comfort to Queen Elizabeth, who was facing fears over her own future and that of the succession. A theatrical depiction of a past king deposed and murdered could not have made easy viewing for an ageing monarch.

The Queen was to find Shakespeare's next history play far more entertaining. *Henry IV Part 1* introduced Shakespeare's greatest comic creation, one of those immortal characters whose name alone bestows instant recognition. Swaggering reprobate Sir John Falstaff is the real hero, although the ostensible topic of this play is the rebellion of the Percy family against King Henry. While war features strongly, the most memorable scenes take place among the teeming lowlife of the Boar's Head Tavern in Eastcheap, a familiar landmark in Elizabethan London from the days of Richard II to its eventual destruction in the Great Fire of 1666. The Boar's Head is the favourite haunt of Falstaff and his 'dissolute crew',[52] Poins, Bardolph and Mistress Quickly (not to mention Pistol and Doll Tearsheet, who we meet in *Henry IV Part 2*). Of all the history plays, *Henry IV Part 1* is most recognisably set in contemporary London.

Falstaff was originally named 'Sir John Oldcastle', the character being based on the 'Sir John Oldcastle' who appeared in the original source for the text, *The Famous Victories of Henry V*. Shakespeare was forced to make a name change when Lord Cobham, a descendant of Sir John Oldcastle, objected to the characterisation of his ancestor. Sir John 'Jockey' Oldcastle had been an intimate of the Prince of Wales, but was executed for his Lollard beliefs. Burned at the stake on the orders of Henry V, Sir John became a Protestant martyr.

Falstaff returned in *Henry IV Part 2*, as the rebellion against Henry IV continued, led by Archbishop Scroop, Mowbray and Hastings. The rebellion is quashed and, following the death of Henry IV, Prince Hal succeeds to the throne, while Falstaff naively assumes he will be promoted for all his loyal service to the future king. But far from it; instead, in a cruel about-turn, Hal callously discards Falstaff with an arrogant 'I know thee not, old man,' and orders him to be thrown into the Fleet prison. Even faced with this massive betrayal, Falstaff remains as faithful as a kicked dog. 'Do not you grieve at this. I shall be sent for in private to him . . . I shall be sent for soon at night.'[53] But Falstaff has been most royally dumped. Greater love hath no man than that he will lay down his friend for his own reputation. *I know thee not, old man.* In the opening scenes of *Henry V*, the audience is informed that Falstaff has died. Of a broken heart, perhaps.

But in the end, Falstaff survived, achieving a mythical longevity thanks to the Queen, who was so delighted with the character that she demanded Shakespeare bring him back from the dead and write a play about 'Falstaff in love'. Eventually, Shakespeare complied, and Falstaff was resurrected, at Her Majesty's pleasure, in *The Merry Wives of Windsor*.

Considering the oppressive censorship of Elizabeth I's London, Shakespeare took considerable risks in the Second Tetralogy. After the less than complimentary depiction of poor Richard II came the critical portrait of Prince Hal, the future national hero. Shakespeare might have given us a Prince Hal as a lively young man, courageous but much given to nightlife, fancy dress and practical jokes. Instead, Shakespeare presents a calculating individual, truly Machiavellian in his willingness to manipulate and exploit his friends for the greater end of statecraft. A man who deliberately plays up his drunken antics so that he will emerge all the brighter when he succeeds to the throne, discarding Falstaff when he becomes expendable. Hal is also so eager to become king that as his father, Henry IV, lies dying, he takes the crown from the pillow and tries it on, only to be mortified when his father awakes. Uneasy lies the head that wears the crown, indeed. But Henry IV himself is ambivalent about his own claims to the throne. 'God knows, my son, By what by-paths and indirect crook'd ways I met this crown.'[54] This is a melancholy descant upon the insecurities of kingship, taking us back once more to the terrors experienced by the elegiac Richard II, as he envisages the malevolent jester Death mocking his royal status:

> For within the hollow crown
> That rounds the mortal temples of a king
> Keeps Death his court and there the antic sits,
> Scoffing his state and grinning at his pomp[55]

This is a man who knows that the death of kings will be inevitable, untimely and cruel. 'Some slain in war. Some haunted by the ghosts they have deposed. Some poison'd by their wives. Some sleeping kill'd. All murder'd.' Because at the end of it, this 'antic death' is waiting to deal the *coup de grace*, this Death who 'Comes at the last and with a little pin Bores through his castle wall, and farewell king!'[56]

If this is an unhappy note upon which to end, it is worth remembering that Shakespeare's kings achieved triumphs as well as tragedies. As King Henry V, Prince Hal will go on to redeem himself, in spectacular fashion, as England's national hero, thus redeeming the nation itself. And with the great history play *Henry V*, Shakespeare and the Chamberlain's Men would open their new theatre in the last year of the dying century. But before such a play could be written and performed, Shakespeare and his company would have to fight many battles of their own.

ALL THE WORLD'S A STAGE

If this were played upon a stage now,
I could condemn it as an improbable fiction.

Twelfth Night, Act 3 Scene 4

In spite of James Burbage's endless debts and enduring financial headaches, the Theatre was going from strength to strength. By 1595, it had consolidated its position as one of London's leading playhouses. Burbage had succeeded in creating a new art form, the play at the playhouse which you had to pay to get in and see. In the course of a few short years, theatre-going had become the most popular pastime in Elizabethan London. From the twin sites of Shoreditch, home of the Theatre and the Curtain, and Bankside, site of the Rose and the Swan, London was approaching the height of the theatre boom. From its humble beginnings in inn-yards, and exclusive private performances at Court and the Inns of Court, drama had become the exciting new form of entertainment. Out of a population of 200,000, around 15,000 Londoners a week paid upwards of a penny, sometimes as much as a shilling, to attend the theatres. At 'the play', men and women learned 'what is happening abroad; indeed men and womenfolk visit such places without scruple, since the English for the most part do not travel much, but prefer to learn foreign matters and take their pleasures at home.'[1] Part blockbuster, part comic review, theatres were the first form of mass entertainment. Audiences were captivated by a heady combination of sensational storylines, larger-than-life characters, life-threatening dilemmas, satirical sketches, philosophical musings, social comment and knockabout comedy. As an art form, theatre could scarcely fail, although towards the end of this decade its future would hover in the balance as one satirical play, *The Isle of Dogs,* almost saw the theatres shut down for good.

Over at the Theatre, James Burbage should have been delighted with the outcome of his venture. However, new troubles loomed for the Burbage clan. While poets were 'plentiful as blackberries'[2] then, it was theatres that were scarce. By 1595, with the lease on the Theatre expiring, James Burbage began to look elsewhere for new premises. Opening another theatre on Bankside was not an option. Philip Henslowe's Rose was already there, and doing great business. So was the Swan, which had opened that year. The last thing Bankside needed was another theatre. In order to expand his empire, Burbage would have to turn away from the liberty of Bankside to another, very different, liberty. Instead of the liberty of Bankside which gave haven to the lowlife and the outcasts of London, or the liberty of Shoreditch which was too far from the city, Burbage alighted upon a royal liberty, crammed with the nobility and the well-to-do, many of them connected with the Court. This was the liberty of Blackfriars, the site of an old abbey destroyed during the Reformation, its name deriving from the black robes of its Dominican monks.

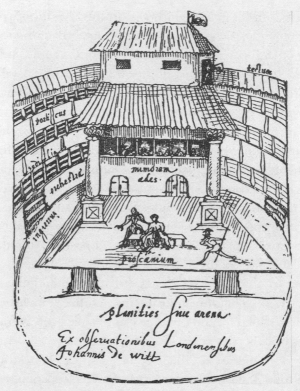

This drawing of the Swan Theatre by Johannes De Witte, showing how an Elizabethan auditorium would have looked.

Originally built outside the city walls, Blackfriars had later been enclosed within them, and yet was not officially part of the city. After the Dissolution, Blackfriars had become Crown lands, and though the land was leased to tenants, the Crown remained in control. Burbage anticipated that Blackfriars, as a better class of neighbourhood, would have few of the apprentices' riots and drunken outbursts that had marred the precincts of the Theatre. Burbage's new venture would not, strictly speaking, be the first theatre at Blackfriars. That honour had fallen to an earlier Blackfriars Theatre which opened in 1576. This theatre had been built for the Children of the Chapel Royal, child actors from the Queen's chapel who sang and performed plays, and it had been popular with other boys' companies, such as the Earl of Oxford's troupe. Expensive and exclusive, the theatre had closed in 1583 following a legal dispute over the lease.

From Sir William More of Loseley, the MP who owned the land upon which Blackfriars Abbey had stood, Burbage purchased a derelict suite of rooms for £600. Burbage intended to remodel these chambers into an indoor theatre, with roofs overhead to protect the patrons from all weathers. The location of this new theatre in Blackfriars also meant that his audience would be drawn from the immediate neighbourhood instead of having to walk across the fields to Shoreditch or cross the river to get to the Rose. Most importantly, chandeliers bearing hundreds of flickering candles meant that plays could be staged in the evening, and patrons would not be required to return home before dark.

Burbage had tremendous ambitions for this new theatre. He put his heart and soul into it. He wanted it to be ready before the lease ran out on the Theatre, so he could transplant his company of brilliant players to the new theatre at once before they could be forced out by a grasping landlord. This new theatre would require a great deal of rebuilding, with stone and lime for walls and pillars, and wood for the stage, benches and boxes. The decorations too must be new, rich and courtly like the staterooms of Whitehall and Hampton Court, and impressive by candlelight, like the great halls of Oxford and Cambridge and the Inns of Court. Burbage effectively made the new theatre his home, taking up residence to manage his new construction project. But any celebratory mood that Burbage entertained at this point was marred by the death of Henry Carey, Lord Hunsdon, the patron of the Lord Chamberlain's Men, on 23 July 1596. This death, which represented yet another blow to Burbage's professional life, was followed less than six months later by a terrible personal sadness, the death of his daughter Ellen, who was buried at St Anne's, Blackfriars, on 13 December. When his son succeeded to the title, Burbage transferred his allegiance to the new Lord Hunsdon; sadly, this individual was neither as benevolent nor as powerful as his father, and the Queen chose not to make him Lord Chamberlain, for the time being at least – the company briefly had to become 'Lord Hunsdon's Men'. Instead, the Queen appointed Lord Cobham, who was no friend of players. It was Lord Cobham who had taken such great exception to Shakespeare's portrayal of his ancestor, Sir John Oldcastle, so that Shakespeare had been obliged to change 'Sir John Oldcastle', 'my old lad of the castle' into 'Sir John Falstaff'. Cobham's appointment represented another blow for Burbage. He was already at odds with the Corporation of the City of London, and the Earl of Essex (who *was* a friend to players) had left the country. In 1596 Thomas Nashe observed that 'The Players are piteously persecuted by the Lord Mayor and the Aldermen, and however in their old Lord's time they thought their estate settled it is now so uncertain they cannot build upon it.'[3]

Yet another attack upon Burbage came from another quarter. While Burbage was already at odds with Myles, from whom he leased the land for the Theatre, and with Giles Alleyn in Holywell, it was now a woman who threatened his new enterprise at Blackfriars. The Dowager Lady Elizabeth Russell dreaded the prospect of Blackfriars becoming contaminated by the evils which surrounded the public theatres in the liberties. This interfering busybody took it upon herself to circulate a petition against Burbage's plans which would be submitted to the Privy Council. While

Elizabeth Russell did not obtain many signatures from members of her own rank and class, she rallied enough opposition to submit the petition to Lord Hunsdon, James Burbage's master, who must have groaned aloud when he recognised her name. Most names upon the petition were those of insignificant local tradesmen but one stands out: Richard Field, printer, publisher of Shakespeare's *Venus and Adonis* and *The Rape of Lucrece*. If Shakespeare had learned of this *volte-face* by his own publisher, it must have hit him hard. '*Et tu, Brute?*' To add insult to injury, Field was a Stratford man.[4]

The petition effectively put an end to James Burbage's dream. Here was a beautiful new theatre, curtained, closed and warm, waiting for the Lord Chamberlain's Men when their lease ran out at the Theatre, and they were forbidden to use it.

Despite Burbage's woes, which, combined with the imminent loss of the Theatre must have cast a shadow over the Lord Chamberlain's Men, the company thrived. Shakespeare, their star writer, and Richard Burbage, the leading man of his day, combined to draw in capacity audiences, day after day. During this period Shakespeare proved that, as a dramatist, he was without any serious rival. He was hitting his creative stride with a series of comedies that proved every bit as popular as his history plays. Indeed, in many ways, the comedies were the flipside of the histories, and said as much about contemporary London life as the dark Senecan tragedies.

Performed from around 1591 onwards, these comedies consist of *The Comedy of Errors*, *Two Gentlemen of Verona*, *Love's Labour's Lost*, *The Merchant of Venice*, *The Taming of the Shrew* and *A Midsummer Night's Dream*. These played to capacity houses at the Theatre and the Curtain; even more significantly, they were performed at Court before Queen

Elizabeth herself. *Love's Labour's Lost* and *A Midsummer Night's Dream* represent Shakespeare's first real romantic comedies, while *Romeo and Juliet* could best be described as a 'romantic tragedy', with Shakespeare proving that he could move his audience to tears with a tale of star-crossed lovers. Between 1591 and 1598, Shakespeare proved himself to be a virtuoso; there was not one genre in the existing canon that he could not take on, adapt and make his own. He had found his own voice, and it was a distinctive one.

The word 'comedy' derived from the Greek *komos*, meaning revel or singing. By the 1590s, Elizabethan comedy had evolved from a combination of the knockabout inn-yard buffoonery, high-minded Court entertainments performed by university students and young men from the Inns of Court, and the Italian *commedia dell'arte,* a form of improvised street-theatre imported from Italy. *Commedia dell'arte* sprang from the Venetian carnival tradition, played outdoors by actors in grotesque masks representing standard types including the young lovers (*inamorate* and *inamorati*), servants (*zannis*), slippered pantaloons and blustering army officers (*miles glorioses*). Originating with the high-jinks of Shrove Tuesday, the last day of fun before the abstinence of Lent, *commedia dell'arte* is really the origin of our pantomime. Added to this, the university wits such as John Lyly and Thomas Nashe had taken on the more elevated model of *commedia eruditia*, learned comedy written and performed by and for scholars, characterised by 'a foolish extravagant spirit full of forms, figures, shapes, objects, ideas, apprehensions, motions, revolutions'.[5] Shakespeare's comic model was a mash-up of all these existing traditions. It is easy to imagine Titania and Bottom or Katherina and Petruchio barnstorming their way across a rickety scaffold outside an inn, while *Love's Labour's Lost* is a brilliant parody of the pretentious students who constituted Lyly's core audience. Somewhere between the pantomime tradition and the pyrotechnic brilliance of the university wits, Shakespeare's own comedy was born. What he lacked in Ben Jonson's biting cynicism, those vicious Volpones and Moscas, Shakespeare made up for in recognisable types and comic situations. Jonson's satire was hugely popular with the university wits, but too dangerous for Shakespeare in an age of censorship. Just how dangerous it was for Jonson will be seen later in this chapter, with the disastrous production of *The Isle of Dogs*. Shakespeare's concern instead was the human comedy, and a typical play from this period featured the constant struggles of a young man trying to find his way despite numerous setbacks, in a plot derived from an existing theatrical genre, played out against a backdrop of bawdy humour, physical comedy and slapstick. Here was the opportunity for Will Kemp, the capering clown, to dance his famous jigs and divert a robust drunken audience. Two of Shakespeare's earliest comedies, *Two Gentlemen of Verona* and *The Comedy of Errors,* are typical examples of this approach. Derived from Plautus, the plots of both plays turn upon the chaos which ensues when identical twins are mistaken for one another; in *The Comedy of Errors,* a girl – played of course by a boy – is dressed as a boy, causing much sexual confusion. This device involved a suspension of disbelief from the audience, but Elizabethan playgoers were happy to go along with the illusion. The performance was all about entertainment, with no pretence at realism. *Pyramus and Thisbe,* the mechanics' play which forms the play within a play in *A Midsummer Night's Dream*, is a spoof of existing love tragedies, *Romeo and Juliet* included. The comedy intellectuals in *Love's Labour's Lost*, resolving to abandon women and retreat into the forest, are straight out of Lyly.

But even at his most comic, Shakespeare cannot resist allowing more serious themes of cruelty and death to seep through the comic fabric. At the end of *Love's Labour's Lost,* a newly mature Don Adriano de Armado observes that 'the words of Mercury are harsh after the songs of Apollo'.[6] *The Comedy of Errors* is played out beneath the threat of execution. *Two Gentlemen of Verona* has a subplot about rape, questionable at the time and unacceptable to audiences today. Profoundly dark materials form the basis of two of Shakespeare's most famous comedies, *The Taming of the Shrew* and *The Merchant of Venice.* One play appears to celebrate misogyny while the second represents a triumph of anti-Semitism, and it is unlikely that modern theatre-goers would regard either of these works as 'comedies'. By any standards, these are difficult plays. Or 'problem comedies', to conflate two existing categories of Shakespeare's drama. Nobody dies, but there is a sense in which these plays are tragedies of the human spirit. Katherina and Shylock survive to the end of their narratives, but their personalities are effectively snuffed out, Katherina's by apparent submission to her husband and Shylock's by forced religious conversion. The real dramatic tension comes from the conflict between the audience's sympathy for Katherina and Shylock, and their treatment at the hands of their fellow characters.

The Taming of the Shrew was one of Shakespeare's earliest plays, written between 1590 and 1594 and based on an earlier play, *The Taming of a Shrew*, which in its turn was based upon the 'shrew-taming' literature of the day. These sources included Gascoigne, Ariosto and many ballads and stories. 'The battle of the sexes', as it used to be called, was to become one of Shakespeare's central themes, from the quarrel between Oberon and Titania in *A Midsummer Night's Dream* to *Much Ado About Nothing*'s sparring Beatrice and Benedick,

right through to the tragic consequences of sexual jealousy
in *Othello* and *The Winter's Tale*. Given that Katherina is one
of Shakespeare's most spirited female creations, and a far
more interesting character than her insipid sister Bianca, it
is difficult to accept that Shakespeare's version of the shrew-
taming tale was just blatant misogyny. This is, after all, the
writer who created the witty Beatrice, the wise Viola, and
the volatile Cleopatra. Rather than relishing Katherina's
humiliation, the audience is invited to be appalled by it.
Playing the shrew certainly provided the actor far more
opportunity to express his range and, more importantly, to
gain the sympathy of the audience. While it is tempting to
accept a modern interpretation of the play, that Katherina's
apparent submission is an elaborate trick to turn the tables
on Petruchio, *The Shrew* is still a play which divides audiences. As it was intended to do. Shakespeare's objective, as
a writer, was to create compelling drama, not a series of
morality plays.

This ambiguity, and a willingness to engage with themes
that were not strictly comic, is at the heart of Shakespeare's
most controversial 'comedy', *The Merchant of Venice*. The
play is billed as a comedy, even though the premise itself is
unfunny: the debtor will be agreeing to his own death if he
acquiesces to the demand for a pound of flesh, and Shylock
will effectively become his murderer. Shylock himself appears
at first glance to be a viciously anti-Semitic stereotype, unsympathetic, materialistic and full of contempt for his Christian
counterparts. A close relation, in many respects, of Marlowe's
Barabas, *The Jew of Malta*.

Most curious of all, *The Merchant of Venice* portrays a Jew
for an audience who had probably never actually met a Jew.
Officially, there were no Jews in England at the time, as they
had been expelled from the country in 1290 on the orders of

Edward I. However, a handful of Jews did visit England from time to time, for trade purposes, and a tiny Jewish community known as Marranos eked out a secret existence in London, living below the radar and practising Christianity to escape persecution. Hostility against Jews, whether they had actually been encountered at first hand or not, was a toxic legacy of medieval Christianity. The most famous Jew in London in the early 1590s was Dr Lopez, physician to Queen Elizabeth, and his terrible fate sheds light upon *The Merchant of Venice*.[7] Rodrigo Lopez (1525–94) was a Portuguese doctor who arrived in London in 1559 and became a physician at St Bartholomew's Hospital. Popular and successful, Dr Lopez numbered among his patients some of the most eminent individuals of the day, including Sir Robert Dudley, the Earl of Leicester, and the Queen's spymaster Sir Francis Walsingham. Although a rumour circulated that he had distilled poisons for Sir Robert Dudley, Lopez rose to the pinnacle of his career in 1586 when he became physician-in-chief to the Queen. Wealthy and popular, Lopez had become a pillar of the establishment. A practising Protestant, he lived in a splendid house in Holborn and sent his son to Winchester College. However, in October 1593 a Spanish plot to poison the Queen was uncovered, and the Earl of Essex accused Lopez of being involved. Despite Lopez's protests, and the Queen's unwillingness to believe his guilt, Lopez was arrested on 1 January 1594 and tried at the Guildhall. This trial created a great sensation at the time, and there are references to it in Dekker's *Whore of Babylon* and Middleton's *A Game at Chess*. After being put on the rack, Lopez is said to have 'confessed' to agreeing to poison the Queen in return for 50,000 ducats, but it must be borne in mind that this confession was obtained under torture. The Queen was unwilling to accept Lopez's guilt and delayed his execution but finally, on 7 June, Lopez was hanged, drawn and quartered. According to William Camden, the Tudor historian, Lopez protested on the scaffold that he loved the Queen as much as he loved Jesus Christ, but the crowd simply laughed at him, taking this as further evidence of his guilt.[8] Lopez's death was particularly barbaric and he underwent appalling suffering at the hands of an incompetent executioner. A similar dreadful fate awaited Shylock if he took his 'pound of flesh' from Antonio. All in all, a curious background for a comedy.

The Merchant of Venice was, of course, set in that Italian city because it had what London lacked, an established Jewish community with usury their only profession. Shylock is at first an uncompromising figure, but his attitudes are not surprising given the way he is treated by his so-called Christian fellows. He is understandably aggrieved, a bitter outsider like Marlowe's Barabas. But, because this is Shakespeare, and none of his characters are two-dimensional, Shylock is also a sympathetic figure, who feels that he has been harshly treated by Antonio. 'He hath disgrac'd me . . . laugh'd at my losses, mock'd at my gains, scorned my nation . . . and what's his reason? I am a Jew.' In response, Shylock advances a compelling argument for respect:

Hath not a Jew eyes? hath not a Jew hands, organs, dimensions, senses, affections, passions? fed with the same food, hurt with the same weapons, subject to the same diseases, healed by the same means, warmed and cooled by the same winter and summer, as a Christian is? If you prick us, do we not bleed? if you tickle us, do we not laugh? if you poison us, do we not die? and if you wrong us, shall we not revenge? . . . The villainy you teach me, I will execute, and it shall go hard but I will better the instruction.[9]

Further proof that Shylock is not simply an updated version of Avarice can be found in the genuine heartbreak he suffers when his daughter, Jessica, runs away with Lorenzo, taking his fortune with her. Bitterness at losing his daughter to a Christian, and losing his money too, is understandable. But then Shakespeare adds an extra twist that makes one wince on Shylock's behalf, when he discovers that Jessica gave away one of her mother's rings in exchange for . . . a monkey: 'It was my turquoise; I had it of Leah when I was a bachelor: I would not have given it for a wilderness of monkeys.'[10]

The conclusion of *The Merchant of Venice* is no easier to accept than Katherina's apparent retreat into wifely compliance. To escape execution, Shylock must agree to undergo forced conversion, to abandon his faith and his cultural identity just to stay alive. A terrible fate indeed, but less ghastly perhaps than that endured by Dr Lopez, or indeed by Barabas, *The Jew of Malta,* who falls into a cauldron and is boiled alive.

The Merchant of Venice and *The Taming of the Shrew* are problem comedies for modern audiences. But when Shakespeare was writing, there was no concept of political correctness. A plot was a plot and the offensiveness or otherwise of the material considered irrelevant. Given the controversy over 'seditious' material, the Marprelate conspiracy and the fates of Christopher Marlowe and Thomas Kyd, little would have been left to write about if Shakespeare had chosen to avoid the disquieting themes of anti-Semitism and misogyny. As it was, both plays provided dramatic storylines with plenty of opportunity for fine writing and distinctive acting without upsetting the Lord Chamberlain.

Despite the triumph of Shakespeare's plays, James Burbage had become something of a tragic figure by 1597. Burbage had spent a life of incessant hard work, constantly thwarted and frustrated in all his enterprises. He was not young and his body was not as tough and resilient as his spirit. Finally, battered, bruised, and defeated in his attempts to open his Blackfriars theatre, Burbage died, aged sixty-seven. He was buried at St Leonard's, Shoreditch, on 2 February 1597, just six weeks before the termination of the Holywell lease. Despite the fact that he was less successful than he deserved to be, Burbage did more for the development of the British stage than all the other actor-managers put together.

The loss of their father was a terrible blow for Richard and Cuthbert Burbage. Richard's career was in the ascendant, thanks to his roles in Shakespeare's dramas, but both sons had relied on their father to direct the business. To make matters worse, James Burbage died intestate. Fortunately, relations between the brothers were amicable. Cuthbert had been given the Theatre in 1589 and continued to run it. Richard, who had informally been given the Blackfriars theatre by James before his death, continued to administer it and take a rent from Nathaniel Giles and Henry Evans while they ran it as a boys' company. Burbage left little in terms of goods and chattels at the house in Holywell, and the sons were content to let their mother go on living there, taking care of her as well as their own families. One small comfort was the fact that their master, Lord Hunsdon, had finally been appointed Lord Chamberlain on 17 March 1597, so once again they became 'the Lord Chamberlain's Men'. But any mood of celebration was eclipsed by the death, that summer, of Cuthbert's baby son, James, named in honour of his grandfather and buried at St Leonard's Church on 15 July.

Just over a week later, these bereavements, enough to test the mettle of the most resilient men, were followed by another crippling blow. On 28 July 1597, the Lord Mayor of London published a letter of complaint against the theatres in which he referred to: 'divers apprentices and other servants, who have confessed unto us that the said Stage Playes were the very places of their rendezvous appointed by them to meet with such others as were to join with them in their designs and mutinous attempts, being also the ordinary playes for masterless men to come together to recreate themselves.'[11]

At first glance, this appears to be a routine letter from the authorities complaining about the theatres, yet another instalment in the relentless campaign against plays and players conducted by the combined forces of the Privy Council, the Corporation of London and the Puritans. However, this letter had more profound implications, accusing the theatres of engendering 'mutinous attempts', otherwise known as sedition, a crime punishable by death. With this in mind, the Lord Mayor's letter concludes with a recommendation for 'the final suppressings of the saide stage-playes as well at the Theatre, Curten and Bankside, as in all other places in and about the City'.[12]

One wonders what on earth could have happened to provoke such a savage outcry. Despite the routine criticism from the authorities, and the genuine need to close the theatres during outbreaks of plague, this letter was more severe than usual. After all, by 1597 theatre had become popular entertainment. It delighted the apprentice and the gentleman alike. Respectable women had even begun to attend the playhouses, albeit chaperoned by their menfolk. What could possibly have gone wrong?

For an answer to this question, it is necessary to introduce a promising young part-time actor-cum-bricklayer named Ben Jonson. Described memorably by John Aubrey as 'a staring Leviathan with a face like the cover of a warming pan and a terrible mouth',[13] Jonson was a gifted writer with a strong personality but limited acting skills. Educated at Westminster School, Jonson had been destined for Cambridge

University, but a lack of funds saw him turn instead to his stepfather's trade of bricklaying. Jonson loathed it and, as soon as he was able, enlisted as a soldier and fought against the Spanish in the Low Countries. If Jonson mentioned in a tavern that he had killed a man in combat, nobody was going to argue with him. Jonson might have hated bricklaying, but he possessed the bluff manner and powerful physique of the typical builder. Combined with a razor-sharp wit and a classical education, Jonson was perfect for the new trade of acting, even if his grasp of iambic pentameter left much to be desired.

On 28 July 1597, Jonson signed to the Admiral's Men under Philip Henslowe at the Rose, for what looked like the start of a promising career. Henslowe even gave Jonson an advance on his wages, meticulously recorded in his diary. 'Lent unto Benjamin Jonson player the 28th of July 1597 in ready money the sum of four pounds, to be paid it again whensoever either I or any for me shall demand it.'[14]

On the afternoon of the very same day that he had signed his contract with the Rose, Jonson appeared on stage at the Swan, with the Earl of Pembroke's Men, in a play he had co-written with Thomas Nashe. Entitled *The Isle of Dogs,* a reference to the former island in the East End of London which traditionally housed the royal kennels and offered immunity from debt, this play was a scurrilous topical satire. With gleeful abandon, Jonson and Nashe ripped the government to shreds, egging each other on to ever more outrageous feats of vitriolic wit. Both men were masters in the art of the vicious parody, with Jonson believing that political satire served a moral purpose while Nashe wrote like a vicious human squid, squirting ink at any who crossed him. All that is known of the play is that it contained slanderous and seditious material and lampooned many of the great and good of the day. Halfway through the performance, the Swan was raided on the orders of Sir Richard Topcliffe, a rabidly anti-Catholic investigator and torturer, and the cast arrested and thrown into gaol. Ben Jonson and his fellow actors, Gabriel Spenser and Robert Shaw, were flung into the Marshalsea, while Thomas Nashe fled London for his native Norfolk.

Regrettably, not one copy of *The Isle of Dogs* has survived. Given the furore which surrounded its one and only production, the play was never printed and any manuscripts were instantly committed to the flames. Jonson's debut had turned into a nightmare. He was only twenty-five and *The Isle of Dogs* was his first play. But he proved to be a resilient prisoner, embracing the role of the hardman, later recalling with pride 'the tyme of his close imprisonment' when his interrogators could get nothing out of him apart from an 'Aye and No'.[15]

The Isle of Dogs furore was potentially catastrophic for London's theatre world. Who needed plague when you had Nashe and Jonson appearing together on the same bill? *The Isle of Dogs* had given the authorities yet another excuse to close the theatres, and worse.

On 28 July, the same day that the Lord Mayor of London condemned the 'mutinous' attitude of apprentices visiting the theatres, the Privy Council wrote to the Justices of Middlesex stating that the Queen herself had demanded the closure of the playhouses on the grounds that there were 'very great disorders committed in the common playhouses, both by lewd matters that are handled on the stages, and by resorte and confluence of bad people'. As a result, the Queen had ordered that 'no plays shall be used within London or about the Citty, or in any publique place, during this tyme of summer until All Hallowtide next'.[16] This was bad enough, but not without precedent. But what came after this must have shocked London's impressarios to the core and Philip Henslowe to the core. The Privy Council demanded that:

those playhouses that are erected and built only for suche purposes shall be plucked down namelie the Curtain and the Theatre near to Shoreditch, or any other within that county . . . and likewise that you do send for the owner of the Curtain Theatre, the Theatre, or any other common playhouse, and enjoin them forthwith to pluck down the stages, galleries and rooms that are made for people to stand in, and so to deface the same as they may not be employed again to such use; which if they shall not speedily perform, you shall advertise us that order may be taken to see the same done, according to her Majesties pleasure and commandment.[17]

Not only did the authorities want a ban on performances until 31 October, All Hallows, but they actually wanted to see the playhouses 'plucked down'. This terrible command-ment was a potential death blow for the Burbages. It looked as though James Burbage's legacy was about to be destroyed without compensation, robbing his family of their means of support. Cuthbert Burbage responded by using a legal subter-fuge to obtain a stay of execution for the Theatre, quite possibly accompanied by a bribe. Some theatres, such as the Swan and the Curtain, chose to flout the prospect of imminent destruction, blithely ignoring the edict and staying open.

For Philip Henslowe at the Rose, *The Isle of Dogs* debacle was a considerable blow. At a stroke, he had lost a promising newcomer, Jonson, and two of his best actors, Shaw and Spenser, to gaol and possible execution. Henslowe's response was to sign up other players to the Admiral's Men over the summer, in preparation for the autumn season. On 3 October 1597, the Privy Council relented and instructed the Keeper of the Marshalsea to release Spenser, Shaw and Jonson. On 11 October, performances began again at the Rose. Henslowe recorded this in his notebook: 'The 11th October began my Lord Admiral's and my Lord Pembroke's Men to play at my house, 1597. In the name of God, Amen.'[18]*Amen*, indeed: not so much a religious platitude as an audible sigh of relief. Sadly, just a year later, Ben Jonson was to try Philip Henslowe's patience once again.

Over the following year, Ben Jonson's writing talents came to the fore and he was much valued by the Admiral's Men. The author Francis Meres records that Jonson was considered 'the best for tragedy',[19] but his satirical skills were also in the ascendant, even after the debacle of *The Isle of Dogs;* 1598 would see a positive reception for Jonson's *Every Man in his Humour*. However, as Jonson's star rose, so another actor's reputation sank. Gabriel Spenser, Jonson's cellmate in the Marshalsea, had come across to join him with the Admiral's Men but a bitter feud had developed between the pair, and their relationship plummeted to new depths over the following year. As the 26-year-old Jonson scaled the professional heights, the unpopular Spenser sank deeper into drink and developed an implacable hatred of Jonson. Unpopular among the actors, Spenser had a reputation as a troublemaker, and worse.

Two years earlier, on 3 December 1596, Spenser had been present at the house of Richard East, along with a man named James Feake, between five and six in the evening. According to witnesses, 'insulting words had passed' between Spenser and Feake. Feake had seized a copper candlestick, which he threatened to throw at Spenser, whereupon Spenser seized his sword and stabbed Feake in the right eye, penetrating the brain and inflicting a mortal wound. Poor Feake 'languished and lived in languor at Holywell Street' for three days before he died. Despite being accused of murder, Spenser was not executed, or required to forfeit any goods. Perhaps the three days between the fight and Feake's death gave Spenser the opportunity to assemble friendly witnesses to testify that Feake had provoked him. It was a violent age and men such as Spenser did not hesitate to resort to their weapons if the opportunity demanded it. But nemesis came for the actor two years later.[20]

On the evening of 22 September 1598, Ben Jonson encountered Spenser in Hoxton Fields in Shoreditch, just around the corner from the Curtain Theatre. The men quarrelled and Spenser challenged Jonson to a duel. Fighting came naturally to both men. Jonson had been a soldier, but as an actor Spenser had trained for fight scenes. All Englishmen had the right to bear arms, and fencing was regarded as a vital accomplishment and an extension of one's masculinity, as indicated in these lines from *The Merry Wives of Windsor*: 'I bruised my shin th' other day with playing at sword and dagger with a master of fence.'[21] Elizabethan youths flocked to the fencing schools, and every thrust and parry was watched and noted by an army of aficionados, as described in *Romeo and Juliet*:

He fights as
you sing prick-song, keeps time, distance, and
proportion; rests me his minim rest, one, two, and
the third in your bosom: the very butcher of a silk
button, a duellist, a duellist . . .
ah, the immortal passado! the punto reverso! The hai! . . .
The pox of such antic, lisping, affecting fantasticoes . . .
these strange flies, these fashion-mongers, these
perdona-mi's![22]

Swordplay was an everyday occurrence in Elizabethan London, part of the throbbing violent pulse of the time, with its own macho ethic and accompanying black humour. When Mercutio is wounded by Tybalt with characteristic brio he makes light his injuries: 'No, 'tis not so deep as a well, nor so wide as a church-door; but 'tis enough, 'twill serve: ask for me to-morrow, and you shall find me a grave man.'[23]

So here stood Jonson, the provoked, and Spenser, the provoker, with weapons drawn, about to fight to the death. The protagonists were equally matched in terms of skill, and the fight between Jonson and Spenser must have been as theatrical as any performed on stage. Once violence is imaginatively recreated, it gains its own momentum. Did this skirmish start as a drunken taunt, a play-fight between two hot-headed hell-raisers? In terms of weapons, it was scarcely a fair fight. Spenser's sword was ten inches longer and it was only the fact that he had been drinking all day that gave Jonson the advantage. As Spenser staggered about waving his sword, Jonson swiped back at him; within minutes, Spenser was dead at his feet.

Although he maintained that Spenser had struck first, wounding him in the arm, Jonson was charged with 'feloniously and wilfully' slaying Gabriel Spenser with 'a certain sword of iron and steel called a rapier, of the price of three shillings, which he then and there had and held drawn in his right hand.'[24] According to witnesses, Jonson inflicted a six-inch wound to Spenser's right side which killed him instantly. Despite claiming to have been acting in self-defence, Jonson was arrested and taken to Newgate Gaol, and was charged with murder. For all his genius, it looked as if Jonson's final performance was to be upon the scaffold at Tyburn. But Jonson had one trump card left. As a former pupil at Westminster School, he possessed one item which nobody could take away from him, and that was his education. Jonson's life was saved by a legal loophole which permitted the literate man to escape sentence 'by benefit of clergy',[25] on the grounds that any man with a working knowledge of Latin was a cleric and therefore immune to secular law. The benefit of clergy posed no difficulty for Jonson, who was required to do nothing more than recite an extract from Psalm 51 which began '*Miserere mei*' or 'Have mercy upon me, O Lord'. This stratagem saved so many prisoners from the gallows that it became known as 'the neck verse'. Jonson emerged from Newgate with an 'x' branded on his thumb to prevent him claiming benefit of clergy a second time. This was a lasting reminder of his imprisonment, but he had at least escaped with his life.

Philip Henslowe was horrified by this turn of events. Writing to Edward Alleyn on 26 September 1598, he told him: 'Since you were with me I have lost one of my company, which hurteth me greatly, that is Gabriel, for he is slain in Hogsden Fields by the hands of Benjamin Jonson, bricklayer.'[26] Jonson, no doubt, would have been hurteth greatly to be referred to as a bricklayer, the trade which he so despised.

Meanwhile, as 1598 drew towards its close, the year grew increasingly darker for the Burbage brothers. Their patrons had become weaker. The Earl of Southampton had fallen out of favour with Queen Elizabeth, after secretly marrying her maid of honour, Elizabeth Vernon. Even the Earl of Essex was not in the same favour as he used to be, and suspected of preparing his own rebellions against the crown. Although the authorities had relented in February and permitted the Lord Chamberlain's Men and the Admiral's Men to perform at the Curtain and the Rose, the Theatre remained, in theatrical parlance, 'dark'. Deserted and lonely, the forlorn shell of the Burbages' hopes and dreams inspired this sorry comparison in Guilpin's *Skialetheia,* 1598:

'But see yonder, one Who like the unfrequented Theater
Walkes in dark silence and vast solitude.'[27]

In the 1598 edition of Stow's *Survey of London,* the historian
refers to Holywell and an old priory long since pulled down,
as a place 'where many houses are built for the lodging of
noblemen, of strangers born and other'. Stow speaks of the
Church of St Leonard's, Shoreditch, the actors' church, and
'near thereunto two public Houses for the acting and Shewe
of Comedies, tragidies and Histories for recreation whereof
one is called The Curtain and the other the Theatre both
standing on the Southwest side towards the Field'.[28] This
was Stow's last printed reference to the Theatre. By the time
the next edition came out, the Theatre was gone.

THE GREAT GLOBE ITSELF

Can this cockpit hold
The vasty fields of France? Or may we cram
Within this wooden O the very casques
That did affright the air at Agincourt?

Henry V, Prologue

Towards the close of 1598, the Burbage brothers suspected that Giles Alleyn, owner of the land upon which the Theatre stood, intended to tear down their beloved theatre. With the Burbages' patrons out of favour, it would be a simple matter for Alleyn to destroy the Theatre, allowing him to recoup his losses, cancel the lease and install a new tenant on the land. Cuthbert Burbage even heard rumours that Alleyn had engaged a party of housebreakers to join him in demolishing the Theatre after Christmas, on some day to be decided by him.

But the Burbage brothers were ready for Alleyn. Realising that there was no hope of saving the Theatre, they could at least salvage the materials from which it had been built, and

erect a new theatre elsewhere. Cuthbert Burbage looked
south, to the liberty of Bankside. It was not an ideal site,
since there were already two theatres there, the Rose and the
Swan. But Cuthbert Burbage knew they had no choice. He
found a suitable site near St Saviour's Church, west of Dead
Man's Place and south of Maiden Lane, and he arranged
with its owner, Nicholas Brend, to take a long lease on it of
£14.10s a year, commencing from 25 December 1598.

On 28 December, Cuthbert and Richard Burbage arrived
at the Theatre, accompanied by players from the Lord
Chamberlain's Men and an army of volunteers and labourers,
one of whom, referred to only as 'WS' or 'William Smith'
in the resulting court records, may have been a pseudonym
for Shakespeare himself. Under the direction of master
craftsman Peter Street, the men set about tearing down the
Burbages' beloved Theatre. This task was not as easy as they
had expected. The original Theatre had been constructed in
1576 by the mortise and tenon method, with each piece of
timber fitting into its neighbour with a tapered wooden peg,
like an elaborate three-dimensional jigsaw. As each peg
locked into place, the construction had become stronger and
more secure. Over twenty years since the building of the
Theatre, the joints had stiffened and it was difficult to take
the timbers apart without splitting the wood.

Word of the Burbages' audacious scheme soon got about,
and Giles Alleyn's men arrived to stop the destruction, causing
uproar. It was probably Alleyn's own men who did most to
destroy the grass, afterwards valued at 40 shillings in Alleyn's
complaint. In his subsequent lawsuit, Alleyn claimed that
Cuthbert Burbage and his comrades 'did riotously take downe
and carry away the said Theatre by confederacy with others
armed with unlawful and offensive weapons, as namely
swords, daggers, bills, axes and such like'.[1] Alleyn also alleged

that the Burbages and their supporters became aggressive when 'divers of your said subjects servants and farmers peacefully going about to procure them to desist, they violently resisted, to the great disturbing of the peace, and terrifying of your said subject's servants'.[2] The Burbages' inspired response to averting the destruction of their theatre had inevitable legal consequences. Giles Alleyn charged Peter Street and Cuthbert Burbage with stealing the theatre and sued the Burbages for £800 in damages. In a typical example of the law's delays, Alleyn vs Burbage dragged on until the summer of 1602 and proved to be emotionally draining and time-consuming. When the case eventually went in Burbage's favour, he was able to cast the millstone of Alleyn's lawsuits from around his neck. At least there was some comfort in the fact that Alleyn had to pay all costs.

These days, it is players who are regarded as the temporary element of theatres and the building itself which is considered to be fixed. But in this case, the Lord Chamberlain's Men moved, like a snail, with their house on their back. To tear it down was one task: to remove it was quite another. The most straightforward way to transport the Theatre would have been by ripping it apart and moving the timber across London Bridge on a series of lumbering carts. But the gates of London Bridge were shut at night, and tolls were charged at all times for 'wheelage and passage'.[3] Any attempt to take the remains of the Theatre over London Bridge would meet with questions and delays at many points. Instead, the Burbages chose to go by water, starting from Peter Street's wharf at Bridewell Stairs, where the timber was loaded onto barges, ready to be sailed across the Thames at high tide. Moving the timber, pillars, and other parts of the building down the steps to the wharf was the hardest part of the task, and much of the materials must have been destroyed or stolen

in the process. And once Cuthbert had succeeded in his
Herculean task of carrying his dead Theatre to the other side
of the river, there it lay, an unsightly pile of debris to the
west of Dead Man's Place, while the new year was ushered
in as the old year passed away.

The transportation of the Theatre was a great and novel
concept, heroically designed and executed through the dark
night and cold grey dawn of midwinter. But so too was the
rebuilding work. This task must have stretched every nerve
and sinew, although the Burbages were not working alone
on the project. They had borrowed money and enlisted five
influential friends – Augustine Phillips, Thomas Pope, John
Hemmings, William Kemp and William Shakespeare – and
formed a company of 'sharers' who would each take a cut
of the eventual proceedings. Cuthbert Burbage contributed
building materials and all his savings, convinced that within
a very short time the new theatre would rise like a phoenix
from the ashes of the old.

A tidal reach of the Thames, Southwark was an unpropi-
tious place for building, as it was prone to flooding. In winter,
when the marshes froze, apprentices skimmed across them,
on skates fashioned from bone. Peter Street had his work
cut out for him in reconstructing a theatre here, 'flanked
with a ditch, and forced out of a marsh'.[4] But the actors,
including Shakespeare himself, worked alongside him, as it
was in their interests to get the new theatre built as quickly
as possible. No theatre meant no money, and Cuthbert
Burbage's ambitious plan was to construct the new theatre
within twenty-eight weeks. Reassembling the previous
theatre was a demanding task, since the timber was already
'seasoned' or hardened and more difficult to work with.

Although described as 'circular', like a globe, the new
theatre was not round at all. Wood does not lend itself easily

to circular constructions[5] and the frame had to be strong
enough to support the three tiers of galleried seating
surrounding the open yard. The new theatre had twenty
sides, and was 100 feet (30 metres) in diameter. Street's first
task was to address the problem of the marshy ground, and
ensure good foundations and adequate drainage. The foundations were laid by digging trenches in the outline of the
outer and inner walls of the gallery. These were filled with
'clunch' or limestone from the Thames Estuary. On top of
the stone foundations went brick walls, wide enough to hold
the oak 'groundsills' or horizontal base timbers of the giant
wooden frame up out of the damp ground. Bedded in lime
mortar, with the grain laid horizontally along the brick walls,
the oak groundsills acted as a barrier against the rising damp.
But water was also a problem from another source. In wet
weather, the roof of the gallery dripped, so a funnel to catch
rainwater was constructed to channel the water away into
the ditch surrounding the theatre and thence into the
Thames. As was traditional in Elizabethan England, the roof
was thatched, with the thatch coming from the reeds which
grew plentifully in the surrounding marshes.

As the reconstruction of the Theatre indicates, the
Elizabethans were resourceful builders and quick to recycle
any serviceable materials. To fill in the yard in front of the
stage, Street's men spread a thick layer of hazelnut shells,
discarded by the local soap works where the nuts had been
harvested for their fat. These shells, spread across the yard
or pit, served as an unusual form of industrial landfill, topped
with a layer of ash and clinker.[6]

Once the foundations had been sunk and the timber frame
constructed, the walls were filled in with a layer of wooden
laths plastered with a mixture of sand, slaked lime and animal
hair, used by the resourceful builders as a valuable layer of

insulation. Outside the theatre, the limewashed walls appeared plain and serviceable. But once admitted inside those walls, the playgoers were guaranteed an awesome spectacle, a theatre which was to become the glory of Bankside.

It has been suggested that Peter Street designed the new theatre along the classical models of the Roman architect Vitruvius (*c*.80–15 BC). It is more likely that this theatre was based on James Burbage's previous structure and the bear garden which stood nearby. In terms of layout, the structure was similar to the old Theatre, with a rectangular stage, five feet high, projecting halfway out into the yard and circular galleries of seating, protected from the elements by a thick thatched roof. In the back wall of the stage were two side doors, flanking a central opening covered with hangings. Above the stage was a balcony, upon which musicians tuned up their instruments. The appearance of this new theatre far surpassed that of its predecessor. The pillars, painted to look as if they had been carved from the finest Italian marble, 'would have deceived even the most cunning'.[7]

The stage was covered by a roof consisting of three parts, a thatched gable, an attached prentice roof covered in lighter oak boards and a decorated ceiling referred to as 'the heavens'. The ceiling of the heavens was painted midnight blue and divided into panels decorated with stars, the sun, the moon and the signs of the zodiac, bringing to mind Lorenzo's admiring description of 'the floor of heaven . . . thick inlaid with patines of bright gold'[8] or Hamlet's reference to 'this brave o'erhanging firmament, this majestic roof fretted with golden fire'.[9] Above the balcony there were images of the gods who influenced the affairs of men, and at either end stood Mercury and Apollo, the gods of eloquent speech, and the bare-breasted muses of Comedy and Tragedy. On the front of the heavens the winged figure of Fame blew her trumpet. This may be the origin of the term 'the gods', used in theatres to this day to describe the uppermost seats. The heavens were supported at the front by a massive crossbeam, the largest piece of timber in the entire building, resting on two thick pillars.

Terms such as 'the heavens' and 'the gods' are significant. For the Elizabethans, the theatre was a sacred space, reflecting their view of the universe. The gods lived in the heavens, mankind – represented by the players – occupied the temporal realm of the stage, and ghosts and demons lurked in the cellarage beneath the stage, otherwise known as 'hell'. It was from there that ghosts and demons would emerge, including the ghost of Hamlet's father.

By the end of May 1599, the new theatre was ready to open. Records from this period refer to a *'domus'* or 'dwelling' occupied by one 'Willielmi Shakespeare' and others, a reference either to the new theatre or to a home owned by Shakespeare in the neighbourhood.[10] The prospect of Shakespeare building a house close by his new theatre is highly likely. But before this new theatre could open, it needed a new name. Wise beyond his years, Cuthbert Burbage decided that this astonishing enterprise would no longer simply be known as 'the Theatre'. There were plenty of theatres around now and the name had lost its distinction. This new playhouse would demonstrate its scale and ambition in its very name. This playhouse would be known as the Globe, after the figure of Hercules carrying the globe on his back, just as Burbage's company had carried their theatre across the river to Bankside. When the Globe opened, a flag depicting Hercules with the globe and the Latin motto *totus mundus agit histrionem* fluttered in the breeze. Nothing could have been more appropriate for the Globe than a Latin tag meaning 'All the world's a playhouse' or, to quote Jacques in *As You Like It,* 'all the world's a stage'.[11] What Hercules had done in a fable, Burbage's company had done in reality. And now it was from the north bank that London could gaze, awestruck, upon this spectacular creation which was its own advertisement. The Globe Theatre was the most magnificent theatre London had ever seen and could hold up to 3,000 spectators.

It was here that Shakespeare would be free to create and Richard Burbage free to interpret his creations. What a wide world was in that little space, 'Thyself a world, the Globe thy fittest place!' It was here that Burbage, with his extraordinary range, brought so many of Shakespeare's characters to life. From 'young Hamlet though but scant of breath crying revenge for his dear father's death', to 'King Lear and Romeo begetting tears for Juliet's love'. From Harry as Prince and King, to Crookback, Brutus, Malvolio, Shylock and 'Othello the grieved Moor, made jealous by a slave, Who sent his wife to fill a timeless grave.'[12] One anonymous admirer recalled that:

> Oft have I seen him leap into a grave
> Suiting ye person (which he seemed to have)
> Of a sad lover, with so true an eye
> That then I would have sworn he meant to die.[13]

The esteem in which Burbage was held indicates the degree to which actors, and acting, had developed over the past two decades. Not only were theatres better, grander and more elaborate, but so too was the dramatist's art and the players' skill. Just as the bombastic roaring of Thomas Kyd and his imitators gave way to silver-tongued soliloquies, so the strutting tear-throats exemplified by Edward Alleyn gave way to the protean, mercurial Burbage. So confident had Shakespeare become in his powers that he could parody bad acting mercilessly, from the am-dram antics of Bottom, demanding a villain's role that would be 'a part to tear a cat in, to make all split!'[14] to Hamlet's disparaging remarks to the players:

> But if you mouth it, as many of your players do, I had as lief the town-crier spoke my lines . . . O, it offends me to the soul to hear a robustious periwig-pated fellow tear a passion to tatters, to very rags, to split the ears of the groundlings, who for the most part are capable of nothing but inexplicable dumbshows and noise. I would have such a fellow whipped for o'erdoing Termagant. It out-Herods Herod. Pray you, avoid it.[15]

Hamlet's directorial style, as he rehearses his players for a production designed to prick the conscience of the king, verges on the patronising. But it provides an insight into the existing canon of acting, when a formal repertoire of gestures and movements indicated the mood of the player. Many of these gestures are still familiar today, from head-scratching and beard-stroking to reflect puzzlement or interest, a hand across the heart to indicate sincerity, or covering the face and wringing the hands to express despair. In rhetoric, of course, the art was in the language itself. For players, the task consisted of 'personating' or bringing the role to life through a combination of word, voice, movement and gesture. Elsewhere in his canon, Shakespeare is well aware of the dangers of overacting. In *Troilus and Cressida,* Ulysses speaks of the 'strutting player whose conceit Lies in his hamstring, and doth think it rich To hear the wooden dialogue and sound 'Twixt his stretched footing and the scaffoldage'.[16] And in *Richard III,* Buckingham boasts that he can:

. . . counterfeit the deep tragedian;
Speak and look back, and pry on every side,
Tremble and start at wagging of a straw;
Intending deep suspicion, ghastly looks,
Are at my service, like enforcèd smiles;
And both are ready in their offices,
At any time, to grace my stratagems.[17]

The Globe Playhouse, surrounded by fields, as envisaged by Wenceslaus
Hollar c.1638.

The Chamberlain's Men celebrated the triumphant opening
of the Globe Theatre with a rousing production of *Henry V*.
What better choice for this magnificent new theatre than
a play celebrating the life of England's great warrior king?
A play of epic grandeur, crammed with colourful characters, battles and romance, the perfect play for the perfect
venue. The subject matter appealed to the public mood of

militant patriotism and the backdrop of national unease at the time of the second Armada of 1597 (which was thwarted by bad weather), when Londoners really felt as if the Spanish were beating at their door. By May 1599, England was on a war footing.

> The soldier and the sailor, frankly both,
> For London's aid are all in readiness
> To venture and fight by land and sea.[18]

Over the course of the decade, the threat of war with Spain had steadily increased and the national mood had become correspondingly aggressive. The hostility of London audiences towards Spain and Roman Catholicism 'found mirrors on stage'. From 1587 onwards, the content of drama was 'all masculine affairs of war and military history'.[19] The heroic historical plays were living monuments to England's past, designed to play in big outdoor playhouses and fit the militantly patriotic mood: 'Now all the youth of England are on fire . . .' The romantic, the playful, the feminine had been laid aside:

> . . . And silken dalliance in the wardrobe lies
> Now thrive the armourers, and honour's thought
> Reigns solely in the breast of every man.
> They sell the pasture now to buy the horse[20]

'The warlike Harry' had already become a popular character on the London stage, familiar to audiences as Prince Hal from *Henry IV Parts 1* and *2*, his exploits conducted against a recognisable backdrop of the Boar's Head Tavern and Gadshill, a reflection of the scenes of London lowlife Elizabethan audiences witnessed on their way to and from the theatre. In *Henry IV Part 1* there is already some indication that he was born for greatness:

> I saw young Harry with his beaver on,
> His cushes on his thighs, gallantly arm'd,
> Rise from the ground like feather'd Mercury,
> And vaulted with such ease into his seat
> As if an angel dropp'd down from the clouds
> To turn and wind a fiery Pegasus,
> And witch the world with noble horsemanship.[21]

Ostensibly, *Henry V* appears to be a celebration of the heroic virtues of kingship and the divine right of kings, proper governance and the established social order, a rhetorical fanfare to flatter the old Queen, written by a Tudor humanist who believed in the absolute power of monarchy. A work of propaganda, designed to stiffen the sinews and summon up the blood on the eve of war. But one has only to watch the play to realise that it is far more complex than that. Henry is not some two-dimensional hero one might encounter in an old revenge tragedy. Instead, Henry's character is a triumph of psychological realism. The callous treatment of Falstaff at the end of *Henry IV Part 2* prepared audiences for this. In *Henry V*, the king becomes harsher still, capable of threatening the citizens of Harfleur that they will be at the mercy of 'the fleshed soldier ... hard of heart', mowing down infants and violating maidens. Unless the town surrenders, its 'shrieking daughters' will be raped and 'naked infants spitted upon pikes'.[22] But he is also capable of great tenderness, offering 'a little touch of Harry in the night'[23] to his men on the eve of battle, and is compassionate towards his vanquished foes. All in all, Henry is a man, deeply flawed and conflicted and human, just like the audience.

This ambivalence extends towards the theme of war itself.

While the battle scenes play to the crowd and can be enjoyed in a spirit of macho bravado, with audiences roaring approval to the rallying cry of 'God for Harry, England, and Saint George!'[24] *Henry V* raises questions about the abject cruelty of war and violent death. Consider these lines on the aftermath of the Battle of Agincourt, when Mountjoy, the French herald, has come to retrieve the bodies of the French dead for burial:

> To look our dead, and then to bury them;
> To sort our nobles from our common men.
> For many of our princes – woe the while! –
> Lie drown'd and soak'd in mercenary blood;
> So do our vulgar drench their peasant limbs
> In blood of princes; and their wounded steeds
> Fret fetlock deep in gore and with wild rage
> Yerk [kick] out their armed heels at their dead masters,
> Killing them twice.[25]

What price glory now? There is a horror of war in this play, as well as a celebration of Henry as a national hero. The men in the audience, potential recruits or old soldiers, were bracing themselves for action, while the women had their own fears. Women faced the civilian consequences of war, the loss of husbands, fathers, sons and brothers, and the potential threat of rape and murder by a marauding army of occupation. Every person in that audience at the Globe was a potential sacrifice to 'the sword of war'.[26]

As a celebration of past military glories, *Henry V* would do great box office and show off the magnificent new Globe. This was Shakespeare's opportunity to consolidate his role as England's dramatic chronicler. But in an age when props and scenery were limited, Shakespeare's challenge was to bring such an epic to life.

> When Burbage played, the stage was bare
> Of fount and temple, tower and stair;
> Two backswords eked a battle out;
> Two supers [extras] made a rabble rout;
> The throne of Denmark was a chair.[27]

How could any company conjure up the voyage to France or re-enact the Battle of Agincourt with a cast of eight principals, four hired men and two or three apprentices? Wasn't this the kind of thing Ben Jonson parodied, when he made this sarcastic allusion to *Henry VI*: 'With three rusty swords And help of some five-foot-and-half-foot words Fight over York and Lancaster's long jars And in the tiring-house bring wounds to scars,'[28] creating a picture of soldiers rushing back to their dressing room (tiring-house) and daubing themselves with fake blood.

In certain respects, theatrical convention was on Shakespeare's side. The audiences that flocked to the new Globe did not anticipate theatrical realism, or expect to see the Chamberlain's Men hold the mirror up to nature. They expected to be entertained, with skirmishes and speeches, comedy and tragedy, and they understood that this could only be achieved by a leap of the imagination. By appealing to the audience to participate with a self-deprecating defence of the limitations of Elizabethan stagecraft, the Chorus begs for a 'Muse of Fire' but makes do with his jobbing actors and the unworthy scaffold of the Globe's stage:

> Can this cockpit hold
> The vasty fields of France? Or may we cram
> Within this wooden O the very casques
> That did affright the air at Agincourt?[29]

Given that even the Globe had no more to offer in the way of battle scenes or sea voyages than the open stage and some limited special effects, the Chorus appeals to the audience to enter into an imaginative contract with the players to suspend its disbelief while the actors or 'ciphers' work upon the audience's imagination. The audience is asked to: 'Think, when we talk of horses, that you see them, Printing their proud hoofs i' the receiving earth.'[30]

At the beginning of Act III the Chorus implores the crowd to visualise Henry's fleet embarking majestically across the English Channel, with cabin boys climbing the rigging and Harfleur hoving into view, a city 'upon the inconstant billows dancing'.[31] Before the Battle of Agincourt the Chorus excuses what is about to follow by confessing that:

> And so our scene must to the battle fly,
> Where – O for pity – we shall much disgrace
> With four or five most vile and ragged foils
> Right ill-disposed in brawl ridiculous
> The name of Agincourt.[32]

But, however feeble the rendition may appear, it is intended to remind us of what occurred at Agincourt, 'Minding true things by what their mockeries be'.[33]

Following the English triumph at the Battle of Agincourt and Henry's successful wooing of Princess Katherine, daughter of the Dauphin, the army returns to London. Once again, the Chorus finds himself apologising for the failure of realism, since, due to the lack of time and numbers, the scenes 'cannot in their huge and proper life Be here presented'.[34] And once again the audience is asked to visualise the huge numbers waiting to greet the returning English fleet, the Mayor of London and all the citizens swarming out into the streets to welcome King Harry back. At this point, Shakespeare allows himself one of his rare topical references to recent events, comparing the account of Harry's triumphant return with the scenes that might ensue if the Earl of Essex disembarked in London having put down the Irish rebellion:

> Were now the general of our gracious empress [The Earl of Essex],
> As in good time he may, from Ireland coming,
> Bringing rebellion broached on his sword,
> How many would the peaceful city quit,
> To welcome him![35]

In May 1599, when *Henry V* was first performed at the Globe, the Earl of Essex was in Ireland confronting rebel leader Hugh O'Neill, 2nd Earl of Tyrone (1550–1616). By September 1599, this reference had become a poignant one, when the military expedition ended in disaster.

The summer of 1599 saw the Globe embark on a successful season. With Shakespeare enriching the repertoire with an inimitable series of plays, and a succession of eager Londoners crossing the river to enjoy the new attractions, it could hardly fail. There were two shows during the summer months, the first at 2pm until around 5pm, and the second ending no later than sundown, so that theatre-goers could return home before dark. The average play of 2,500 lines was supposed to take two hours – the 'two hours traffic of [the] stage'[36] – but one can only conclude that the texts were heavily cut, as a full performance of *Richard III* in its 3,700-line entirety or the 4,000 lines of Hamlet would take three hours. Either that, or performances lasted longer than the statutory two hours stipulated by the Lord Chamberlain back in 1594.

The Globe Theatre proved irresistible to the 'clamorous fly'[37] of lawyers, students, courtiers, apprentices, servants and foreign visitors who flocked to the playhouse at the rate of 3,000 a day. Many were regular visitors, such as the Earl of Southampton and his friend the Earl of Rutland, who both went to see plays every day. The popularity of playgoing is reflected in *Of Well Penn'd Plays* as John Marston takes the opportunity to satirise the stage-struck:

> Luscus, what's played today? Faith, now I know,
> I set thy lips abroach, from whence doth flow
> Naught but pure Juliet and Romeo.
> Say, who acts best? Drusus, or Roscio?
> Now I have him, that ne'er of ought did speak
> But when of plays or players he did treat.
> H'ath made a commonplace book out of plays,
> And speaks in print, at least whate'er he says
> Is warrented by Curtain plaudities;
> If e'er you heard him courting Lesbia's eyes,
> Say, courteous sir, speaks he not movingly
> From out of some new pathetic tragedy?
> He writes, he rails, he jests, he courts, what not,
> And all from out his huge long scrap'd stock.[38]

A view of the Thames showing the second Globe and the bear garden by Claus Visscher c.1616.

Managing a theatre, of whatever size or status, is a demanding task. Indeed, the bigger the theatre, the greater requirement for an efficient and reliable staff. Given that the Chamberlain's Men had become the most successful company in London, the smooth running of the Globe depended not only upon the actors but the front of house staff and the unseen heroes backstage. Front of house were the 'gatherers' who collected the money from the public in collection boxes and stored it in the 'box office'. As in today's theatres, eating and drinking (before, during and after performances) provided a vital source of income, and it was the task of the gatherers to oversee the sales of beer, hazelnuts, 'pippins' (a kind of small apple) and even tobacco. Backstage, there were three types of assistant at the Globe. Most lowly of all was the Stage Keeper – a cleaner, handyman and general factotum. At the Hope Theatre, where Ben Jonson's *Bartholomew Fair* was first staged (1614), it was the task of the Stage Keeper to gather up the apple cores so they could be fed to the bears which appeared there every fortnight. In *Bartholomew Fair,* it falls to the Stage Keeper to come on before the play begins and beg the audience to have patience as the first player due on stage has a hole in his black silk stocking. While the player's laddered stocking is being attended to, the Stage Keeper reflects upon the shortcomings of the current actors before informing the audience, 'And yet I kept the stage in Master Tarlton's time, I thank my stars. Ho! An' that man had lived to have played in *Bartholomew Fair*, you should ha' seen him!'[39]

This monologue is interrupted by the Book Holder, who briskly reminds the Stage Keeper that his duties consist of sweeping the stage and gathering up the apple cores, for the Stage Keeper is the most humble position in the theatre, like Puck: 'I am sent with broom before To sweep the dust behind the door.'[40]

The Book Holder had a far more valuable role. Their task was to receive the original manuscript or 'the book', as it is still called, from the dramatist and then arrange with the scrivener, or professional scribe, for at least one whole copy to be made. The book had to be submitted to the Master of the Revels for his 'allowance' or permission to perform, and was returned to the Book Holder with any subversive or seditious content censored. The scriveners then had to transcribe the entire play and make separate copies of the actors' script on long scrolls with the cues marked. It is from these scrolls or 'roles' that the term 'role' originated for an actor's part. No actor had a complete text of the whole play, as that would have been ruinously expensive. Instead, the company had a briefing from the dramatist so that the players had some understanding of the narrative and the significance of their roles. The Book Holder also had to provide another aid for the players in the form of 'The Plot', a summary of the action scene by scene with all the entrances and exits marked on it which was pasted up on the wall of the tiring house.[41] The Book Holder was not the same thing as the prompt, although there were prompts, and Shakespeare seems to have had a dim view of actors who dried:

> Like a dull actor now
> I have forgot my part and I am out
> Even to a full disgrace.[42]

The most important role backstage was that of the Tire Man or wardrobe master, who was responsible for tending to the players' costumes and doing running repairs, such as darning a stocking or sewing a torn garment if there was no time to send it out to the seamstresses. Costumes were extremely valuable, so the Tire Man's role was a responsible one. A fine cloak might cost £20, and the actual fabrics – the silk, damask, satin and velvet required for gowns in a range of gorgeous colours, cloth of gold, azure, tawny, carnation, crimson – were very costly. With so little scenery, so few props, costumes played a vital part in creating the theatrical illusion. As Bottom reminds his players when their play is 'preferred' for the Duke of Athens' wedding feast, it was essential to look the part:

> Get your apparel together, good strings to your beards, new ribbons to your pumps; meet presently at the palace; every man look o'er his part . . . let Thisbe have clean linen; and let not him that plays the lion pair his nails, for they shall hang out for the lion's claws. And, most dear actors, eat no onions nor garlic, for we are to utter sweet breath; and I do not doubt but to hear them say, it is a sweet comedy.[43]

The Tire Man's responsibilities also included theatre lighting in its most primitive form – flaming torches. The threat of fire was a serious one in Elizabethan London, particularly in a theatre built of wood with a thatched roof, so any torches brought on stage had to be handled with care. Subsequently, at the Blackfriars, the Tire Man would be in charge of the candles used to illuminate the indoor theatre.

The summer of 1599 saw Londoners flock across the river to see the new theatre for themselves, much to the delight of the Thames watermen, who ferried them over the Thames in their wherries. Among their passengers on 21 September 1599 was young Thomas Platter, who recorded his visit to the Globe for posterity. 'Daily at two in the afternoon, London has two, sometimes three plays running in different places, competing with each other,' noted Thomas, 'and those which play best obtain most spectators.'[44]

Shortly before two of the clock, on the afternoon of 21 September 1599, Thomas stepped nervously into a rowing boat moored on the north bank of the Thames. A Swiss doctor completing his education in England, Thomas was embarking on a visit to the Globe with a group of friends. This was to be one of the highlights of his tour. To cross the river, Platter and his friends boarded a wherry, a water taxi which could carry five passengers, rowed by a waterman with a pair of sculls. As Platter wobbled into his seat, he could see the distinctive outline of the Globe across the river, flanked by the bear gardens and a mass of taverns.

Platter sat nervously as the waterman bellowed 'Westward Ho!' and the wherry pushed off from the shore. Even on a warm day, the Thames was a choppy, tidal river, vividly described by one contemporary as a 'long, broad, slippery fellow, always in motion'.[45] Embarking on a crossing of the Thames was not for the faint-hearted, but it was the most direct route to the Bankside and a means of avoiding the gridlock of coaches on London Bridge. Looking about him, Platter could see dozens of other wherries, all making the same journey across the river for the afternoon performances at the Globe, the Rose and the Swan, and the Thames was alive with boats and barges and ships rocking at anchor. Platter gasped in horror as a fellow passenger told him that the heads of executed traitors were displayed at the south end of London Bridge, but his waterman was gruffly dismissive. For him, London Bridge was a dangerous eyesore. Not only did it rob him of trade, but its arches created dangerous currents. Men had drowned trying to shoot the rapids between the arches and negotiate the steep drop in the water level on the other side.

Now the Globe was growing closer as the wherry sped towards Bankside, and Platter found himself setting foot on the south bank with a frisson of excitement. Not only was he visiting the most famous and popular theatre in London, something to boast about when he returned home, but he might also sample the other delights Bankside had to offer. At last, Platter and his friends were standing outside the Globe itself.

Thomas Platter and his young companions had a choice of admission prices. They could pay the one English penny for standing room only below the raised stage. A further penny gained admission to one of the covered galleries that surrounded the stage, and yet another penny guaranteed cushioned seating. With the average artisan's wage at six shillings a week, a penny or so to get into the Globe was not bad value. The most expensive seats were in the Lords' gallery, a VIP area for the most important guests, obtainable for a sixpence.

Opting for the gallery, the young men crowded through the narrow doorway and filed into the first tier. Settling down on the hard wooden bench, they looked about them and gawped. Nothing of the Globe's smooth, pale exterior could have prepared them for this awesome spectacle. The pillars, so exquisitely painted that they appeared to be carved out of marble; the starry heavens; and the sounds and sweet airs of musicians tuning up above the stage. The enormous, rustling, chattering, shifting, many-headed creature that was the audience, thrust into the narrow galleries or churning about the yard. The Globe seemed to be a great place to pick up women, Platter noted, as predatory young men circled the yard, running their eyes across the gallery until they had spotted their prey, before descending on them like ravens on carrion. The crowd itself contained all sorts and conditions of men, and women too. Gallants in stiff frilled ruffs and huge hats decorated with feathers, jewels dangling from their ears. Law students from the Inns of Court, ladies in 'vizards' or masks who were quite evidently whores, prising themselves into the galleries, while girls of lesser status worked the yard, crushed in among the groundlings. A supporting cast of pickpockets, coney-catchers, scroungers, idlers and ne'er-do-wells circulated yard and gallery, thriving in the atmosphere of noisy carelessness, dipping into a pocket or slitting the string of a purse. Wenches pressed through the throng with baskets of pippins, nuts and gingerbread on their plump arms, or glided through the crowd with flagons of ale as men parted respectfully to make way for the precious cargo.

A pall of thick tobacco smoke hung over the scene, as men and women alike sucked on little clay pipes; it seems the English were notorious for lighting up on all occasions, at the play, in the taverns or elsewhere. 'It makes them riotous and merry and rather drowsy, just as if they were drunk.'[46] Thomas Platter rather enjoyed the scent of tobacco, but other grosser odours assailed him, the inevitable result of around 3,000 people packed together in a small space. Faint from the reek of bad breath, stale beer and sweaty bodies plastered together, he recalled Dekker's comments about the 'garlic breathed stinkards so glued together in crowds with streams of strong breath that when they came forth their faces looked as if they had been par-boiled'.[47] Ever the medical student, Thomas wondered idly where all that beer went? There appeared to be no privies or jakes at the Globe. Soon he had his answer. Men shouldered their fellows roughly aside, to pee outside, or sometimes inside, if they did not make it out of the yard in time. Women made water where they stood, the more genteel resorting to a flat dish, carried for the

purpose (Thomas was astonished to see) beneath their volu-
minous skirts. Stunned by this discovery, Thomas turned his
attention back to the stage, where the actors were about to
make their appearance.

There were no printed programmes, but a board at the
side of the stage announced the title of this afternoon's performance: *The Tragedy of Julius Caesar,* written by William
Shakespeare and given by his company, the Lord Chamberlain's
Men. Excellent, thought Thomas, settling into his hard
wooden seat on the bench. A topical theme promising statecraft, politics, swordplay and war, Machiavellian ambitions
brought low by the Wheel of Fortune, tyrants destroyed and
a tragic outcome. As an educated man, Platter was familiar
with the classics and recognised that the tragedy about to be
played out before him reflected popular anxieties regarding
the ageing Queen who had no viable heir. But this was no
dry scholars' debate about Roman history or whether it could
ever be morally acceptable to assassinate a despot. The
moment the company of fifteen actors set foot on stage,
Thomas knew he was watching a sophisticated drama,
although he sat up sharply, slightly taken aback that the cast
wore elaborate, expensive contemporary dress, and not
Roman togas.[48] It seemed the audience did not object to seeing
Julius Caesar in a doublet and hose, despite the location being
Rome in 44 BC, any more than they objected to anachronisms
such as a clock striking, so why should he? The crowd did
not give a fig for such details. Their hearts and minds were
wholly given over to the compelling scenes before them.

The audience recognised the archetypes: Julius Caesar, the
charismatic but arrogant leader; the conflicted Brutus intent
on assassinating him for the public good; and the triumphalist
Mark Antony turning the assassination to his own advantage.
As the tragedy played itself out the audience became

entranced. This was the theatre of enchantment, of shared experience, of captivating spectacle. With the audience crowded up against the stage, so close they could almost touch the performers, with lightning-swift changes of scene and no intervals the actors made rapid transitions from mood to mood, producing a cumulative emotional impact as first Caesar and then Brutus moved inexorably towards their fates. The audience were active participants, shouting, hissing, booing. As the ghost of Caesar appeared to Brutus on the night before battle, even the pickpocket sitting next to Thomas froze open-mouthed as he was slipping his fingers under a lady's cape.

Special effects were basic but effective: Julius Caesar died in a pool of blood, thanks to the pig's bladder of gore hidden inside his doublet; to create the atmosphere of a battle happening just offstage, drums were beaten and cannons fired. Londoners on the north bank of the Thames did not need to see the black flag flying from the roof of the Globe. They could tell a tragedy was playing from the sounds of battle floating across the river.

After Brutus had fallen on his sword and the tragedy had been concluded, the actors returned to take a bow. Writing later in his diary, Thomas described it as 'an excellent performance, and when the play was over they danced very marvellously and gracefully together as is their wont, two dressed as men and two as women'.[49]

Stunned but elated, Thomas and his friends stood up, stretched and shuffled towards the exit, pushing and jostling with the crowds back onto Bankside. They debated a while whether to go off in search of food, drink, girls, or take a wherry back to the city. Thomas stopped to relieve himself against a post and fend off the advances of a merry young whore as his friends weighed up the advantages of going to the tavern now, while they were still full of excitement, or holding back until they had crossed the Thames. Thomas himself could scarcely speak. This performance had been one of the greatest experiences of his life, and he was still trying to put it into words for his diary, little knowing that his trip to the theatre would be immortalised for centuries to come. Thomas had been to the Globe and seen Shakespeare's magic for himself at first hand. Whatever else happened that evening, this was enough.

8

GUNPOWDER, TREASON AND PLOT

When the hurly-burly's done,
When the battle's lost and won.

Macbeth, Act 1 Scene 1

For Londoners, indeed for all who lived under the sovereignty of Elizabeth, the turn of the century would prove a freakish time of dire combustion and confused events. The first decade alone was to be marked by two sensational attempts to overthrow the monarchy, both ending in despair for their protagonists. The Earl of Essex's failed rebellion and the doomed Gunpowder Plot would provide an exciting but hazardous backdrop for the players at the Globe and a dangerous environment for writers. In another development, the writers themselves would be at loggerheads, in a dispute dubbed 'the war of the theatres' and best summed up by Guildenstern's verdict that 'there has been much throwing about of brains!'[1]

At the end of the chapter about Shakespeare's history plays, I concluded with Richard II's reflection upon the fate of kings. 'Some . . . deposed, some slain in war . . . some poisoned by their wives, some sleeping killed – all murdered.' Shakespeare was aware of the essentially fleeting nature of royal power. 'Not all the water in the rough rude sea can wash the balm off from an anointed king', but power is transitory. Ultimately, Death trumps all kingship; Death pricks the bubble of life in the hollow crown and the monarch is gone. Farewell, king![2]

This chapter is about two attempts to destroy the monarchy, in the form of the Essex rebellion and the Gunpowder Plot, and the impact these seismic events had upon Shakespeare, his contemporaries and the Globe. For one, mercifully brief, moment it looked as though the Lord Chamberlain's Men might be flung into gaol, or make one last appearance not upon the scaffold of the stage but upon the scaffold of the gallows.

In May 1599, Shakespeare made a rare topical allusion to the Earl of Essex's campaign in Ireland, drawing flattering comparisons with Henry V's magnificent return from Agincourt. Shakespeare confidently predicted a victory procession for Essex 'the conquering hero', promoted to general, 'from Ireland coming, Bringing rebellion broached on his sword'.[3] At the time, this forecast appeared reasonable enough. Essex, who had appointed himself Lieutenant of Ireland, had left London to cheers in March 1599 at the head of 16,000 troops, the largest expeditionary force ever sent to Ireland, at a cost of £290,000 per annum, twice the budget of the war in the Low Countries. His mission was to put down the rebellion of the Irish chieftains led by Hugh O'Neill, Earl of Tyrone. It was anticipated that the rebellion would be crushed instantly, but the English had underestimated the resources of the Irish, who had recruited soldiers from Scotland and Spain to fight for their cause. Essex's initial strategy had been to confront

O'Neill in Ulster, but instead he took his men into Southern Ireland where, unable to outwit the native cunning of the Irish rebels, the campaign became a disaster and the Irish won several victories. Instead of facing O'Neill in battle, as he had hoped, Essex was forced to make a truce with the rebel leader. This truce was regarded as humiliating and that it undermined the authority of the Queen.

Essex's homecoming on 28 September 1599 was a hollow mockery of Henry V's triumphal entry into London. Far from returning from Ireland as the conquering hero, Essex hastened to Nonsuch Palace in Surrey, burst into the Queen's bedchamber and begged for her forgiveness. For this indecorum, and for his failure in Ireland, Essex was put under house arrest and ordered to retire from public life. Humiliated and disgraced, Essex had lost both the trust of the Queen and his income too, when the patent which granted him the tax on sweet wine from his estate in the Canaries was withdrawn.[4] Lord Cecil, the Queen's advisor, who nursed an implacable hatred for Essex, guaranteed that he would never hold a position of power again. Essex's situation had become desperate, and, in the words of Sir John Harington, who had accompanied him to Ireland, Essex shifted 'from sorrow and repentance to rage and rebellion'.[5]

But Essex was not entirely without resources, and he had many influential friends. In all his campaigns, Essex had secured the loyalties of his officers by conferring knighthoods. By the end of his doomed Irish campaign, more than half the knights in England owed their rank to Essex. The rebels even joked that Essex 'never drew sword but to make knights'.[6] This practice of conferring knighthoods had enabled Essex to build up a formidable power base. Soldiers admired him as a fellow professional, despite the disastrous conduct of the campaign in Ireland. Puritans regarded him as their champion at a time when popular feeling had turned against the Queen and her government. But Essex also had two powerful and ruthless enemies: Lord Cecil and Sir Walter Raleigh, who hated him bitterly.

The moment he was freed from house arrest on 26 August 1600, Essex retreated to his mansion on the Strand to regroup. Among Essex's supporters was James VI, King of Scotland and potentially next in line to the throne. Essex began to draw up plans to challenge the authority of Lord Cecil, remove the Queen from office and place James on the throne instead. He was supported in this initiative by a faction of powerful Catholic noblemen including Essex's stepfather, Sir Christopher Blount, and Sir Charles Percy, of the distinguished Northumberland Percy family (his ancestor, Harry 'Hotspur' Percy, had famously taken up arms against Henry IV and been slain at the Battle of Shrewsbury). The Earl of Southampton, Essex's close companion, encouraged him in this endeavour, and by the winter they had been joined by courtiers fallen out of favour and disaffected Midlands peers. Essex House swiftly became a hotbed of rebellion, with Puritan preachers haranguing anyone who would listen and Essex himself speaking slightingly of the Queen he had once adored, sneering that now she was an old woman, her mind was as crooked as her body.[7] Some great upheaval was surely at hand. Public alarm among the superstitious increased when, four days before Christmas, London was rocked by an earthquake.

After Christmas, Essex received a caution from the Lord Keeper warning him that he would never regain the Queen's favour if he continued to receive so many disreputable men. This fell on deaf ears; Essex retorted haughtily that he saw no reason to reject anyone who came to visit him in good will.[8] Essex's visitors were one thing; even at this point the

Queen might have softened towards her former favourite if Essex had appeared suitably contrite. However, it was Essex's reading matter which really contributed to his downfall. In 1599, Sir John Hayward had published his controversial volume *The First Part of the Life and Reign of King Henry IV* with a dedication to Essex as '*futuri temporis expectatione* – great thou art in hope, greater in the expectation of future time' – a thinly disguised suggestion that it was Essex who was truly heir to the throne.[9] The book, which included an account of the deposition and death of Richard II, was inflammatory, given the war with Ireland and the anxieties over Queen Elizabeth's succession. Attempts to suppress and burn the book on the orders of the Bishop of London were unsuccessful and it continued to circulate, while the author was committed to the Tower of London on a charge of treason and remained in gaol until Elizabeth's death. The Queen was particularly sensitive regarding parallels between the reign of Richard II and her own life. Reputedly, when looking upon historical records from the Tower of London, Elizabeth's eyes had fallen upon a reference to Richard II. Wryly, the Queen remarked: 'I am Richard, know ye not that?'[10]

Elizabeth I made this comment to William Lambard, the Keeper of Records at the Tower, in 1601, but the sentiment behind it dates back far earlier and was the reason that she found the abdication scene from *Richard II* so painful. Although there is no evidence that Shakespeare deliberately set out to draw a comparison between the two monarchs in his own play, the similarities between Elizabeth I and Richard II were startling, and painfully apparent to contemporary audiences.

Like Richard II, the Queen was regarded as having been 'basely led by flatterers',[11] sycophantic courtiers and overpowerful ministers such as her secretary, Sir Robert Cecil, causing her to commit great faults to herself and the state. Like Richard, the Queen had oppressed her people with grievous taxes, 'And quite lost their hearts', and had alienated her noblemen by fining them 'For ancient quarrels'.[12] She had become unpopular with Puritans for her tolerance towards Catholics, and unpopular with Catholics for not being lenient enough towards them, and permitting the draconian anti-Catholic legislation introduced by the late Sir Francis Walsingham.

Queen Elizabeth also resembled Richard II in another specific particular. Like Richard, she was childless, and uncertainty surrounded her successor, although James VI of Scotland, son of Mary, Queen of Scots, possessed the best claim to the throne in terms of genealogy and the greatest degree of support among the general population. Like Richard II, the Queen had become increasingly unpopular towards the end of her reign. No longer Gloriana, Astrea or the Faerie Queen, Elizabeth was mocked as a bad-tempered old woman in a red wig. The combination of a poor harvest in 1599, rising food prices and steep taxes had left thousands destitute. Families starved while masterless men roamed the country, and the spectre of civil unrest grew daily, as Elizabeth's subjects feared a complete breakdown of the social order.

When the Queen asked Lambard, 'I am Richard, know ye not that?' Lambard responded: 'Such a wicked imagination was determined and attempted by a most unkind gent. The most adorned creature that ever your majesty made.'

Elizabeth replied: 'He that will forget God will also forget his benefactors; this tragedy was played 40tie [sic] times in open streets and houses.'[13]

On first reading this exchange, it is tempting to assume that the Queen had made a reference to Shakespeare's play,

Richard II, and that the 'unkind gent' Lambard refers to is Shakespeare. That is certainly the most obvious interpretation. At the request of the Lord Chamberlain, the abdication scene in which Richard gives up his crown to Bolingbroke had been omitted from printed copies of *Richard II* during the 1590s to appease the Queen's sensibilities.[14] But if this man is Shakespeare, then the reference to 'the most adorned creature' is puzzling. While Shakespeare and the Chamberlain's Men were popular at Court, and the leading acting company in London, Shakespeare had not been noticeably adorned. He did not even have a knighthood. The 'adorned creature', or perhaps 'adored creature', can only be the Earl of Essex, and while Elizabeth's comments could be true of Shakespeare's play about Richard II, it is also possible that this entertainment played in open streets and houses was another play based on Hayward's book. Whatever interpretation readers chose to accept, the fact was that being in possession of Hayward's text – 'that treasonable book'[15] – would prove damning for Essex. The Earl had lost sight of the fact that his primary benefactor was the Queen herself.

On 6 February 1601, Essex despatched his steward Sir Gilly Meyrick to the Globe, accompanied by Blount and Percy. Meyrick offered the Chamberlain's Men forty shillings on top of the box office to revive *The Tragedy of King Richard II* in its entirety, complete with the abdication scene.[16] The Chamberlain's Men found themselves in something of a quandary. If they agreed to stage the entire play, against the Queen's wishes, the company could be charged with treason. The calamity of *The Isle of Dogs* was still fresh in their minds and the last thing the Globe needed was a raid with half the company arrested and dragged away to the Marshalsea. The Chamberlain's Men did not wish to lose their hard-won status as the best company in London. However, the Earl of Essex remained a powerful and influential patron and his companion, the Earl of Southampton, was an even more significant figure. Shakespeare had dedicated *Venus and Adonis* to him, and Southampton had been instrumental in establishing Shakespeare's early career as a poet. To affront the Earl of Essex would have been career suicide; in the end, the company were 'content to play it'[17] as requested.

And so it was on the afternoon of Saturday 7 February 1601 that *The Tragedy of King Richard II* was performed at the Globe. A number of Essex's supporters were in the audience, including Sir Christopher Blount, Sir Charles Percy and Lord Monteagle, a staunch Roman Catholic who was nevertheless loyal to the crown. The men had dined at Gunter's, by the Temple, and taken a wherry across the Thames.[18] Essex himself was not at the Globe. He had received a summons to appear before the Privy Council but refused to go on the grounds that his life had been threatened and it was too dangerous to leave the house.[19] But Essex did not need to be at the Globe. He had not commissioned a revival of *The Tragedy of King Richard II* for his own enjoyment. His motives were not aesthetic but keenly political. Essex had asked for the play to be performed as a means of whipping up audience sympathies in his favour. With Londoners on his side, his bid for power would be more favourably received. For the Earl of Essex, once Elizabeth's favourite, intended to depose the Queen and seize power.

If Essex had hoped for riots that night, he was sadly disappointed. Unlike the production of *A Knack to Know a Knave* at the Rose in June 1592, which had been followed by riots, the production of *Richard II* passed off without incident. Those members of the public who had turned out enjoyed their 'two hours' traffic of the stage', cheered, jeered, drank, smoked and departed. If any regular had questioned why the play had been put on his fellows would no doubt have commented that a history is always pleasing stuff.

On the following morning, 8 February, the Lord Keeper, Sir Thomas Egerton, and members of the Privy Council including the Earl of Worcester, Sir William Knollys and the Lord Chief Justice appeared at the gates of Essex House. As they entered the courtyard they found the Earl of Essex at the centre of a great tumult of activity, along with Lords Southampton, Rutland, Sandys and Monteagle. The Lord Keeper explained that he had been sent by the Queen to ask Essex if he had a particular grievance, and to give him a fair hearing. Essex conducted the privy councillors to his library and promptly took them prisoner.[20]

It was time for Essex to show his hand. He left Essex House with a party of around 200 men and marched towards the house of Sheriff Smyth in Fenchurch Street. The sheriff had promised to join him with a force of a thousand men. As he entered the city, Essex shouted: 'For the Queen! For the Queen! A plot is laid for my life!'[21] People turned out of their houses to watch as Essex and his men marched past, but nobody offered to join them.

Meanwhile, the news had reached the Palace of Whitehall. A barricade of carts was hastily erected and the Lord Admiral assembled a small army, while Lord Cecil hurried to the city and proclaimed that Essex and his accomplices were traitors. When Essex arrived at Sheriff Smyth's house, the sheriff left by the back door and offered his services to the Lord Mayor instead. Essex appealed desperately to the rapidly diminishing crowds, telling them that the country was being betrayed and there was a plan to put the Spanish Infanta on the throne. Nobody came to join him and, worse still, his own supporters began to drift away as fervour cooled into prudence. Deciding to return to Essex House and bargain for his freedom with his hostages, Essex led his company down Fenchurch Street only to find a barricade at Ludgate Hill and a band of pikemen and musketeers waiting to stop him. As Essex's party tried to smash their way through, Sir Christopher Blount was injured and the musketeers opened fire. Realising that the situation was hopeless, Essex's men retreated to the river and took a boat up to Essex House. They arrived to find the house surrounded and their prisoners gone. The privy councillors had been released and it was only a matter of time before Essex and his men were arrested. Essex's wife and sister were still inside with their gentlewomen, shrieking in terror with every exchange of fire. Essex and his followers held out until nine o'clock in the evening, with desultory sniping on both sides, until they had to admit defeat and were forced to surrender.[22]

Essex and Southampton went on trial for treason on 19 February 1601 before a jury of their peers. The trial lasted from nine in the morning until seven at night, as the prisoners pleaded for their lives while their fellow peers smoked their pipes and drank their beer. Both earls were found guilty and condemned to death, but Southampton was reprieved and his sentence commuted to life imprisonment. He was sent to the Tower, where he remained until the accession of James I. The remaining rebels, including Sir Christopher Blount and Sir Gilly Meyrick, were brought to trial eight days later and condemned to death.[23]

Some days before Essex's execution, Captain Thomas Lee, who had served under Essex in Ireland, was apprehended as he kept watch on the door to the Queen's chambers. His plan had been to confine her until she signed a warrant for the release of Essex. Captain Lee, a devoted supporter of Essex, had acted as a go-between with the Ulster rebels. Lee was tried and executed the following day.[24]

The Tower of London. The Earl of Essex was beheaded here on Ash Wednesday 1601 following his disastrous attempted rebellion.

On 24 February, Shrove Tuesday, the Queen signed the Earl of Essex's death warrant before going to watch a play. Next day, Essex was beheaded on Tower Green. He went to his death bravely, and with great piety. Ironically, Essex had once pardoned his executioner, Thomas Derrick, when the latter went on trial for rape. Essex had offered Derrick his freedom if he consented to becoming an executioner at Tyburn. Derrick, who had the melancholy distinction of giving his name to a type of gallows, made a bad job of this particular execution. It took three strokes to sever Essex's head from his body. Watching the scene through a cloud of tobacco smoke from his room in the Tower was Essex's greatest rival, Sir Walter Raleigh. A tragic hero, whose hubris had been his downfall, Essex had resembled Henry V in at least one respect. Much lamented by many, he proved 'too famous to live long'.[25]

Elizabeth had indulged Essex, her 'adorned creature', as much as she could have done, and nearly paid with her life for being a foolish old woman. An observer reported in 1602 that 'Her delight is to sit in the dark and sometimes with shedding tears to bewail Essex.'[26]

Essex's abortive rebellion placed the Chamberlain's Men in a difficult position. Immediately after his arrest, the company feared that they could be regarded as traitors, threatened with prison or even execution. The Privy Council summoned Augustine Phillips, one of the leading actors, to explain why the Chamberlain's Men had decided to stage *Richard II* on 7 February, and for an hour or two the entire company held its breath. By way of explanation, Phillips told privy councillors that the Chamberlain's Men had been reluctant to put on the play when requested, because it was 'so old and so long out of use that they should have a small company [audience] at it'.[27] Fortunately, the council chose to accept Phillips's version of events and no further action was taken. The Chamberlain's Men were considered innocent and on Shrove Tuesday, the same day the Queen signed the warrant for Essex's execution, they performed at Court. The name of the play is not known, but perhaps, with her bitter wit, the Queen asked to see *Richard II*.

Although the Chamberlain's Men had escaped prosecution and were playing at Court, the time seemed right to distance themselves both from the Queen and any association with the disgraced Essex. The Chamberlain's Men went on tour, possibly as far as Scotland, a tour which would, three years later, provide Shakespeare with local colour and authentic Scottish turns of phrase when he came to write *Macbeth*. Shakespeare may well have derived all his knowledge from Holinshed's history of Scotland, but his information has the ring of truth: the unexpectedly mild climate of Inverness, the blasted heath on the way to Forres, lines such as 'How far is't called to Forres'[28] all indicate a grasp of the Scots idiom that seems tellingly authentic. It was in Scotland that the Chamberlain's Men first became associated with a mysterious individual known as Lawrence Fletcher, 'the English

Comedian'.[29] Reputedly an actor, Fletcher appears to have done very little actual acting but a lot of touring. Fletcher was a particular favourite of James VI, leading to suspicions that his true role consisted of spying for James. Perhaps it was here, on tour in Scotland, that the Chamberlain's Men began to forge links with the Scottish king. James was the closest thing to an heir that Elizabeth had. It made good business sense for the Chamberlain's Men to endear themselves to her likely successor.

Back at the Globe, there were no further repercussions from the Essex rebellion. Indeed, judging from this scene from *The Return from Parnassus,* performed at Christmas at St John's College, Cambridge, the Lord Chamberlain's Men had consolidated their position. In this undergraduate comedy, two stage-struck students, Philomusus and Ingenioso, audition at the Globe before Richard Burbage and William Thomas Kemp. The scene opens as Kemp and Burbage are discussing the limitations of the university play:

> KEMP: Few of the university pen playes well; they
> smell too much of that writer Ovid, and that writer
> Metamorphosis, and talk too much of Proserpina
> and Jupiter. Why here's our fellow Shakespeare
> puts them all down – ay, and Ben Jonson too.[30]

Earlier in the play, another character refers to Ben Jonson in more critical terms as 'so slow an inventor that he were better betake himself to his old trade of bricklaying'.[31]

After the students have introduced themselves, Kemp extolls the benefits of the acting profession:

> But be merry,
>   my lads, you have happened upon the most excellent

vocation in the world for money: they come north
and south to bring it to our playhouse; and for
honours, who of more report than Dick Burbage,
and Will Kemp; he is not counted a gentleman,
that knows not Dick Burbage, and Will Kemp;
there's not a country wench that can dance 'Sel-
lengers Round,' but can talk of Dick Burbage, and
Will Kemp.[32]

After a successful audition, the students are informed that
they will become successful, as long as they take heed of their
instructor. 'Thou wilt do well in time, if thou wilt be ruled
by thy betters, that is by myself, and such grave Aldermen
of the Playhouse as I am,'[33] Kemp tells them.

This portrait of Kemp and Burbage shows the Chamberlain's
Men consolidating their position as the most successful
company in London, at the most successful playhouse, with
audiences coming from north and south to bring money to
it. On a sadder note, it fell to the authors of the *Parnassus*
plays to provide an epitaph for Thomas Nashe, who was
dead by 1601.

Let all his faultes sleepe with his mournfull chest
And there for ever with his ashes rest.
His style was wittie, though it had some gall,
Some things he might have mended, so may all.
Yet this I say, that for a mother witt,
Few men have ever seene the like of it.[34]

The Lord Chamberlain's Men appeared to have consolidated
their hold on the London theatre world. However, almost
as soon as the Essex conspiracy had been resolved, another
threat appeared, from an unexpected source. To give some

idea of the nature of this threat, allow me to quote from another play, this time *Hamlet*.

During Act 2 Scene 2 of *Hamlet*, the Prince of Denmark asks the courtier Rosencrantz about the company of travelling players who have appeared at Elsinore. Rosencrantz tells Hamlet that the actors are the same company which he had always admired, 'Even those you were wont to take such delight in, the tragedians of the city.'

Somewhat surprised that the actors have been reduced to touring, Hamlet asks if the company still has the same cachet: 'Do they hold the same estimation they did when I was in the city? Are they so followed?' to which Rosencrantz replies, 'No, indeed, are they not.'

Astonished, Hamlet asks if this is because the players have grown 'rusty'.[35] Rosencrantz explains that the actors have been driven to touring after having their licence to perform withdrawn following some misdemeanour. This may of course be a veiled reference to the potential disgrace of the Chamberlain's Men with the staging of *Richard II*. As the tragedians have lost ground, says Rosencrantz, a new company has become the latest craze: 'There is, sir, an aery of children, little eyases, that cry out on the top of question, and are most tyrannically clapped for't: these are now the fashion . . .'[36]

This reference to a children's company, a brood of 'little eyases' or baby hawks, shrilling at the tops of their voices, dates from between 1598 and 1602, when Shakespeare's *Hamlet* was first performed. It is a topical reference to the competition the Chamberlain's Men were facing from an unexpected source, that of the Blackfriars Theatre.

Previously, in 1597, when James Burbage's heart had been broken by his failure to work the Blackfriars as a theatre, it seems to have been left unused. It may have been borrowed for private entertainments, for fencing classes or other purposes, but one can only surmise. On the death of William Hunnis, the Master of the Children of the Chapel Royal, on 6 June 1597, Nathaniel Giles was appointed to train up children to sing in the Queen's Chapel and perform plays before the Queen. Giles teamed up with one Henry Evans, who took a lease of the Blackfriars Theatre from Richard Burbage for £40 a year, and they began to run a private theatre, at which the children performed.[37] It became fashionable and successful. The rougher elements were excluded, prices were high, and the luxuries that had been designed by James Burbage to entice audiences to come and see his son Richard perform were enjoyed by those who came to hear the children instead. The Blackfriars attracted the more affluent classes away from the Globe, and other public theatres where anybody could go. Understandably, the Globe players were wounded by the successes of the child actors.

In 1600, the Blackfriars experienced difficulties of its own, in what became known as the 'Clifton Case'. Nathaniel Giles's patent to take up children as apprentices had a proviso, under which any child performers must not be 'the sons of gentlemen'.[38] But Giles or Evans disobeyed this stipulation and took up children who did not have singing voices but who did possess good acting skills. On 13 December 1600, James Robinson, acting as a talent scout for Giles, seized a boy called Thomas Clifton as he was walking to school. Clifton's father, a Norfolk squire, retrieved his son, complained to the Privy Council and instituted legal proceedings against Giles and Evans.[39] Evans made over his lease to his son-in-law, a new directorate was formed and the children of Blackfriars went on as a company stronger than ever.

Ben Jonson, John Marston, George Chapman and others wrote plays for the children which included music, singing, dancing and masques, more like comedy revues than the strong meat over at the Globe. Following the Bishops' Ban of 1599, it was no longer legal to publish satire in verse or prose. The only outlet was the stage, and audiences warmed to this topical entertainment, which combined Court gossip with the news of the day. It was at the Blackfriars that the so-called 'War of the Theatres' broke out between Jonson and his rivals John Marston and Thomas Dekker, who referred to it as the 'Poetomachia'. The 'war' began after Jonson, a merciless satirist, received a dose of his own medicine when Marston pilloried him as the arrogant 'Chrisoganus' in *Histriomastix* (1599). Jonson struck back by parodying Marston's verbose style in *Every Man out of His Humour* (1599), a play acted by the Lord Chamberlain's Men. Marston responded with *Jack Drum's Entertainment* (1600), acted by the Children of Paul's, satirising Jonson as Brabant Senior, a cuckold. Jonson's riposte followed with *Cynthia's Revels* (1600), acted by the Children of the Chapel.[40] In this play, Jonson satirises Marston as 'Hedon', a 'light voluptuous reveller' and Dekker as 'Anaides'.[41] He also made fun of the child actors themselves:

> Having paid my money at the door, with much ado, here I take my place and sit down: I have my three sorts of tobacco in my pocket and my light by me and thus I begin. (At this he breaks his tobacco.) By this light I wonder that any is so mad as to come to see these rascally tits' plays – they do act like so many wrens or pismires [ants] – not the fifth part of a good face amongst them – and their music is abominable . . . By this vapour, an t'were not for tobacco, I think the very stench of 'em would poison me, I should not dare to come in at their gates. A man were better visit fifteen jails or a dozen or two of hospitals than venture to come near them.[42]

The battle continued with Marston attacking Jonson in *What You Will* (1601) and Jonson responding with *The Poetaster* (1601), performed by the Children of the Chapel, with the character representing Marston vomiting all the bombastic and ridiculous words he has ingested. In *Satiromastix* (1601), Dekker completed the sequence, vilifying Jonson as 'Horace', an arrogant and overbearing hypocrite.[43]

Despite the fact that Jonson's plays were performed by Shakespeare's company, the Lord Chamberlain's Men, Shakespeare's characteristic response was to watch this rivalry from the sidelines, commenting on it obliquely in this scene between Hamlet, Rosencrantz and Guildenstern:

> ROSENCRANTZ: Faith, there has been much to do on both sides; and the nation holds it no sin to tar them to controversy: there was, for a while, no money bid for argument unless the poet and the player went to cuffs in the question.
> HAMLET: Is't possible?
> GUILDENSTERN: O, there has been much throwing about of brains.[44]

In the spirit of bear-baiting, courtiers fanned the flames of jealousy for their own entertainment, provoking controversy to the point at which the poet and the player resorted to fisticuffs. Subsequently, scholars have debated the true nature of the 'War of the Theatres'. In retrospect, the 'war' may have been professional rivalry between theatre companies, a genuine debate between three successful writers or a publicity stunt from which everyone benefited.

The 'war' certainly provided some much-needed distraction from the gloom which had descended upon the country in the opening years of the new century. By 1603, the old Queen was sixty-nine, and frail, although refusing to bow to the indignities of age. There were rumours of plague and outbreaks of plague and constant anxiety about who would succeed when Elizabeth was gone. Showing little concern for her own preservation, the Queen wore summer clothes in February while the rest of her Court huddled in furs. But following the death of her closest friend, Catherine Howard, Countess of Nottingham, on 25 February, Elizabeth lost the will to live. Refusing all medicine, she slipped into a coma on 19 March. The Queen finally died on 24 March, with Essex's ring upon her finger and his name carved upon her heart.[45] According to diarist John Manningham, the Queen departed this life as mildly as a lamb, or like an apple dropping from the tree.[46]

'She came in with the fall of the leafe, and went away in the Spring: her life, (which was dedicated to Virginitie), both beginning and closing up a miraculous Maiden circle: for she was borne upon a Lady Eve, and died upon a Lady Eve . . . Three places are made famous by her for three things, *Greenwich* for her birth, *Richmond* for her death, and *Whitehall* for her Funerall.'[47]

These were the words of Thomas Dekker, in *The Wonderful Year,* but his fellow writers remained strangely silent, despite being exhorted to mourn in an English broadside ballad of 1603:

> You poets all, brave Shakespeare, Jonson, Greene,
> Bestow your time to write for England's Queene.
> Lament, Lament, Lament you English peeres,
> Lament your loss, possessed so many years,
> Return your songs and sonnets and your lays,
> To set forth sweet Elizabeth's praise.[48]

Chettle, in his *England's Mourning Garment*, wrote:

> Nor doth the silver-tongued Melicert [Shakespeare]
> Drop from his honied muse one sable tear
> To mourne her death, who graced his desert,
> And to his layes opened her Royall ear.
> Shepherd, remember our Elizabeth,
> And sing her rape, done by that Tarquin, Death.[49]

This admonishment seems to have gone unheeded. Perhaps Shakespeare's thoughts were with his old patron, the Earl of Southampton, who was still in the Tower. While the poet Michael Drayton, Shakespeare's fellow Warwickshireman, hastened to welcome the new king with his poem,[50] the players bided their time. The death of the Queen had serious implications for the Lord Chamberlain's Men, who feared they might lose royal patronage.

But the new King appeared to bring peace and joy. He freed the Earl of Southampton on 10 April 1603 and had barely reached London before he began to make sweeping changes. James removed the power to select plays and patronise players from the noblemen. Henceforth, the privilege of selecting plays and players would be restricted to the King himself. Finally, and this must have come as a great relief to Shakespeare and his fellow sharers, James chose the Lord Chamberlain's Men as his own company. With their name changed to the King's Men, Shakespeare's players would still enjoy royal patronage. This came at a price, however. James insisted that the mysterious Lawrence Fletcher, the 'English clown' and possible spy, was to be their chief. It is not recorded how the company at the Globe responded to this intrusion or how Fletcher fitted into their ranks, and little more is heard of him. But Fletcher did at least bring with him the Royal Patent. The new King came to London on 7 May 1603 and on 17 May the Privy Seal for their patent was signed. It was granted on 19 May. This patent, *pro Laurentio Fletcher et Willielmo Shakespeare et aliis,* informed all 'Justices, Mayors, Sheriffs, Constables and other Officers and Loving Subjects' that 'wee of our Speciall Grace' had licensed and authorised . . .

> . . . these our Servants, Laurence Fletcher, William Shakespeare, Richard Burbage, Augustine Phillipps, John Hemings, Henry Condell, William Sly, Robert Armyn, Richard Cowly, and the rest of their Associates, Freely to use and exercise the Art and Facultie of playing Comedies, Tragedies, Histories, Enterludes, Morals, Pastoralls, Stage Playes and such others . . . for our Solace and Pleasure, when we shall think good to see them.[51]

The King's Men were licensed 'to show and exercise publically to their best Commoditie, when the Infection of the Plague shall decrease, within their now usual house called the Globe within our county of Surrey, as also within any Town Halls, Moot Halls or other convenient places within the Liberties and Freedom of any other City, Universitie, Town or Borough within our said Realmes and Dominions.' This patent informed the authorities that when on tour the King's Men should be allowed to perform without any 'Letts, Hindrances or Molestations' and also to aid and assist them 'if any Wrong be to them offered'.[52]

The status conferred on the players by becoming the King's Men was enormous. By virtue of this patronage, the actors took rank as grooms of the Royal Chamber (although they were only paid when they rendered services), wore the King's livery, and held certain privileges such as immunity from arrest while on the King's service, except for treason or great crimes. Any problems with debt were referred to the Lord Chamberlain, and the patent carried them all over the country, protecting them while in London from civic interference. They also had the additional protection of the Earl of Southampton, now safely out of the Tower and in attendance to the King. The King's Men also had an increased source of revenue thanks to their new-found status. Ironically, this source of income came from plague, which in previous years had reduced the company's takings. It was plague which halted the King's royal progress through the country from the latter part of 1603, forcing James to hold Court at Wilton, Winchester and Basing during most of October, November and December. Letters and proclamations indicate that the King was not willing to wait until Christmas to see his players. King James sent a warrant to John Hemmings to bring one of his plays to the Court at Wilton on 3 December 1603, in return for His Majesty's reward of £30 to cover 'the paynes and expense of himself and the rest of the company coming from Mortlake in the county of Surrey unto the Court aforesaid'.[53] This was generous indeed. The King's Men were also given immunity from the financial impact of the plague, being given the right to claim compensation during periods when the Globe was closed by plague. A warrant signed at Hampton Court on 8 February 1604 shows that Richard Burbage was presented with £30 'for the maintenance and relief of himself and the rest of his company being prohibited to present any plays publically in or near London by reason of the great peril that might growe through the extraordinary concourse and assemblie of people to a newe increase in the plague, till it shall please God to settle the city in a more perfect health'.[54] In the same month they were paid £20 for two plays presented before His Majesty on Candlemas Day at night and on Shrove Sunday at night. The King's Men went from strength to strength, and the nagging lawsuits which had blighted the life of James Burbage became a thing of the past.

In August 1604 the King's Men were appointed to attend on the Spanish Ambassador at Somerset House, 'for the space of 18 days, viz, from the 9th day of August 1604 till the 27th day of the same, as appeareth by a bill thereof signed by the Lord Chamberlyne £21.12s'.[55] It is possible that, among other plays, they performed *Love's Labour's Lost*, which might have appealed to a Spaniard. The play had been revived that year to entertain the King's wife, Queen Anne, and her brother, as indicated in a letter from January 1604:

> Sir, I have sent and bene all thys morning hunting for players, juglers and suche kinde of creatures, but fynde them hard to fynde, wherefore leaving notes for them to seeke me, Burbage is come, and says there is no new playe that the Queene hath not seen, but they have revyved an old one cawled 'Loves Labore Lost' which for wytt and mirthe he says will please her exceedingly. And this is appointed to be played tomorrow night at my Lord of Southampton's, unless you send a writ to remove the *Corpus cum causa* to your house in Strand. Burbage is my messenger ready attending your pleasure.[56]

Love's Labour's Lost was clearly an old favourite, but a different type of play was required now, a play shrouded in mystery and controversy. At some point in January 1604 the King's Men performed a play entitled *The Tragedy of Gowrie* in which King James I himself was impersonated upon the stage. The play was ordered to be suppressed, on the grounds that it was not considered fit to represent contemporary people or events. We do not know if it was by Shakespeare, but it is almost certain that it inspired *Macbeth*, a play designed to impress the king who had done so much for the company.

Relations between the Globe and the Lord Mayor and the Corporation of London had become more favourable by this time, since the King's patronage allowed the corporation to see the players as they really were, as professional actors and not a rowdy gang of vagabonds. On one occasion they enlisted Richard Burbage to honour Henry, James I's oldest son, on his investiture as Prince of Wales. The playwright Anthony Monday (1560–1633) wrote the speeches and designed an elaborate pageant during which Richard Burbage and John Rice were required to ride two giant fish down the Thames. For this the players were paid £17.10s.6d, and, in recognition of 'their pains', the actors were permitted to keep the taffeta and silk robes which had adorned them throughout the performance, for use on other occasions.[57] As a royal patron, James was nothing if not generous.

In May 1605, the King's Men lost Augustine Phillips, the actor and musician who had been called to give evidence to the Privy Council after the controversial revival of *Richard II*. Phillips left a generous will, with bequests to his fellow actors. His executors, John Hemmings, Richard Burbage, and William Sly, each received a silver bowl worth five pounds. Shakespeare, Henry Condell, and Christopher Beeston each received a thirty-shilling gold piece, while twenty shillings each went to Lawrence Fletcher, Robert Armin, Alexander Cooke, Richard Cowley and Nicholas Tooley. To his former apprentice, Samuel Gilburne, Phillips willed his clothes, a common practice among actors when costumes were so valuable, including his 'mouse-colored' velvet hose, his black taffeta suit and white taffeta doublet, his purple cloak, his sword and dagger, and his bass viol. Phillips's apprentice,

James Sands, got forty shillings and his musical instruments, a cittern, a bandora, and a lute. The remaining five pounds was to be split among the company's hired men. Phillips's widow made an unwise second marriage to a man named John Witter, forfeiting her inheritance by doing so. The second marriage eventually ruined her and her children and ended in legal proceedings.[58]

The dying months of 1605 were dominated by the extraordinary news of an audacious assassination attempt. In November 1605, just hours before the State Opening of Parliament, Catholic convert Guido or 'Guy' Fawkes was discovered in the labyrinth of tunnels beneath the Palace of Westminster with thirty barrels of gunpowder. Fawkes's intention had been to blow the Houses of Parliament sky-high and everyone in it, including:

[our] Sovereign Lord the King, the excellent, virtuous and gracious Queen Anne, his dearest Wife, the most noble Prince Henry, their eldest Son, and future Hope and Joy of England; and the Lords Spiritual and Temporal, the Reverend Judges of the Realm, the Knights, Citizens and Burgesses of Parliament, and divers other faithful Subjects and Servants of the King in the said Parliament . . . and all them, without any respect of Majesty, Dignity, Degree, Sex, Age or Place, most barbarously, and more than beastly, traitorously and suddenly to destroy and swallow up.[59]

King James I himself later declared that had this plot succeeded, the explosion would have cracked open the earth which would have 'destroyed and defaced, in the twinkling of an eye, not only our present living Princes and people, but even our insensible Monuments . . .'[60]

The Gunpowder Plot had been devised by a group of fanatical Catholic recusants, led by Sir Robert Catesby, who intended to assassinate King James and place his daughter, Princess Elizabeth, on the throne. Under torture, Guy Fawkes revealed the names of his seven co-conspirators, all of whom were hanged, drawn and quartered. Guy Fawkes was executed in Old Palace Yard, opposite the Palace of Westminster, along with Thomas Wintour, Ambrose Rookwood and Robert Keyes on 31 January 1606. Dragged from the Tower of London by horses, the men were hanged, cut down and disembowelled while still breathing. Fawkes was the last to die, but escaped the worst excesses of his execution by flinging himself from the scaffold before he could be hanged and breaking his neck.[61]

The failure of the Gunpowder Plot created old stirrings of anxiety among Shakespeare's family and friends. Ben Jonson, a one-time Catholic, had frequently drunk with the plotters in the Mermaid Tavern. Perhaps Shakespeare reflected on his father's secret Catholic past, and any errands he might have run for him, delivering messages to recusant networks, and shuddered. Sir Robert Catesby, the ringleader, had been a Warwickshire man, and Shakespeare's daughter, Susanna, may already have displayed recusant leanings; she was later accused of recusancy in 1606. In the febrile climate of post-Gunpowder Plot anxiety, anti-Catholic feeling ran riot. King James informed his people that: 'the Jesuits are the worst and most seditious fellows in the world. They are slaves and spies . . . they have always been the authors and instruments of all the great disturbances which have taken place.'[62]

Not only were Jesuits considered spies, but in some quarters they were even regarded as witches. As prejudice fanned into paranoia, the time was right for a play about magic, but not the mischievous country magic of Shakespeare's youth

that had enchanted *A Midsummer Night's Dream* with a sprin-
kling of faery dust. This magic was composed of 'toil and
trouble',[63] the evil spells of malevolent old witches who spent
their time killing swine and deluding weak men into seizing
the crown. A Scottish play about witchcraft for a Scottish
king obsessed with witchcraft. 'Screw up your courage to the
sticking place,' Shakespeare may have muttered, reaching for
his quill. 'And we'll not fail.'[64]

King James's preoccupation with witchcraft was well documented. He had become obsessed with the topic following
his own extraordinary experiences in 1589. In this year, James
was betrothed to Anne of Denmark, but a series of violent
storms kept the couple apart and prevented them from
marrying. When James eventually reached Denmark and
married Anne, the admiral of the Danish fleet declared that
the storms had been caused by Danish witches intent on
drowning the couple. Six witches were tried and executed
in Denmark in May 1590. James accepted this extraordinary
interpretation of events and went even further, claiming that
his cousin and rival, Francis Stewart, the Earl of Bothwell,
had conspired with a coven of witches in North Berwick to
have James and his queen drowned on their return from
Denmark.[65] The Earl of Bothwell was arrested on charges
of high treason and went on trial with over seventy other
accused, who were tortured into admitting that they conjured
up the devil, who 'licked them upon their privy parts' and
gave them a special mark to indicate that they were his servants. Finding 'the mark of a witch' was a humiliating and
degrading ordeal for such women, particularly as any mole
or wart might be interpreted as satanic in origin.[66]

James personally supervised the witch trials, taking a
particular interest in the case of Agnes Sampson, a local
midwife. Agnes was taken to Holyrood Palace, chained to a

wall, and tortured with a device known as a 'witch's bridle' – an instrument with four sharp tongues pressed into her mouth. After she had been shaved all over and the 'devil's mark' found upon her privates, Agnes confessed to fifty-three counts against her of conspiring to drown the King by creating violent spells with the following method:

> Agnes Sampson confessed that at the time when his Majesty was in Denmark she took a Cat and christened it, and afterward bound to each part of that Cat, the chiefest parts of a dead man, and several joints of his body, and that in the night following the said Cat was conveyed into the midst of the sea by all these witches sayling in their riddles or Sieves and so left the said Cat right before the Town of Leith in Scotland, this done, there did arise such a tempest in the Sea as a greater hath not been seen; which tempest was the cause of the perishing of a Boat . . .
>
> . . . it is confessed that the said christened Cat was the cause that the King's Majesty's Ship at him coming forth of Denmark, had a contrary winde to the rest of his Ship and further the said witch declared, that his Majesty had never come safely from the Sea, if his faith had not prevailed above their intentions.[67]

This account, from the contemporary pamphlet *Newes from Scotland,* is accompanied by a woodcut of four witches around their cauldron, one inspiration for the three weird sisters, and the leaking craft may well be the inspiration for the First Witch's claim that she will go to sea in a sieve, to boil up storms.

To give him his due, even King James was not entirely convinced of Agnes's guilt at this point of the trial and accused her of lying. In response, Agnes said that she would tell him something that would leave him in no doubt that she was telling the truth.

> And thereupon, taking his Maiestie a little aside, she declared unto him the very words which passed between the Kings Maiestie and his Queene at Oslo in Norway the first night of their marriage, with their answer each to other: whereat the Kinges Maiestie wondered greatly, and swore by the living God, that he believed that all the Devils in hell could not have discovered the same.[68]

With this, the King believed that Agnes had not been lying and that she was indeed a witch. Agnes was garrotted and then burned at the stake on Castlehill, and her ghost is said to haunt Holyrood Palace. Around 3,000 to 4,000 'witches' died in Scotland between 1560 and 1707.[69]

King James had become so fascinated by witchcraft that he even published a book on the subject, *Daemonologie, In Form of a Dialogue, Divided into three Bookes* (1597). The King justified witch-hunting and executing witches on the grounds that: 'The feareful abounding at this time in this countrie, of these detestable slaves of the Devil, the Witches or enchanters, hath moved me (beloved reader) to dispatch in post, this following treatise of mine . . . to resolve the doubting . . . both that such assaults of Satan are most certainly practised, and that the instrument thereof merits most severely to be punished.'[70]

Shakespeare's inclusion of the witches in *Macbeth* was another way of flattering his patron, as well as responding to the eternal public fascination with the supernatural. Witchcraft was a common topic in Shakespeare's time, and most representations of witches in plays were of poor, ugly old women (as were most of those actually accused of witchcraft), the reverse of the ideal of female beauty and virtue. The witches in *Macbeth* or 'the three weird sisters' live up to this representation with their 'skinny lips' and 'choppy' fingers.[71] Witches in Shakespeare's England were feared and loathed, as it was believed they would deceive people and lure them to their downfall.

Witches were believed to have 'familiars', demonic creatures 'either in likeness of a Dog, a Cat, an Ape, or such-like other beast',[72] which followed them around and did their bidding. In *Macbeth*, the First Witch has a cat familiar named Graymalkin (grey Mary) and the Second Witch has a 'paddock' or toad, which calls or croaks to her.

In addition to reflecting King James's obsession with witchcraft, *Macbeth* flattered the King in another significant respect. King James was commonly believed to be descended from Banquo, the Thane of Lochaber, the historical counterpart of Shakespeare's Banquo, the friend who Macbeth betrays and has murdered. With this in mind, the witches' prophesy that Banquo's ancestors will be kings takes on a new meaning. It is referring to Banquo's descendant, James Stuart, King of Scotland and England. Thus the escape of Fleance, Banquo's son, from Macbeth's murder plot echoes James's own escape from the Gunpowder Plot and affirms the House of Stuart as legitimate rulers.[73]

In another oblique reference to the Gunpowder Plot, there is a scene at the beginning of Act 2 Scene 3, where the porter amuses himself by pretending he is the gatekeeper of Hell, letting in the new arrivals.

Who's there, I' th' name of Beelzebub? – Here's a farmer, that hang'd himself on the expectation of plenty . . .
    Who's there, I' th' other devil's name? Faith, here's an equivocator, that could swear in both the scales against

either scale; who committed treason enough for God's sake, yet could not equivocate to heaven. O, come in, equivocator.[74]

'Equivocator' was a pejorative term for a Jesuit, as Jesuits were particularly associated with equivocation, a means of avoiding the sin of lying by instead implying something untrue through ambiguous phrasing. The insistent reference to equivocation is taken by many scholars to be an allusion to the Jesuit Father Garnet, also known as 'Farmer Garnet', who was hanged, drawn and quartered for his role in the Gunpowder Plot and was deeply criticised for equivocating. Garnet had heard confession from Robert Catesby, one of the plotters, which revealed his intention to kill the King, but obeyed the seal of the confessional by keeping it secret. Garnet's defence of equivocation was extremely damaging in his trial, and the porter's light-hearted remarks seem to be playing on popular derision of the priest.[75]

With *Macbeth,* Shakespeare succeeded in flattering his new king, creating an unforgettable tragic hero and commenting indirectly on sensationally topical issues. In other words, the Lord Chamberlain's Men might have changed their name to the King's Men, but it was business as usual. It must have seemed as though nothing could prevent Shakespeare and the King's Men from being the best company in London. But soon enough, Shakespeare and the King's Men would meet their own nemesis, in the form of death, and the great Globe itself fall prey to 'dire combustion and confused events'.[76]

CHIMES AT MIDNIGHT

Our revels now are ended . . .

The Tempest, Act 4 Scene 1

It is tempting to read the sense of an ending into Shakespeare's later plays, a dying fall, an elegiac recognition that the author was bound for the kingdom of perpetual night. The plays have a valedictory quality, and resonate with farewells. 'The bright day is done, and we are for the dark.'[1]

> Fear no more the heat o' the sun,
> Nor the furious winter's rages;
> Thou thy worldly task hast done,
> Home art gone, and ta'en thy wages:
> Golden lads and girls all must,
> As chimney-sweepers, come to dust.[2]

Such retrospective judgements are tempting to scholars and general readers alike, but there is no real evidence that Shakespeare felt he was approaching the end of his

life, or was about to make a last farewell to all his greatness. A less such subjective interpretation would be that
Shakespeare and his contemporaries were responding to
the sable-black mood of the period, a sombre era which
produced the dark Jacobean tragedies of Webster, Tourneur
and Middleton. Plays like *The Revenger's Tragedy, The
Duchess of Malfi* and *The White Devil* were a testament to
the times, just as Thomas Nashe's *Litany in Time of Plague*
had expressed the universal mood fifteen years earlier.
Writers had been seized by a collective sense of *lacrimae
rerum* or 'there are tears for things'.[3] Despite the relative
stability of King James I's regime, these were difficult
times. A particularly virulent outbreak of plague killed
over 7,500 people between 1608 and 1609.[4] The winter of
1608 was so cold that the Thames froze, and the ice was
so solid people could walk across from one side to the
other. While this offered many opportunities for bacchanalian revels, frost fairs, ice-skating, bull-baiting, horse
races and tippling, the downside was an unbearable,
creeping cold. Fowls, fish and birds, exotic plants and
vegetables perished. Deer parks were destroyed as the
animals starved to death, and fuel became so expensive
that the poor begged for sea coal and firewood. In London,
the air was so cold and still that smoke from coal fires
hovered in a suffocating layer at ground level.

The cold weather caused acute food shortages, while
political dissent led to riots in the Midlands caused by
proposals to enclose common land. One of the most significant riots in 1607 had been led by 'Captain Pouch', also
known as John Reynolds, a tinker from Desborough,
Northamptonshire.[5] Telling his supporters that they would
never go hungry as long as they followed him, Captain
Pouch led his thousand-strong band against the King's

forces after a local landowner announced his intention of enclosing a piece of land called 'The Brand', originally part of Rockingham Forest. The rebels, including women and children, were put down by the King's forces, and fifty men were hanged for treason, Captain Pouch among them. When his famous pouch was opened, they found nothing inside apart from a piece of green cheese.[6] Riots, caused by food shortages, dominate the opening scenes of *Coriolanus* when an angry mob, determined to die fighting rather than perish from starvation, descends upon the Roman senate demanding grain 'ere we become rakes'.[7] Shakespeare himself stood accused of hoarding grain for profit in time of scarcity, an unappealing indictment, although one would have expected nothing less of the shrewd businessman he appears to have become.[8]

Against this turbulent backdrop, Shakespeare suffered his own personal grief, losing his brother Edmund and his mother. In this context the exhortation to 'Fear no more the heat of the sun' suggests that it was not his own death that preoccupied him, but the loss of family. Shakespeare had already buried his son Hamnet, who had died aged eleven in 1596, and he knew the distinctive grief of a bereaved parent. It has often been claimed that previous generations, accustomed to a high mortality rate, were more accepting of the death of a child. These lines from *King John* indicate that parental bereavement is always impossible to bear, whatever the historical period:

> Grief fills the room up of my absent child,
> Lies in his bed, walks up and down with me,
> Puts on his pretty looks, repeats his words,
> Remembers me of all his gracious parts,
> Stuffs out his vacant garments with his form.[9]

Shakespeare's younger brother Edmund, also an actor, was buried at St Saviour's on the last day of 1607. He was just 27. A year later, their mother, Mary Shakespeare, died in Stratford, and was buried on 9 September.

This first sad decade of the new century required festivities to distract a depleted unhappy nation from its own grief. *The Winter's Tale*, operatic in its scale; the astonishing *Pericles*; and *The Tempest*, incorporating all that Shakespeare had learned of the masque and exploiting to the utmost the resources of the Blackfriars Theatre. Indeed, the very Blackfriars itself, for by 1608 the Burbages had finally taken control of this wonderful indoor theatre after an extraordinary series of events.

At the start of 1608, the King's Men had settled down artistically with King James as their new patron. The Globe flourished, although Shakespeare's latest tragedy, *Antony and Cleopatra*, had not been as successful as might have been hoped. While audiences had responded appreciatively to the Roman political drama *Julius Caesar*, this tale of Mark Antony's doomed middle-aged love affair failed to elicit the same response. Nevertheless, the King's Men continued to attract audiences, until the Globe was closed by an outbreak of plague. Although some income was guaranteed by playing for the King and at private celebrations, the company needed to increase its revenue in order to fill the coffers. As the cold seeped into their bones from the frozen Thames, Shakespeare and the Burbages began to consider the benefits of an indoor theatre, where they could play during the winter months. A winter home where the action might be punctuated by dazzling masques, with gods and goddesses descending from the flies as *deus ex machina*. An indoor theatre warmed by the flattering glow of candlelight, where such plays might be re-enacted as those which graced royal palaces, the Inns of Court and the smoke-blackened panelled halls of Cambridge colleges. An indoor theatre might also escape being closed by the pestilence. It was time to take back the Blackfriars.

Henry Evans, who was renting the Blackfriars for his boys' company, had begun to negotiate with Richard Burbage over surrendering the lease in 1604, but talks had stalled when the company had been reconstituted as the Children of the Queen's Revels,[10] with Queen Anne as patron. The performances were lively and audacious, becoming ever more satirical in nature. In 1605, the children performed a comedy called *Eastward Ho* by George Chapman, Ben Jonson and John Marston. Following the 'war of the theatres', Jonson and Marston had clearly resolved their differences sufficiently to write together.

The supposedly anti-Scottish sentiments expressed in this play provoked outrage from the Court, although by modern standards the remarks seem innocuous enough. On facing a life in the colony of Virginia, Golding the apprentice is told he might encounter 'only a few industrious Scots, perhaps, who indeed are dispers'd over the face of the whole earth. But, as for them, there are no greater friends to Englishmen and England, when they are out on't, in the world, than they are.'[11] This reference to the Scottish diaspora hardly seems insurrectionary but Queen Anne withdrew her patronage and Chapman, Jonson and indeed some of the children were sent to gaol. They faced not the death penalty, but the unpleasant prospect of having their ears cut off and their noses split. Marston fled, and Chapman and Jonson were later freed thanks to the intervention of the Duke of Suffolk. Despite this offence, the play was not banned, Blackfriars remained open and the children continued to perform. The playwrights continued to write topical satires and the children continued to perform them, without mincing their words. The final straw for the authorities came in 1608, with Chapman's *Tragedy of Byron,* a political satire based on events in France. In a thinly veiled reference to the doomed Earl of Essex, Byron was portrayed as a military commander whose pride brought about his downfall and execution. One scene in particular echoed a notorious incident when Queen Elizabeth had slapped the Earl of Essex across the face.[12] In the play, it is the French Queen who slaps her husband's mistress across the face, in a scene later cut from the printed edition. The French Ambassador, Antoine Lefèvre de la Boderie, was outraged by the play, and by way of apology the Children of the Chapel were banned. On 9 August 1608, the lease of Blackfriars was surrendered to Richard Burbage for a 21-year lease at £40 per annum. This was the opportunity the Burbage brothers had been waiting for. There was only one company in London which could exploit the potential of the Blackfriars and, as Cuthbert Burbage later recalled, 'it was considered that house would be as fit for ourselves'.[13] Richard Burbage formed a company of sharers from his partners at the Globe, and took on some of the older children. The other children, faced with losing their venue and their livelihood, swiftly rallied and started a new company at Whitefriars. Finally, the King's Men had rid themselves of their little eyases.

The Blackfriars Theatre gave the King's Men a new lease of life. At last, old James Burbage's original venture had been fulfilled and the actors had an indoor theatre. Richard Burbage was the landlord, and James I their patron. With two stages at his command, Burbage could choose his plays and his roles in a way that very few actors could. He could work summer and winter, by daylight and by candlelight.

He still had Shakespeare by his side, the esteemed 'bending author' and fellow actor willing and ready to find themes and subjects which suited his genius. Not only could Shakespeare exploit this new venue to its utmost, but he was developing new skills. Old Shake-scene had not lost his touch; rather, he was keen to explore the technical developments offered by the indoor theatre combined with new ways of writing. Always versatile, Shakespeare adapted to the times. His role became that of a consultant, working with other, younger writers. There may have been a practical reason for this, caused by faltering health. Handwriting experts have suggested that later samples of Shakespeare's writing indicated the onset of debilitating disease, such as Parkinson's. If this is the case, Shakespeare's output would have been diminished, the great 4,000-liners a thing of the past. But Shakespeare's expertise and dramatic skill remained stronger than ever, making him the ideal script doctor. Although he was spending increasingly longer periods of time at his house in Stratford, New Place, consolidating his business affairs and trying to resolve his daughters' tribulations, there is no indication that Shakespeare was preparing to leave London for good. The concept of retirement was an alien one to Shakespeare and his contemporaries, who worked until they dropped. Those who live by the pen never truly retire.

Pericles, the first of these collaborations, is also the first imperfect play in the series referred to as the 'romances', fantastic fairy tales that defy the conventional laws of dramaturgy. In *Pericles, Cymbeline, The Winter's Tale* and *The Tempest,* audiences are required to suspend their disbelief to the utmost and believe they are watching tales of long-lost children, shipwrecks, sixteen-year gaps in the narrative, magic, cannibals, and a statue coming to life, all taking place in exotic lands such as Tyre (now in Lebanon), Ancient Britain, Bohemia and Bermuda. If downtrodden, gloomy Londoners longed to be taken out of themselves, then this was the fare that they needed. In effect, Shakespeare's audiences were being asked to believe in miracles, just as previous generations had accepted and enjoyed the mystery plays and interludes of Shakespeare's youth.

Pericles, Prince of Tyre was probably co-written with George Wilkins (d. 1618), a dramatist and petty criminal who kept an inn, and possibly a brothel, in Cow Cross. It is thought that Wilkins wrote the first two acts of the play, around 835 lines, and Shakespeare contributed the remaining three acts. Wilkins, a violent thug who had been prosecuted for kicking a pregnant woman in the belly, seems an unlikely writing partner. The most obvious explanation is that Shakespeare was asked to complete the project while Wilkins was in gaol.[14] One of the most notable features of the play is the inclusion of an elaborate masque. While the masque in *Pericles, Prince of Tyre* had worked well in the outdoor theatre of the Globe, the Blackfriars offered the possibility of ever-more elaborate masques.

There had always been a masque element in Shakespeare's plays, from the amateur dramatic presentation of *Pyramus and Thisbe* given by the 'rude mechanicals'[15] in *A Midsummer Night's Dream* to the dumb show performed by the players in *Hamlet,* devised to reveal the killing of Hamlet's father. There is a masque in *Romeo and Juliet* and *Henry VIII* would also include a masque when it was first staged in 1613. Masques had been performed at Kenilworth in 1575, when the Earl of Leicester ostentatiously welcomed the Queen to his castle, and were a mainstay of royal entertainments. By the Jacobean period, they had become more elaborate, incorporating music, dance and narrative. The chief distinction between masques and plays was that masques were performed only once, on one occasion, while plays could be repeated endlessly. Masques were dominated by music and display and, most notably of all, by female semi-nudity. While women were forbidden to tread the boards as professional actors, aristocratic ladies were permitted to perform in these entertainments which took place in the privacy of the Court. The pleasure-loving, vivacious Queen Anne appeared in a masque about the Twelve Goddesses, in a very short skirt, so that according to one observer, 'we might see a woman had both feet and legs which I never knew before'. These were not professional productions. The participants often slurred their lines, forgot their lines, and were so drunk they fell over. When Anne's father, the King of Denmark, visited England he was profoundly shocked to witness scenes of intoxication, with his own daughter leading the proceedings glassy-eyed and hiccoughing.[16] The court masques were redeemed by the ingenious and beautiful designs of the architect Inigo Jones, but the performances often left authors in despair. Ben Jonson, who wrote *The Masque of Blackness* for Queen Anne, was horrified when he discovered that the Queen and her ladies intended to black up for the occasion. 'It was her Majesty's wish,' he wrote later, 'to have them blackamoors.'[17] Rather than adopting masks, as had been the custom, this was achieved by covering Anne and her women with black body paint when the masque was performed at Whitehall in January 1605. Perhaps it was the extravagance of these events, and the fact that they were only performed once, which deterred Shakespeare from writing specific masques. As it was, the indoor theatres, smaller and more intimate, offered sufficient protection to incorporate elements of the masque, without dispensing with his most significant ingredient, that of language.

The Winter's Tale seems to have been designed for the Blackfriars but could play just as well in the Globe. It is likely that the play was performed at both venues, with adjustments for indoor and outdoor performances. By any standards, it is an extraordinary play, 'tragical-comical-pastoral', as if Shakespeare was combining some elements of his youth – an old wives' tale, a text from Robert Greene, and a *bear,* for heaven's sake – with his later developments, the psychological accuracy of Leontes's jealousy, the awful death of a child, themes which belong to the mature tragic period of *Othello* and *Hamlet.* The clue is in the name. *The Winter's Tale* is a pantomime, with its demon king, Leontes, its fairy godmother, Paulina, its love interest and even its 'saucy' language, complete with a reference to the 'dildos' carried in his pack by Autolycus the pedlar. *The Winter's Tale* has all the stuff of traditional winter entertainment, including an animal. *Exit, pursued by a bear* remains the most famous stage direction in theatre history. A real bear, borrowed from the nearby bear garden, might have been used in performances at the Globe, but this would have proved impractical. Never mind the old adage of never working with children and animals, one can only imagine the damage that could be inflicted by a live bear, lose on stage.

The Winter's Tale certainly qualifies as a masque, or even an opera, an emerging genre at the time (Monteverdi's *L'Orfeo* appeared in 1607). It is certainly a new type of play, moving away from the dictates of Senecan tragedy into a more fluid, imaginative realm. The audience travels from the tragic consequences of Leontes's pathological jealousy, the death of his young son Mamillius and the apparent death of Hermione to the comic pastoral sequences. Indeed, with its fairy-tale storyline, element of tragedy, romantic reunions and extraordinary healing, and its restorative transformation scene, *The*

Winter's Tale is the closest Shakespeare ever comes to that great twentieth-century art form, the West End musical. *The Winter's Tale* is interesting for another reason. The original 'book' was Robert Greene's *Pandosto*. Years after being vilified by Robert Greene as the upstart crow, the vastly successful Shakespeare raided one of his novels for inspiration. Was this by way of homage? It seems unlikely. Shakespeare was a magpie of a writer. Like Autolycus, he was 'a snapper up of unconsidered trifles'.[18]

The Winter's Tale was performed at Court in 1611. In hindsight, the death of Mamillius, Leontes's son, seems tragically apt. In 1612 Henry, Prince of Wales, died of typhus and the country was plunged into mourning. Henry had, after all, been first in line to the throne, and had been compared with King Arthur, creating a fashion for medieval chivalry, for the lost world of Malory and Spenser. With Henry's death, Queen Anne was plunged into melancholy. Her love of dancing, drinking and display were gone, and masques held little fascination for her now. Broken-hearted, Anne retreated from Court life.

Of all the romances, it is *The Tempest* which is most artificial, and the most suited to an indoor theatre. Set on a desert island, the play includes a shipwreck, a monster (Caliban), an enchanter (Prospero), a witch (Caliban's mother Sycorax), and makes absolutely no attempt at realism whatsoever. It is the desert island itself which most intrigues, showing Shakespeare prepared to write about the New World, as well as the Old. *The Tempest* reflects the popular fascination with the lands which were being discovered at the edge of the world, and their exotic inhabitants. Inspiration for *The Tempest* came from *The Bermuda Pamphlets,* describing a wreck in the Bermudas in 1609. In May of that year, a fleet of nine ships with 500 colonists under Sir Thomas Gates and

Sir George Somers set out to John Smith's colony in Virginia, but on 25 July the *Sea Adventure*, which carried both Gates and Somers, was separated from the rest of the fleet by a storm during which 'the heavens were obscured and made an Egyptian night of three days perpetual horror'. The ship was driven towards the coast of the Bermudas, 'hardly accessible through the environing rocks and dangers'; the crew had no choice but to run their ship aground. When 'neere land' the ship became wedged between 'two rocks, where she was fast lodged and locked for further budging'. But all on board safely reached the beach, and they managed to save most of the ship's stores.[19]

The other ships, with one exception, safely reached Virginia and, ultimately, Gates and Somers set out for Virginia the following May and reached it safely. The story of their adventures travelled to England in the autumn of 1610, by which time it had been assumed that they were all dead. The news that Gates and Somers had survived their ordeal had enormous dramatic appeal, as did the travellers' tales of Sir Anthony Shirley, written up by William Parry, in which Shirley talked about strange new lands inhabited by wild animals, wild men and cannibals, the anagrammatic inspiration for Caliban. Michael Drayton's *Polyolbion,* meanwhile, included an illustration of a race of men in New Guinea with no heads at all, whose faces were on their chests![20]

Half-man, half-monster, Caliban is one of Shakespeare's most intriguing characters. The son of Sycorax by 'Setebos' (or the devil), Caliban is portrayed on one level as a practical man with survival skills: 'I'll show thee the best springs; I'll pluck thee berries, I'll fish for thee and get thee wood enough,'[21] and on another as essentially bestial, with his plot to kill Prospero, rape Miranda and people the isle with more

Calibans. But Caliban has a genuine grievance, and once again Shakespeare gives us not a mere monster but an abused slave. Prospero has made himself king of his island but, as Caliban rightly points out,

> This island's mine, by Sycorax my mother,
> Which thou tak'st from me. When thou cam'st first,
> Thou strok'st me, and made much of me; wouldst give me
> Water with berries in't; and teach me how
> To name the bigger light, and how the less,
> That burn by day and night: and then I lov'd thee . . .'[22]

Nor is Caliban without redemption. He is not a brute beast, or a monster, for he can be moved by music:

> Be not afear'd; the isle is full of noises,
> Sounds and sweet airs, that give delight and hurt not.
> Sometimes a thousand twangling instruments
> Will hum about mine ears, and sometime voices
> That, if I then had waked after long sleep,
> Will make me sleep again: and then, in dreaming,
> The clouds methought would open and show riches
> Ready to drop upon me that, when I waked,
> I cried to dream again.[23]

One of the most powerful moments in *The Tempest* comes with Prospero's announcement that he will abandon magic. Just as it is tempting to read elegy and closure into many of his late plays, it is almost impossible to hear this speech without taking it to be Shakespeare's swansong:

> I have bedimm'd
> The noontide sun, call'd forth the mutinous winds,

And 'twixt the green sea and the azured vault
Set roaring war: to the dread rattling thunder
Have I given fire and rifted Jove's stout oak
With his own bolt; the strong-based promontory
Have I made shake and by the spurs pluck'd up
The pine and cedar: graves at my command
Have waked their sleepers, oped, and let 'em forth
By my so potent art.[24]

Surely these are references to the great power of the playwright's art and the director's art: opening graves, and
bringing the dead to life again with the roaring war of the
history plays? Commanding magnificent stage effects, dread
rattling thunder, dimming the noontide sun at the Globe
with the smoke of battle. And now, he is willing to abandon
it all:

But this rough magic
I here abjure, and, when I have required
Some heavenly music, which even now I do,
To work mine end upon their senses that
This airy charm is for, I'll break my staff,
Bury it certain fathoms in the earth,
And deeper than did ever plummet sound
I'll drown my book.[25]

That final line, 'I'll drown my book', with its echoes of
Faustus's desperate promises to burn his books if
Mephistopheles will only spare his life, what else can that be
but Shakespeare bidding his own farewell to arms?

Attractive as it is, such an interpretation proves misguided.
The Tempest may have been Shakespeare's last complete play,
but he would continue to write, collaborating on *The Two*

Noble Kinsmen, *Cardenio*, *Henry VIII* and *Sir Thomas More*.
His writing may have developed a melancholy note, but
Shakespeare clearly had no intention of stepping away from
the theatre for good. It was still his livelihood, and his life.
The book that Prospero offers to drown is not the complete
works of Shakespeare, for these were never gathered
together in his lifetime. Prospero's book is a necronomicon,
a book of magic spells. The model for Prospero, a name
inspired by a London groom, was Dr John Dee, philosopher
and divine, a former tutor to Queen Elizabeth who ended
his days in obscurity, living with his daughter in Mortlake.
The erudite Dee was also a gifted mathematician and
believed by many to be a necromancer of some distinction.
Dr Dee's somewhat mundane plight, reduced to poverty
despite his great gifts, was reflected in a play about an exiled
duke living, with his daughter, on a desert island. Such are
the sources of creativity, though it took Shakespeare to gild
these disparate elements with heavenly alchemy. The 'potent
art' which opens graves and wakes their sleepers may be
that of a great playwright, looking back upon his career.
But in Prospero's case, the reference is to Ovid, and the
enchantress Medea casting her spell.[26]

The Tempest was performed as part of the royal wedding
celebrations for King James's daughter, Princess Elizabeth, and
her new husband, Frederick V, Count Palatine of the Rhine,
when they married on 14 February 1613. The play was a
particularly appropriate choice for a wedding entertainment,
as it includes the 'betrothal masque', in which Miranda and
Ferdinand are exhorted to obey fidelity and chastity. During
the festivities, which lasted for almost two months, the King's
Men appeared fourteen times, making a total of £153.[27]

In the summer of 1613, Shakespeare collaborated with
John Fletcher on a play called *King Henry VIII*. What could

be a more obvious choice for the chronicler of the nation's kings than to round off his sequences of history plays with a drama about Henry VIII? Queen Elizabeth was safely dead, so any remarks about her 'bastardy' as the offspring of an unrecognised marriage between Anne Boleyn and King Henry would go unchallenged. In any case, the play would skate lightly across the surface of contentious events such as Henry's divorce from Catherine of Aragon and the break from Rome, concluding with the birth of Elizabeth, the future Queen. The old King was to be portrayed as the Henry the audience's grandparents had spoken of, a Henry almost within living memory, affable, pleasure-loving but capable of tempestuous, destructive rages.[28] *Henry VIII* would be a magnificent summer production at the Globe, ideal for the open-air setting with its pageantry, fanfares, drums and guns.

A packed house greeted an early production of *King Henry VIII*, or *All Is True*, on St Peter's Day, 29 June 1613. The crowd was in high good humour as the action reached the final scene of Act 1, located in York Place, home of Cardinal Wolsey. In an elaborate set piece, Anne Boleyn was due to enter with 'diverse other Ladies and Gentlemen' to attend a feast where she would meet Henry VIII for the first time and he would fall madly in love with her.[29] It was an elaborate production, designed to outdo every other playhouse in London with magnificent processions and costumes. The diplomat and author Sir Henry Wotton, who was in the audience on that fateful afternoon, described the play with its 'many extraordinary circumstances of pomp and majesty even to the matting of the stage; the knights of the order with their Georges and Garter, the guards with their embroidered coats, and the like: sufficient in truth within awhile to make greatness very familiar, if not ridiculous.'[30]

Offstage, King Henry and his friends lurked, disguised as shepherds, preparing to ambush the cardinal and his guests with a surprise masque. Trumpet and drum were sounded and a cannon fired to announce the unexpected arrival of the king. But at this point the linstock used for lighting the cannon set fire to the thatched roof. As the flames ran around the thatched roof like a tailor throwing his tape measure around a man's waist, the audience gasped in admiration at this audacious special effect. But then, as the smoke darkened and became heavier and the thatch began to crackle and roar, the crowd panicked. Pandemonium ensued as the audience stampeded for the two narrow exits, tumbling over the benches in the galleries, squashing up against each other in the yard.

Out runne the Knightes, out runne the Lordes
And there was great ado
Some lost their hats, and some their swords,
Then out run Burbage too.[31]

The blaze was uncontrollable and within an hour the Globe had been burned to the ground. The fire destroyed 'both beame and snag, And did not spare the silken flag'.[32]

Remarkably, given the fact that around 3,000 people had been in the theatre, everyone escaped safely. Nothing perished, apart from wood and straw and abandoned clothes, good buff jerkins and a few forsaken cloaks. There were no casualties, although one man had his breeches set on fire, 'that would perhaps have broiled him, if he had not by the benefit of a provident wit, put it out with a bottle of ale'.[33]

Once it had been established that nobody had died, the forlorn players gathered to inspect the damage. Here were the 'Foole and Henry Condye, Then with swollen eyes like drunken Fleminges Distressed stood old stuttering Heminges'.[34]

The entire company was distraught, from Shakespeare and the Burbages to the remainder of the King's Men, the gatherers, the Book Holder, the Tire Man and the Stage Keeper. Their dream was in ruins. This little O, this casque, this globe that they had carried across the Thames, lovingly rebuilt, the greatest, most successful playhouse in London, reduced to ashes. How prophetic Prospero's speech seemed now:

> Our revels now are ended. These our actors,
> As I foretold you, were all spirits and
> Are melted into air, into thin air:
> And like the baseless fabric of this vision,
> The cloud-capp'd towers, the gorgeous palaces,
> The solemn temples, the great globe itself,
> Yea, all which it inherit, shall dissolve,
> And like this insubstantial pageant faded,
> Leave not a rack behind.[35]

Our revels now are ended. It was a catastrophe, for Shakespeare and the King's Men. Not only had they lost their theatre, but countless props, costumes and books had been destroyed in the conflagration. Who now can tell what plays were lost to posterity in that fire, plays which might have been gathered into the First Folio had they survived. It was left to Ben Jonson to reproach God for this act of wanton destruction.

> The Globe, the Glory of the Bank,
> Which, though it were the fort of the whole parish,
> Flanked with a ditch, and forced out of a marsh
> I saw with two poor chambers taken in
> And razed, ere thought could urge this might have been.
> See the World's ruins! Nothing but the piles
> Left, and wit since to cover it with tiles.[36]

This catastrophe was an appalling loss for the Burbages and the entire company. But they were accustomed to adversity, and, after shifting their performances to the winter house of Blackfriars, the Burbages set about rebuilding the Globe, and rebuilding it even better than before. King James and his court contributed liberally to the costs, while Matthew Brend, son of Nicholas Brend from whom they had leased the land, extended the original lease for them. By February 1614, the second Globe was in working order.[37]

It is thought by many scholars that the experience of seeing the Globe go up in flames finished Shakespeare as a writer and that with his dream in tatters he decided it was time to go home. Shakespeare's footprint grows lighter at this point, and the written stage directions increase, indicating that he was not around at rehearsals to give verbal directions. Shakespeare certainly spent increasingly longer periods in Stratford, at his fine new home, New Place, but he maintained an apartment at Blackfriars, rather in the manner of a country gentleman keeping a flat in town. In Stratford, Shakespeare spent his time with the men he had known since childhood, the local tradesmen who had once sat beside him at school, the lawyers and the landowners who now greeted him as a fellow gent. His daughter, Susanna, was even married to the local doctor, John Hall. The vagabond actor was a thing of the past, the family's reputation redeemed. With his London fortune and Court connections, Shakespeare was accepted without comment as a local man made good, complete with a coat of arms. The parallel today would be of a veteran musician retiring to a country estate. The wheel had come full circle.

But Shakespeare had not forgotten his old friends. In the spring of 1616, around the time of his birthday on 23 April, Shakespeare hosted a supper with the poet Michael Drayton

and Ben Jonson, who had come up from London especially
for the occasion. Shakespeare had already made his will, and
was considered to be in poor health, but by all accounts this
was a 'merrie meeting' and the local vicar recalled that the
men 'drank too hard'.[38] As with most theatrical reunions,
much drinking was probably involved, uncharacteristically
heavy drinking for Shakespeare, but one suspects he had
already heard the chimes at midnight. Perhaps the evening
ended with a late-night visit to the nearest tavern, despite
warnings that the air was cold and Shakespeare should be
taking more care of himself at his time of life, and where
was his cloak and had he not already had enough to drink?
Clearly, these warnings went unheeded, for on 23 April,
Shakespeare died. Given the elegiac nature of his later work,
it is tempting to hope this was an easy passing. Perhaps he
left this world like Falstaff:

A' made a finer end and went away an it had been any
christom child; a' parted even just between twelve
and one, even at the turning o' the tide: for after
I saw him fumble with the sheets and play with
flowers and smile upon his fingers' ends, I knew
there was but one way; for his nose was as sharp as
a pen, and a' babbled of green fields.[39]

Explanations for the cause of death are as plentiful as
Shakespeare scholars, ranging from influenza to tertiary
syphilis and from Parkinson's to typhus, seeping up from
the polluted waters of the river into New Place.[40] Whatever
the causes, Shakespeare slipped away unnoticed by the great
and the good. While Francis Beaumont, who died in the
same year, was buried at Westminster Abbey, Shakespeare
was interred at Holy Trinity, his parish church, on 25 April.

The burial is referred to in the parish records as that of 'William Shakespeare, gent'. Shakespeare's tomb was inscribed with the following epitaph, allegedly composed by Shakespeare himself, although the language seems uncharacteristically crude:

> GOOD FREND FOR JESUS SAKE FORBEARE
> TO DIGG THE DUST ENCLOASED HEARE.
> BLESTE BE YE MAN THAT SPARES THES STONES
> AND CURST BE HE THAT MOVES MY BONES.[41]

Shakespeare's true monument would, of course, be his work. In 1623, two members of the King's Men, John Hemmings and Henry Condell, published the First Folio, containing all the plays of which Shakespeare was considered to be the author, apart from *Pericles*. The book was dedicated to the Earl of Pembroke, the Earl of Montgomery and 'the Great Variety of Readers'.[42] In the introduction, the old actors took the opportunity to salute their late friend's extraordinary talent: 'His mind and hand went together; And what he thought he uttered with that easinesse, that we have scarce received from him a blot on his papers.'[43]

The First Folio also contained a eulogy from Shakespeare's old rival, Ben Jonson, who had been present on that fateful night in Stratford. For all their old antagonism, Jonson recognised Shakespeare's worth and could see his talent for what it was:

> Soul of the age!
> The applause! delight! the wonder of our stage!
> My SHAKESPEARE rise! I will not lodge thee by
> Chaucer, or Spenser, or bid Beaumont lie
> A little further, to make thee a room:

Thou art a monument without a tomb,
And art alive still while thy book doth live
And we have wits to read, and praise to give . . .
And tell how far thou didst our Lyly outshine,
Or sporting Kyd, or Marlowe's mighty line . . .
He was not of an age, but for all time![44]

Less than three years later, on 13 March 1619, Richard Burbage died, his nervous system apparently succumbing to an attack of paralysis. He left behind him a young son, born in 1616, and christened William in honour of Shakespeare. The city and the stage were both shrouded in gloom, as Queen Anne had died less than a fortnight earlier. Burbage, his death somewhat overshadowed by that of the Queen, was buried at St Leonard's in Shoreditch and the entire theatrical world was plunged into mourning. Queen Anne's funeral was postponed until 29 April to allow sufficient preparations for her state funeral, 'to the great hindrance of our players, which are forbidden to play for so long as her body is above ground'.[45]

'Hung be the Heaven's with black, yield day to night,' wrote Thomas Middleton in *On the death of that great Master in his art and quality, painting and playing, R Burbage*:

Burbage the player has vouchsafed to die;
Therefore in London is not one eye dry:
The deaths of men who act our Queens and Kings
Are now more mourned than are the real things.
The Queen is dead! To him no what are Queens?
Queans of the Theatre are much more worth.
Dick Burbage was their mortal God on earth.
When he expires, lo! All lament the man.
But where's the grief should follow good Queen Anne?[46]

Another epitaph, *Upon Mr Richard Burbage, the player,* reflects
that:

> This Life's a play, scened out by Nature's Arte,
> Where every man hath his allotted parte.
> This man hath now (as many men can tell)
> Ended his part, and he hath acted well
> The Play now ended, think his grave to be
> The retiring house of his sad Tragedie
> Where to give his fame this, he is not afraid,
> Here lies the best Tragedian ever played.[47]

The Earl of Pembroke confessed himself so devastated by
the loss that, once the theatres were open again, he could not
bear to attend a play with the French Ambassador's party.
'My Lord of Lennox made a great supper to the French
Ambassador this night here and even now all the company
are at the play, which I being tender-hearted, could not
endure to see so soon after the loss of my old acquaintance
Burbage.'[48]

> He's gone, and with him what a world is dead.
> (Which he revived to be renewed so.)
> No more young Hamlet, old Hieronimo,
> King Lear, the grieved Moore, and more beside
> That lived in him, have now for ever dy'de.[49]

Camden's epitaph is the most economical and pithy of all:

> EXIT Burbage.[50]

Richard Burbage had left his £300 fortune and his lands in
Kent to his wife and executor, Winifred. In time, these

passed to their only surviving son, William. The King's Men soldiered on, maintaining good relations. Despite all adversity there was still the sense that the King's Men were the few, the happy few, the band of brothers. But one by one the old players passed, remembering one another in their wills. Nicholas Tooley, Richard Burbage's old apprentice, died in Cuthbert's house in 1623, leaving the bulk of his estate to the Burbages. When John Hemmings made his will, it was to Cuthbert, 'his loving friend'.[51] Hemmings died on 12 October 1630. Condell had already gone, in 1627. Ben Jonson, Shakespeare's great friend and rival, died in 1637, after a series of strokes. Having been unofficial 'Poet Laureate' from 1616, Jonson was buried upright in Westminster Abbey, in a tiny grave just eighteen inches across. Controversial in death as in life, even Jonson's tomb caused speculation. Did the inscription read 'O Rare Ben Jonson', an admiring epitaph, or did it mean *Orare,* meaning 'arise', a cryptic reference to his one-time Catholic faith? This may be wishful thinking: there is a clear space between the 'O' and the 'R'.[52]

Jonson's burial in the Abbey was remarkable for a mere actor and poet; all the more remarkable for the fact that he had fallen out with the Court following the death of James I in 1625. Unlike King James, his successor, Charles I, was no great friend of the theatre, and it was under his rule that the first steps were taken to close the playhouses. On 8 October 1633, the Privy Council attempted to get the Blackfriars Theatre closed down on the grounds of nuisance, and 'the great inconvenience and annoyance occasioned by the resort and confluence of Coaches to the Playhouse in Blackfriars, whereby the Streets being narrow thereabouts are at those times become impassable to the great prejudice of his Majesties subjects passing that way upon their several occasions and in particular to divers noblemen and Councillors of State whose houses are in that way, whereby they are many times hindered from their necessary attendance upon his Majesty's person and service.'[53] In other words, the privy councillors considered that the playgoers constituted a public nuisance. The council proposed that the Blackfriars Theatre should be torn down, and the owners given appropriate compensation.

During the subsequent valuation it was discovered that Cuthbert Burbage and Richard's son William were the owners. The property was valued at £700, and the Burbages also owned four adjacent tenements. These were estimated at a business rate, making the value even higher. Taking into account consideration of loss to the shareholders, the property all in all was worth around £2,400, something in the region of £24 million today.[54]

The Privy Council then put further pressure upon the Blackfriars Theatre by banning coaches from waiting outside the playhouse, stating that 'it is much more fit and reasonable that those which goe thither should goe thither by water or else on foote'.[55] Any coachman failing to park elsewhere, at St Paul's Churchyard or Fleet Street, would be arrested and thrown into Newgate or Ludgate gaols. One may imagine the outcry from wealthy female playgoers, uncertain about the whereabouts of their carriages in wet weather, at a time when umbrellas had yet to be invented. It was obvious that the Lord Mayor and the Corporation wanted to suppress the Blackfriars Theatre altogether, but this was yet to come.

There was also trouble over at the Globe. Cuthbert Burbage began to run into legal difficulties with his landlord Sir Matthew Brend, son of Nicholas Brend, from whom he had originally leased the site at Maiden Lane. Brend had respected the 31-year lease but now he was uncertain about granting an extension. It seems as if Sir Matthew did not have much faith in the future of theatres. In this case, history would prove him right.

The final blow came from closer to home. Eliard Swanston, the leading actor in Burbage's company, persuaded two of his fellow actors, Robert Benfield and Thomas Pollard, both former boy-actors at the early Blackfriars, to complain with him to the Lord Chamberlain that the bulk of the shares in the Blackfriars Theatre were in the Burbages' hands, and not in those of the actors. As there were no shares available, Swanston wanted the Lord Chamberlain to force the Burbages to part with some of their shares, and to sell them to him and Pollard. The Lord Chamberlain, Sir Philip Herbert, granted Swanston and Pollard's petition, probably because they were considered to be the best actors of their day, before old Cuthbert Burbage had the opportunity to speak.[56] While it seems obvious that the actors had a right to obtain shares in their company, the verdict shocked Cuthbert. In a response, Cuthbert described how he and his brother Richard had inherited his father's theatre, cared for it, tended it, sacrificed themselves for it. Cuthbert was no actor, but his speech on receiving the news has great dramatic power.

'We, your humble suppliants Cuthbert Burbage and Winifred his brother's wife, and William, his son, we ought not in all charity to be disabled in our livelihood,' he began. 'The father of us Cuthbert and Richard was the first builder of playhouses, and was himself in his younger years a Player. The Theatre he built with as many hundred pounds taken up at interest, the Players that lived in these first times had only the profits arising from the doors but now they receive also the coming in at the doors to themselves, and half the galleries from the Housekeepers.'[57]

Swanston did indeed have a healthy income, of around £30 a year, which Cuthbert noted 'will keep him from starving',[58] but Cuthbert objected to sharing any more of the profits with him. At the accusation that Cuthbert was taking profit out of his players' mouths, he replied that he and his late brother were the ones who had suffered the most, keeping the Globe and the Blackfriars open in the face of tremendous adversity.

'He [James Burbage] had a greate suite in lawe, and by his death, the like troubles fell on us his sonnes. We then bethought us of altering from thence, and at like expense built the Globe, with summes of money taken up at interest which lay heavy on us many years, and to ourselves we joined those deserving men Shakespeare, Hemmings, Condall, Phillips and other partners in ye profits of that they call the house.'[59]

Speaking in damning terms of 'these new men that were never bred from children in the King's service', and their attempts to take money off the Burbages 'with oaths and menaces'[60] Cuthbert accused Swanston of putting the Burbage family under excessive strain, when it was all the estate could do to keep going and to ensure that Richard Burbage's widow did not starve. It was more than the family could bear, he concluded. 'Mr Hemming and Mr Condall had their shares of the Blackfriars of us for nothing.'[61] All Cuthbert wanted now, he explained, was the guarantee of a comfortable old age following the labours of his youth. Instead of which, by reason of the Lord Chamberlain's verdict, 'It is we that suffer continually.'[62]

These were the last recorded words of Cuthbert Burbage; indeed, of the Burbage family. Despite Cuthbert Burbage's impassioned plea, the Lord Chamberlain upheld his decision and the scornful Eliard Swanston triumphed over the others.

Cuthbert Burbage died not long afterwards. Did the Lord Chamberlain's decision and the inevitable bad feeling stirred up by the case help to hasten his end? Or was Cuthbert carried away in 1636 by a swift visitation of the plague? The register does not give the cause. It merely says: 'Cuthbert Burbage was buried ye 17th day of September 1636.' Within a fortnight, his wife Elizabeth followed him to the grave. The couple were buried in the same tomb in the chancel of St Leonard's, Shoreditch. According to the historian John Strype, the inscription read, 'Cuthbert Burbage and Elizabeth his wife. They departed in September 1636. *Venimus, Vidimus, Redivivimus, Resurgemus* (We Came, We Saw, We Conquered, We Will Return).'[63]

Four centuries later, James, Richard and Cuthbert Burbage are still remembered as the founders of the Theatre, the Globe and the Blackfriars, as the collaborators of Shakespeare, and for the exceptional part they played in the history of the English stage.

It was just as well that Cuthbert Burbage did not live to see what happened next. Following the death of King James I in 1625, the warm climate of tolerance which had enabled the stage to flourish disappeared, to be replaced by an increasingly puritanical regime. Theatres and playhouses were regarded as little more than brothels, and drama, the greatest English art form, no more than idolatry. In 1642, Parliament suppressed all stage plays in the theatres. When the English Civil War broke out between Parliament and Royalists, the King's Men, bereft of their livelihood, went to fight for their old master King Charles I. One, William Robbins, was killed when Basing House, in Hampshire, fell to the Parliamentarians led by Major General Thomas Harrison. Another, Charles Hart, was made a Lieutenant of Horse, while a William Allen became a Major at Oxford. Eliard Swanston, who professed himself a Presbyterian, was one of the few players

to side with the Puritans. After the war, he took up the trade
of a jeweller and lived in Aldermanbury, near the Guildhall.
The other actors risked or lost their lives for the King.[64]

In 1648, Parliament ordered the destruction of all theatres
and playhouses. The actors were arrested and whipped, and
anyone caught attending a play was fined five shillings. The
second Globe had already been demolished, in 1644, and the
land sold for building. The Cockpit in Drury Lane was
dismantled in 1649, and the second Fortune Theatre also
went in 1649. The Blackfriars was demolished in 1655. At
the Hope, which was not actually pulled down until 1656,
seven bears were taken out and shot.[65] After nearly a century,
the authorities had finally triumphed in their war against
the theatres, and London was, in the theatrical parlance,
'dark'. It was as though Malvolio, that humiliated Puritan
from *Twelfth Night,* had returned triumphant to settle the
score, shaking his fist and shouting: 'I'll be reveng'd upon
the whole pack of you!'[66]

10

THE GLOBE REBORN

And thus the whirligig of time brings in his revenges.
Twelfth Night, Act 5 Scene 1

In the three centuries following the death of Shakespeare, the closure of the theatres under the Commonwealth and their rebirth in 1660 following the Restoration, Shakespeare became preserved in the nation's consciousness as our national poet. The cult of bardolatry sprang up, fanned by luminaries such as Samuel Johnson and Samuel Taylor Coleridge, and eagerly seized upon by those who wilfully misread Shakespeare as the embodiment of cultural conservatism and the notion of Merrie England. By the end of the nineteenth century, Stratford-upon-Avon had become a shrine to all things Shakespearean, exploited by shrewd locals eager to cash in on any association with Shakespeare and his life. This state of affairs horrified one American visitor, a 'Mr James C. Fairfield', who conducted a pilgrimage to the town with the British author Christian Tearle in 1910. Fairfield railed at the commercialism which had already engulfed the birthplace of the 'Swan of Avon', complete with scruffy urchins demanding half-a-crown to tell them all about Shakespeare and a charge of sixpence to park a bicycle near Shakespeare's tomb at Holy Trinity Church, Stratford upon Avon.[1]

Despairing of Stratford, the pair resolved to discover Shakespeare's London instead. But this journey also proved to be a disappointment, although in a different way. None of the buildings associated with Shakespeare had actually survived. The Mermaid Tavern on Cheapside had been destroyed in the Great Fire; the Boar's Head in Eastcheap perished too. As for the playhouses, the Blackfriars, the Rose, the Theatre and the Globe, these were long gone by 1910.[2]

In *Rambles with an American,* an early example of psycho-geography, Fairfield and Tearle explored Bankside in search of Shakespeare's old haunts. This proved to be a melancholy excursion through a shabby waterfront, lined with a forest of masts and cranes. After a brief visit to Clink Street, where Shakespeare once lived, they reached the site of the Globe. But no trace of Shakespeare's original theatre remained. Instead, the pair found Barclay Perkins, the biggest brewery in the world, an immense building which had obliterated many landmarks, including the burial ground of Dead Man's Place.

'This street was certainly here in Shakespeare's time,' said Tearle, 'it was called Maiden Lane then, and the Globe Theatre stood a little to the south-east of where we are standing.' But it was an uninspiring spot. 'There was nothing at all interesting in the buildings that lay on our left hand.'[3]

Mr Fairfield, the 'Chicago Pilgrim' who had travelled to England in search of Shakespeare, was understandably dismayed. He walked up and down Rose Alley, pursing his mouth. 'It was easy to see, that he found it difficult to associate that forlorn prospect with the site of the old playhouse. I was not disposed to be hard on him; for all the buildings

within sight were of a most commonplace character, and
there was a cleared space with a hoarding round it, which
gave the alley an almost desolate appearance.'[4]

More disappointments lay ahead. The Falcon Inn on
Holland Street, where Shakespeare had spent many a night,
had been demolished and replaced with the Epps's cocoa
factory. Nevertheless, Mr Fairfield attempted to invest the
spot with some significance.

> It's pleasant to fancy Shakespeare, slipping away from the
> Falcon crew some summer evening, and strolling along
> that lane as it was in his time, with the wild roses in
> blossom – canker-blooms, he called them:
>> 'The canker-blooms have full as deep a dye
>> As the perfumed tincture of the roses,
>> Hang on such thorns, and play as wantonly
>> When summer's breath their masked buds discloses.'[5]

Tearle, a barrister by training, took a more pragmatic view.
'Surely we ought not to pass the Falcon without crushing
a cup?'

The only cup available turned out to be coffee, not ale, but
over it Tearle attempted to recapture, from unpromising material, Bankside as it must have been. 'As we sipped our coffee
and I thought over what he had told me, I tried to call up the
Surrey side of our recent pilgrimage; but instead of the
Blackfriars Road and the squalid streets that turn out of it,
there wavered before my mind's eye a vague picture of flat,
green water meadows, from which one saw across the river
the London of Elizabeth, all shadowy in a June twilight.'[6]

Later that evening, as they bowled across Blackfriars
Bridge in a hansom cab, Fairfield summed up the true nature
of literary pilgrimage.

'I have often thought,' he remarked meditatively, 'what a privilege it is to be able to visit interesting places like the Bankside whenever you like, and particularly at night-time. The thought has often occurred to me in this city of yours, after dark. It really seems sometimes as if the places had been cleared of people and lighted up for one's especial benefit. I can assure you, sir, I have wandered about Upper Thames Street and the lanes behind Cheapside and between Cornhill and Lombard Street at night-time when the City has been as silent as the grave, and when the thought of its immense antiquity as a dwelling place has quite overcome me. More than once, I have seemed to lose the sense of my own identity, and to be drifting to and fro as a shadow among shadows. Do you know that feeling?' he inquired a little shyly, as if conscious that his remarks were somewhat out of the common. I knew the feeling quite well and I told him so.[7]

And so, it seems, did many other people, anxious to commune with the spirit of Shakespeare by seeking out the places associated with him. By 1909, two plaques had appeared in London, one on the side of the brewery, funded by the Shakespeare Reading Society of London, the other close to Southwark Bridge, showing the Globe in a pastoral setting. This became the site of annual Shakespeare birthday celebrations. In 1912, an alabaster statue of Shakespeare was erected in Southwark Cathedral, while 1923 saw a memorial window to Shakespeare in Curtain Old Church on the site of the original Theatre. In the same year a plaque appeared on the site of Shakespeare's old house in Silver Street. By the 1920s, the Bankside literary walk pioneered by Tearle and Fairchild had become an institution with a standard itinerary, but there was no attempt to recreate the three great theatres of

Shakespeare's era until a former actor, William Poel (1852–1934), drew up plans for a replica of the Globe to be built in Battersea Park.[8] Regarded as something of an eccentric genius, Poel founded the Elizabethan Stage Society and became an authority on Elizabethan staging. Sadly, he never lived to see his Globe built, but sixty years later his plans would be influential in the designs for the new Globe in Southwark, thanks to the pioneering work of another actor and Shakespeare enthusiast, Sam Wanamaker.

In 1949 Wanamaker arrived in London to appear in *Give Us This Day,* a film set in Brooklyn but shot entirely in London, as its director, Edward Dmytryk, and Wanamaker himself had both been blacklisted in the United States for their alleged Communist affiliations. A second 'Chicago pilgrim', like his predecessor Mr Fairfield, Wanamaker was already a confirmed Shakespeare enthusiast, having been inspired by a scale model of the Globe at the Century of Progress Exhibition in Chicago. As a young actor he played his first Shakespeare in a half-size replica of the Globe, donated by the British government, at the 1937 Great Lakes Festival in Cleveland, Ohio. He later recalled that 'it must have been about then that I began to think how to "bring forth so great an object".'[9]

Inspired by Laurence Olivier's film of *Henry V,* the opening scenes of which depict a production of the play at the Globe, Wanamaker visited Bankside to look for the site of the original theatre. While he did not expect to find a full-scale replica of the Globe, he expected some recognition of what the Globe had represented in the history of theatre. But he arrived in Bankside to be confronted with the same enormous brewery that his fellow countryman had found two generations earlier. The only evidence that Shakespeare had once been associated with the spot was the soot-blackened metal plaque on the wall. 'Underneath the plaque was a large pile of garbage, which seemed to sum up the situation,' he recalled. 'I simply could not imagine why the British had done nothing else to mark the site.'[10]

Fired up by the discovery of the plaque and frustrated by British indifference, Wanamaker began to dream of a fitting monument to the genius of Shakespeare and the Globe, an Elizabethan theatre which would revitalise this dismal, semi-derelict area of London. And not just a theatre, but a museum too, with an exhibition space, shops and even hotels. It was a massive project, ambitious in its scope and scale. As Wanamaker first stood staring at that blackened plaque, he did not know that it would take almost fifty years and an extraordinary combination of research, archaeology, crafts-manship and fund-raising to achieve his dream of recreating Shakespeare's own theatre. 'I expected it all to happen very quickly,' Wanamaker admitted in 1969, 'spring up in two or three years, or I probably wouldn't have started it!'[11]

To make his dream a reality, Wanamaker needed a strong team of dedicated experts. While the Burbages had built the Theatre and the Globe with nothing more than their bare hands, actors turned labourers and master carpenter Peter Street, Wanamaker needed historians, scholars and an archi-tect for his project. He recruited academic allies in the form of Professor Glynne Wickham of Bristol University and Professor Terence Spencer, Director of the Shakespeare Institute at Stratford-upon-Avon. For his architect, Wanamaker found a fellow enthusiast in the form of Theo Crosby, who had made it his mission to bring humanity back to city architecture with a balance between old and new, inspired by the Italian cities he had visited during World War Two. Straight away, Crosby realised that the role of the new Globe in the city would be 'as a magnet for visitors to taste the myth of Shakespeare'.[12] Together, Wanamaker and Crosby approached the local council in Southwark with their proposals.

Wanamaker rented a temporary site at Greenmoor Wharf, Emerson Street, and founded the Globe Playhouse Trust. With Charlotte Wanamaker, his wife, he also formed Bankside Globe Developments, to acquire joint ownership of 1 Bear Gardens and numbers 1 and 2 Rose Alley, near the site of the original Hope Theatre.[13]

The World Shakespeare Congress in Vancouver in 1971 unanimously endorsed the merits of the reconstruction of the first Globe. Wanamaker registered the name The World Centre for Shakespeare Studies to carry out the educational aims of the project.[14]

In 1972, Wanamaker launched a programme of events in Southwark, which the press nicknamed 'Stratford-on-Thames'. It included a gala concert in Southwark Cathedral, a six-week summer school, a season of Shakespeare films, and a joint exhibition with Southwark Council entitled 'In the Clink'. The Museum of Shakespearean Stage opened in Bear Gardens, curated by Charlotte Wanamaker and friends. John Player & Sons sponsored a theatre season in a tent at Emerson Street, including Keith Michell in a modern-dress production of *Hamlet*, and on the opening night a good-luck telegram arrived reading: 'Cry God for Bankside, Southwark and Sam Wanamaker!'[15]

Speaking on BBC Radio 4's *The Reunion: The Globe Theatre* in 2012, Diana Devlin said that she received the following friendly warning when she joined the project as organising secretary of the summer school: 'Working for Sam, you will have to prepare large quantities of ready-mixed concrete to support castles in the air.' This proved prophetic for, although there was a tremendous amount of goodwill involved in the project, progress was constantly marred by financial setbacks and even problems with the weather. In 1973 a second John Player season included Julian Glover and Vanessa Redgrave in *Antony and Cleopatra*. But the season was brought abruptly to an end when the tent theatre became waterlogged.[16] Progress continued to be erratic. The Globe Playhouse Trust became insolvent, but the World Centre for Shakespeare Studies survived. In 1974 the North American Chapter of the Shakespeare Globe Centre was established in Chicago. Other international Shakespeare Globe Centres followed. In 1975 the third and last summer season was staged on the temporary site. At this point, funding, always erratic, became a real problem as the Globe project was competing for financial resources with two other major theatres, the National Theatre, which opened in 1976, and the Barbican, which opened in 1982.[17]

In 1979 the Cockpit, a replica of a seventeenth-century theatre, was acquired from the Inner London Education Authority and installed in Bear Gardens. A new company, the Bear Gardens Museum and Arts Centre, was formed to promote educational and arts activities.[18]

In 1981, a preliminary agreement was signed between Southwark Council, Derno Estates and the World Centre for Shakespeare Studies for the development of Greenmoor Wharf on a 125-year lease at a peppercorn rent. As well as a reconstruction of the Globe, the scheme included offices, residential units, a restaurant, pub and shops. Professor Andrew Gurr, the world-renowned Shakespeare scholar, headed an academic committee and theatre historian John Orrell advised the architect Theo Crosby on the authentic reconstruction. The plans also now included the building of an indoor playhouse, a reconstruction of the old Blackfriars Theatre. This would be named the Inigo Jones Theatre, in memory of the Jacobean architect who had contributed so many elaborate stage designs to the masques and plays performed at the original Blackfriars.[19]

In 1982, local authority elections brought in a new council that was unsympathetic to the Derno/Globe agreement. Councillor Tony Ritchie, then deputy leader of Southwark Council, was reported to declare that 'Shakespeare is tosh!'[20] and demanded to know what Shakespeare had ever done for Southwark. Southwark Council reneged on the 1981 preliminary agreement and the Shakespeare Globe Trust sued both the council and Derno Estates.[21]

There was also an element of opposition to the project in academic and critical circles, with the Globe proposals being dismissed as little more than Disney-on-Thames. One detractor even channelled Elizabethan Puritan Philip Stubbes in dismissing the Globe as 'the painted brothel on Bankside!'[22] Polly Hope, artist wife of Theo Crosby, felt that there was distrust of Wanamaker on account of his American background. 'Reconstruction is anathema to the British,' she said on *The Reunion* in 2012, 'it is distasteful to them.' This anathema extended to dismissing the proposal as a tourist trap which would attract Americans. 'If I had a pound for every time at a party somebody said the Americans will love it, it would have been opened in 1986,' added Patrick Spottiswoode, Director for Globe Education.

American money was clearly what the Globe needed if it was to be built at all. Wanamaker's response to the critical disdain and shortage of funds was to initiate a major fund-raising campaign in the USA, with Prince Philip, Duke of Edinburgh, as patron of the project. He set off on a ten-city tour of the United States under the banner 'Brush Up Your Shakespeare', featuring Johnny Dankworth, Cleo Laine, Douglas Fairbanks Jr, Millicent Martin, Michael York and

Nicol Williamson.[23] Wanamaker felt so positive about the future of the Globe that, with the planning agreement yet to be ratified, he organised a dedication ceremony outside the site. This provoked a swift response from anti-Globe campaigners, who protested against the scheme on the grounds that what Southwark needed was housing not tourism, and howled down Wanamaker's argument that the Globe would actually create jobs.[24] There was another blow when the council planning committee opposed the scheme on the grounds that road-sweepers' carts, housed on the proposed site, would be difficult to relocate. One road-sweeper, Charlie Cox, told the press: 'If Shakespeare moves in 'ere, I'm moving out!'[25]

But all was not lost. In 1985 a local campaign for the Globe began to grow, involving staunch support from Councillor Ann Ward and the founding of the Friends of the Southwark Globe. 'I am Southwark-born, I heard you and I want the theatre!' declared Emily Braidwood, local resident.[26] Later that year, the case came to court and a settlement was agreed giving the Trust a 125-year lease of the site. On 25 June 1986, the Globe team signed the lease and building work proper finally began, with a photo opportunity showing Dame Judi Dench at the controls of the digger.

In 1987, an International Shakespeare Week included the official ground breaking ceremony. Prince Philip drove in the first oak foundation post, taken from Windsor Great Park. Other posts were donated by Austria, Canada, China, Czechoslovakia, Denmark, East Germany, Finland, Hungary, Israel, Italy, Japan, Korea, Luxembourg, Malaysia, Mexico, Netherlands, Nigeria, Norway, Portugal, Singapore, Spain, Sweden, USA, USSR and West Germany.[27]

A year later, in 1988, the remains of the Rose Theatre on Bankside were discovered. The archaeology of the Rose had a profound influence on the reconstruction of the Globe. Here was a genuine Elizabethan theatre in jeopardy, and a cause which would naturally attract a tremendous amount of philanthropy. The ever-canny Wanamaker soon appreciated that this was not a threat but an opportunity, and swung into action with a new campaign that urged his backers to 'Save the Rose! Build the Globe!' But it was the Rose which attracted more funding; 500 years on, it seemed that the Rose and the Globe were rivals once again. Meanwhile, by 1990 the Globe was £2 million in debt and the foundations had filled with water. A production of *The Tempest* in a tent on the site only went ahead after the team spent five hours a day baling out the water.[28]

By 1991, the picture had grown darker, with the project about to be wound up. There was nothing to be seen but a deep hole full of water. It was then that inspiration struck. Theo Crosby realised that the secret of this project was to build the Globe 'as if it were a pleasure not a business' and create forward momentum.[29] To get the project under way, Theo Crosby initiated a 'self-build' scheme. The International Shakespeare Globe Centre hired tradesmen directly and funded the work in phases, £25,000 at a time. As the public saw the timbers rising, it really would be a case of 'build it and they will come'.[30] In 1992 the master builder Peter McCurdy, a specialist in the restoration of Elizabethan buildings, and the architect Jon Greenfield began to create a new Globe using the same traditional techniques that had been used to build the original one, basing their design on original Tudor plans and the sketch of the old Globe by John Norden. Just as with the first Globe, this playhouse was constructed with a timber frame with mortise and tenon joints fixed with tapered wooden pegs. As the skeletal frame rose beside the Thames, many onlookers must have wondered whether the building was going up or coming down. Once the frames had been locked into place, infilling and plastering began. Although every effort was made to keep the design authentic, twentieth-century safety regulations meant that fireproof sheets had to be sealed between the layers of plaster, capable of withstanding 1,000°C for nearly three hours.[31]

Fire regulations would play a significant part in one of the most distinctive features of the new Globe, the thatched roof. Although thatched roofs are still to be seen in the English countryside, they have been banned in London ever since the Great Fire. If Southwark Council agreed, the new Globe would be the first building in London to have a thatched roof since 1666. This feature could only be achieved with stringent safety standards, including a flame-retardant chemical on the reeds used to make the thatch, fireboard underneath and a sprinkler system capable of drenching the roof within minutes.[32]

The most significant aspect of a playhouse is its stage, and here the designers had to work from a tantalising combination of one contemporary sketch (the drawing of the Swan by De Witte), and the excavations of the nearby Rose Theatre. Stage directions and lines from the plays were also a source of research, as were period details from buildings which have survived the centuries such as Middle Temple Hall and Charterhouse. With diligent research, the architects and builders believe they have come as close as possible to creating a reproduction of Shakespeare's Globe, but inevitably with some twentieth-century refinements. There were no safety regulations in Shakespeare's day, meaning that up to 3,000 people could be crammed into the little O. Today, that figure is closer to 1,200.[33] There were no toilets in the original Globe and no access for the disabled, but such necessities had to be incorporated into the modern design. Shakespeare's playgoers had no objection to standing in the pouring rain, but modern audiences are given plastic ponchos to keep away the elements, although umbrellas are forbidden as they would block the view. In many ways, to attend a performance at Shakespeare's Globe is closer in spirit to attending a gig than visiting a conventional theatre. Anxious that modern ground-lings might want to sit down, and thereby dilute the atmos-phere, the Globe team sluiced the yard down so that the surface would be wet. But they need not have worried. It seems the prospect of standing in the yard for two or three hours does not deter the audience. Instead, they seem to welcome it.

In 1993, the first performance in the shell of Shakespeare's Globe, on a temporary stage flanked by bays, was a short version of *Die Lustige Weiber von Windsor – The Merry Wives of Windsor*, presented by the Bremer Shakespeare Company, in keeping with the international character of the Globe.[34]

In a devastating blow to morale, Sam Wanamaker died of cancer on 18 December 1993. He was seventy-four. Earlier that year, Wanamaker had described the Globe as 'a Holy Grail, a dream, an ambition I will have spent one quarter of my life trying to fulfil'.[35] Tragically, Wanamaker did not live to see the Globe in its entirety, but his dream was at least well on its way to being fulfilled. The following year Theo Crosby died, his monument partly completed; his assistant Jon Greenfield took over as project architect.

In 1995, Mark Rylance was appointed as the Globe's Artistic Director. A 'Workshop Season' on a temporary stage at the nearly completed Globe aroused fierce debate between theatre scholars and practitioners, as Rylance maintained that theatre-going at the Globe was less of a passive experience and more of a crowd-pleaser, a gig which attracted a younger audience.[36] The following year, with the Globe nearing completion, the 'Prologue Season' presented *Two Gentlemen of Verona* and allowed the creative team to test the design of the stage prior to the building of the permanent oak structure. The stage house now had a larger and lighter cantilever which allowed the pillars to be moved closer together and further back towards the *frons scenae* (the back walls of the stage). Experiments were made with the painted decorations of the *frons scenae,* heavens and pillars. The ticket queues were huge, according to Diana Devlin, 'massive, like the first day of the sales!'[37]

In 1997, Charlotte Wanamaker, Sam's widow and his greatest supporter, died. Their daughters Abby, Zoe and Jessica continue to support the project. This year also saw the Gala Opening of the first full season of Shakespeare's Globe, in the presence of Her Majesty Queen Elizabeth II and HRH Prince Philip, Duke of Edinburgh. The opening ceremony also took place in the presence of the first queen. Zoe Wanamaker recalled that one of the most extraordinary moments during the proceedings was witnessing the first Queen Elizabeth appear in the yard on a horse, in front of Queen Elizabeth II.[38]

After so many years of struggle to get the theatre built, 1997 was a milestone in the story of the new Globe. But it was not the end of the journey; if anything, it was only the beginning. The Globe continued to draw flak from academics, critics and even the acting profession. According to current artistic director Dominic Dromgoole, 'When the Globe first opened, the negative catcalling was almost deafening,' recalling the inaugural production of *Henry V.* 'Mark Rylance stepped out on to the stage and delivered the prologue into a culture thick with scepticism and suspicion . . . Critics wondered aloud if the space would ever be more than a "tourist-trap-cum-playpen-for-cranky-academics".'[39]

Shakespeare's Globe as it is today – not for an age but for all time.

Despite this chorus of disapproval, Shakespeare's Globe has become both a commercial and artistic success at a time when many theatres are struggling to survive, and manages to do so without funding from Arts Council England. Dromgoole believes that part of this success is due to the fact that the Globe returns the event to the audience.

The Globe offered productions of Shakespeare in a single shared light, stripped of bells and whistles, productions that put power back into the hands of the spectator . . .

It reminded us that the greatest playwright who ever lived wrote for an audience capable of great joy and irreverence and sensuality . . . a robust and raucous people, happy to welcome outsiders, eager to embrace the new in any form, who would cheerfully congregate in all weathers to hear stories and to celebrate stories. Understanding that we come from this tradition helps us understand who we are today.'[40]

Today, Shakespeare's Globe is internationally recognised as a centre for drama and culture and has played an important part in the revitalisation of this historic part of the capital, making it one of the success stories of London. Since 1997, the Globe has welcomed millions of visitors, who have come to take part in workshops, watch performances, explore the exhibition or experience any of the countless other activities that Shakespeare's Globe provides. The centre continues to be a place of experiment and research, of new writing and innovation, a place where ideas about theatre are challenged every day.

And it is always changing. Even the theatre building itself, though officially completed in 1997, evolves from year to year, as audiences and theatre professionals learn more and more about how it works. There is a dynamic relationship between the building, those who work in it and those who visit which has always driven the process of experiment and change; and it is this same relationship that ensures the excitement of the journey will not end here.

In January 2014, a new 340-seat indoor playhouse, The Sam Wanamaker Playhouse, opened next to the Globe, a replica of the Blackfriars Theatre. Originally intended to be known as the Inigo Jones Theatre, by the time of its opening there was only one person it could possibly be named after. The playhouse is a remarkable tribute to a remarkable man who had the vision and tenacity to see the Globe rise again.

'It took an American, Sam Wanamaker, over two decades of tireless work to get the Globe rebuilt, encountering stubbornness, snobbery and scepticism at every turn,' commented Dominic Dromgoole. 'Sometimes we need an outsider's perspective. Wanamaker ultimately helped show us much about the theatre of the past – which can help us towards a bolder future – but also much about the English character, which had perhaps been lost in the great fog of empire and post-empire.'[41]

The Sam Wanamaker Playhouse was designed by Jon Greenfield, in collaboration with Allies and Morrison. The design is based upon two drawings that fell out of a dusty old book in the library of Worcester College, Oxford, in the 1960s. Once thought to date from the early seventeenth century, and to be by Inigo Jones, these drawings have now been attributed to his pupil John Webb, *circa* 1660. The sketches are believed to be a reasonable indication of what theatres would have looked like half a century earlier. According to Rowan Moore, writing in the *Observer*, the playhouse aims to be an 'archetype' of what such theatres were generally like, rather than a reconstruction of any one in particular. The oak frame, which in Shakespeare's day was the conventional way of constructing a theatre, is 'striking for its smell and warmth, its irregularities and warps, for its closeness to nature.' This is enhanced by the use of 'naked-flame candelabra descending from the ceiling, candles in sconces and, if desired, in the hands of the actors'.[42]

Lighting a timber theatre with candles presents a challenge to health and safety, but safety was achieved by the architects working closing with fire consultant Andy Nicholson and the London Fire Brigade to install a sophisticated smoke detection system. Their contribution was vital: 'without the combination of wood and flame, which makes the interior feel like a kind of boat, floating in shadow, more than half the point of the project would be lost'.[43] The critic Andrew Dickson described the playhouse on the opening night of *The Duchess of Malfi* as being like 'a jewel box shimmering in amber candlelight'.[44]

The verdict of Rowan Moore was similarly positive. Noting that, potentially, 'A candlelit modern theatre would risk looking affected and twee,' Moore commented that in fact 'the Globe's theatres are surreptitiously radical, which saves them from being waxworks. The Globe complex is a peculiar place, and sometimes awkward in its transitions, but it is good-peculiar.'[45]

According to Dromgoole, the Sam Wanamaker Playhouse is in some respects 'the "anti-Globe", a small, intimate, indoor space, hand-crafted from oak and lit entirely by beeswax candles. We have tried to create an indoor playhouse that Shakespeare would have recognised.'[46]

Dromgoole believes that staging productions in the new playhouse will offer . . .

> exhilarating new insight into the plays of Shakespeare and his contemporaries, and the society they were written for, about and within . . . The light produced by candle flames is organic, alive, permanently in slight motion . . . There is a shadowy eroticism to watching people under this light, that unmistakeable whiff of sulphur that eventually caused the anxious Puritans to close down the playhouses in 1642.[47]

To round off this account of the current-day Globe, I asked Dominic Dromgoole what a time-travelling Shakespeare would have made of the new Globe, and indeed the Sam Wanamaker Playhouse, if he arrived on Bankside today. What was the difference between being director of the Globe in 2014, compared with 1613, the year the first Globe was destroyed by fire?

'Good Lord, the differences are infinite,' Dromgoole replied, 'but I suppose what is more surprising are the similarities. London then was much more similar to London now than people would like to admit, a bustling, chaotic, international city, full of stories and an uncertain sense of its own future.

'When the Globe reopened, people thought it would be a financial disaster, and that no one would want to visit such a place, to stand for three hours to watch a Shakespeare [play], to sit on hard benches, to be unprotected from the rain, to watch theatre without sets or lighting or sound. No one thought it could succeed. But the doors opened, and people flocked in.

'Something about big stories told with beautiful and human detail, in a shared light, with no barrier between play, performers and audience, was immediately intoxicating, and a modern audience wanted it as much as an old audience. Citizens' theatre had returned to London, and the biggest and strangest question was why no theatres had been built this way between 1640 and 1995. That is a really hard question to answer.'[48]

I asked Dromgoole what he considered to be the advantages of the Globe as it is now, and he replied, with great enthusiasm, 'The surprise of it, the relish for the language, the refreshment of this old/new way of making theatre, the immediacy of the contact. The disadvantages are the lack of a roof, the unfamiliarity with the language, the academic and critical terror which is provoked by a popular response, and people's fear of populism.'

If Shakespeare and Burbage were in charge now, I asked, what kind of plays would they commission and perform?

'They would commission history plays which told big stories about the past and which obliquely shone a light on the present,' Dromgoole replied, 'contemporary comedies which made people laugh stupidly, adaptations of non-fiction books which were both sensational and profound, and anything with good playable parts in it for their company of actors.'

Telling Dromgoole that I see Shakespeare as a populist, I asked what kind of other media Shakespeare might work in today.

'Shakespeare would love television, would love new media, might find film a bit up itself, and whichever the medium it would be important to him that in a gentle discreet way he was master of his own destiny.'

I can't help thinking that Shakespeare would appreciate the new Globe, named in his honour, packed out with audiences month after month, with productions of his own works, those of his contemporaries, and plays from theatre companies the world over. Experimental, just as he was, weaving together his magic from mouse-eaten histories, classical drama, Italian romances and old wives' tales. James C. Fairfield, the Shakespeare pilgrim from Chicago, would be impressed, as would his guide, Christian Tearle. Some purists might say that if Shakespeare saw the Globe now, he would be turning in his grave. I don't think so. If William Shakespeare ever did put in an appearance, courtesy of Doctor Who's Tardis, he would pause to gather himself, take a deep breath and happily tread the boards once more, taking a turn as the ghost of Hamlet's father or the Chorus in *Henry V*.

Our play is done . . .

I hope, during the course of this book, that I have achieved something in bringing to life the extraordinary story of the Globe playhouse in its three incarnations, the conditions that made it and how it was reborn three centuries later to become the triumph of Bankside once more. I will close in the traditional way, with an appeal for your indulgence and a song. Let me leave you with these lines from Feste: 'Our play is done. And we'll strive to please you every day,'[49] and a final plea from Puck, or Robin Goodfellow:

> If we shadows have offended
> Think but this and all is mended,
> That you have but slumber'd here
> While these visions did appear . . .
> So goodnight unto you all.
> Give me your hands, if we be friends,
> And Robin shall restore amends.[50]

Bibliography

Adams, John Cranford, *The Globe Playhouse: its design and equipment*, Harvard University Press, Harvard, 1943

Addison, Joseph, and Steele, Richard, *The Tatler: With Notes and a General Index; Complete in One Volume*, Desilver, London, 1837 (e-book)

Ankarloo, Bengt, Clark, Stuart, and Monter, William, *The Athlone History of Witchcraft and Magic in Europe*, Athlone Press, London, 2002

Astington, John, *Actors and Acting in Shakespeare's Time*, Cambridge University Press, Cambridge, 2010

Bate, Jonathan, *The Genius of Shakespeare*, Picador, London, 2008

Bate, Jonathan, and Thornton, Dora, *Shakespeare: Staging the World*, British Museum Press, London, 2012

Bednarz, James P., *Shakespeare and the Poets' War*, Columbia University Press, New York and Chichester, 2001

Boas, Frederick S., *Shakspere and his Predecessors*, John Murray, London, 1896

Brett, D. (ed.), *This Earthly Stage: world and stage in late medieval and early modern England*, Brepols, Turnhout, *c.*2010

Brown, Ivor John Carnegie, *How Shakespeare Spent the Day*, Bodley Head, London, 1963

Brown, Pamela Allen (ed.), *Women Players in England, 1500–1660*, Ashgate, Aldershot, 2005

Bullough, Geoffrey, *Narrative and Dramatic Sources of Shakespeare*, 2 volumes, Routledge and Kegan Paul, London, 1957

Burford, E. J., *Bawds and Lodgings*, Peter Owen, London, 1976

Burgess, Anthony, *Shakespeare*, Jonathan Cape, London, 1970

Burgess, Anthony, *Nothing Like the Sun*, Allison and Busby, London, 2009

Burgess, Anthony, *A Dead Man in Deptford*, Vintage Classics, London, 2010

Byrne, Muriel St Clare, *Elizabethan Life in Town and Country*, Methuen, London, 1950

Chambers, E. K., *Shakespeare: A Study of Facts and Problems*, Oxford University Press, Oxford, 1930

Chambers, E. K., *The Elizabethan Stage*, 4 volumes, Oxford University Press, Oxford, 1965

Champion, Larry S., *The Noise of Threatening Drum: dramatic strategy and political ideology in Shakespeare and the English chronicle plays*, Associated University Presses, London, 1990

Cohen, J. M. and M. J., *The Penguin Dictionary of Quotations*, Penguin, Harmondsworth, 1960

Cook, Judith, *The Golden Age of the English Theatre*, Simon and Schuster, London, 1995

Cook, Judith, *Roaring Boys: Shakespeare's Rat Pack*, Sutton, Stroud, 2004

Craik, T. W., *The Tudor Interlude*, Leicester University Press, Leicester, 1958

Cranfill, Thomas M., and Hart Bruce, Dorothy, *Barnaby Rich: A Short Biography*, University of Texas Press, Austin, 1953

Defoe, Daniel, *A Journal of the Plague Year*, Penguin, London, 2003

De Somogyi, Nick, *Shakespeare's Theatre of War*, Ashgate, Aldershot, 1998

Dover Wilson, John, *Life in Shakespeare's England*, Penguin, Harmondsworth, 1968

Dromgoole, Dominic, *Will & Me*, Penguin, London, 2006

Duncan-Jones, Katherine, *Shakespeare: An Ungentle Life*, Arden Shakespeare, London, 2001

Eliot, T. S., *Elizabethan Essays*, Faber & Faber, London, 1934

Fraser, Lady Antonia, *The Gunpowder Plot: Terror and Faith in 1605*, Phoenix, London, 2002

Grantley, Darryll, *London in Early Modern English Drama: Representing the Built Environment*, Palgrave Macmillan, Basingstoke, 2008

Gurr, Andrew, *Rebuilding Shakespeare's Globe*, Routledge, New York, 1989

Gurr, Andrew, *The Shakespearean Stage 1574–1642*, Cambridge University Press, Cambridge, 1992

Gurr, Andrew, *Playgoing in Shakespeare's London*, Cambridge University Press, Cambridge, 1996

Gurr, Elizabeth, *Shakespeare's Globe: The Souvenir Guide*, Shakespeare's Globe, London, 1998

Halliday, F. E., *A Shakespeare Companion, 1564–1964*, Penguin, Harmondsworth, 1964

Harrison, G. B., *Shakespeare at Work 1592–1603*, Routledge, London, 1933

Harrison, G. B., *Elizabethan Plays and Players*, Routledge, London, 1940

Henslowe, Philip, *Henslowe's Diary*, ed. Greg [*sic*], Walter W., Bullen, London, 1904

Herbert, William, *The History of the Twelve Great Livery Companies of London*, published by the author, London, 1832

Holland, Peter, and Orgel, Stephen, (eds.), *From Performance to Print in Shakespeare's England*, Palgrave Macmillan, Basingstoke, 2008

Holmes, Martin, *Elizabethan London*, Cassell, London, 1969

Holmes, Martin, *Shakespeare and his Players*, John Murray, London, 1972

Jonson, Ben, *The Alchemist and Other Plays*, ed. Campbell, Gordon, Oxford University Press, Oxford, 1995

Jorgensen, Paul A., *Shakespeare's Military World*, University of California Press, Berkeley, 1956

Kiernan, Victor, *Shakespeare: Poet and Citizen*, Verso, London, 1993

Kinney, Arthur F. (ed), *Companion to Renaissance Drama*, Wiley-Blackwell, London, 2008

Kohn, George C., *Encyclopedia of Plague and Pestilence*, Infobase Publishing, 2008

Lawrence, William John, *The Elizabethan Playhouse and Other Studies*, Russell & Russell, New York, 1963

Mack, Maynard, *Jacobean Theatre*, Edward Arnold, London, 1950

Manley, Lawrence (ed.), *London in the Age of Shakespeare: An Anthology*, Croom Helm, Beckenham, 1986

Mann, David, *The Elizabethan Player: Contemporary Stage Representation*, Routledge, London, 1991

McMillin, Scott, *The Queen's Men and their Plays*, Cambridge University Press, Cambridge, 1998

More, Sir Thomas, *Selections from his English Works*, ed. Allen, P. S. and H. M., Clarendon Press, Oxford, 1924

Mulryne, J. R., and Shewring, Margaret, *Theatre and Government Under the Early Stuarts*, Cambridge University Press, Cambridge, 1993

Nagler, A. M., *A Source Book in Theatrical History*, Courier, Dover, 2013

Nicholl, Charles, *The Reckoning: The Murder of Christopher Marlowe*, Vintage, London, 2002

Nicholl, Charles, *The Lodger: Shakespeare on Silver Street*, Penguin Books, London, 2007

Oxford Book of English Verse 1250–1958, ed. Quiller-Couch, Sir Arthur, Clarendon Press, Oxford, 1939

Oxford Dictionary of Quotations, 2nd edition, OUP, London, 1968

Raleigh, Sir Walter, *The History of the World*, Temple University Press, 1971

Rowse, A. L., *Shakespeare's Globe: his intellectual and moral outlook*, Weidenfeld and Nicolson, London, 1981

Salgado, Gamini, *Eyewitnesses of Shakespeare: first hand accounts of performances 1590–1890*, Chatto & Windus, London, 1975

Salmon, Thomas, and Sollom, Emlyn, *A complete collection of state-trials, and proceedings for high-treason* (e-book)

Shakespeare, William, *The Arden Shakespeare Complete Works Revised Edition*, Arden Shakespeare, London, 2011

Shapiro, James, *1599: A Year in the Life of William Shakespeare*, Faber & Faber, London, 2005

Shaughnessy, Robert (ed.), *The Cambridge Companion to Shakespeare and Popular Culture*, Cambridge University Press, Cambridge, 2007

Simpson, William, *The Reign of Elizabeth*, Heinemann, Oxford, 2001

Smout, Thomas Christopher, *A History of the Scottish People 1560–1830*, Fontana, London, 2011

Sprague, Arthur Colby, *Shakespearian Players and Performances*, A & C Black, London, 1954

Stopes, C. C., *Burbage and Shakespeare's Stage*, The De La More Press, London, 1913

Stuart, James (King James I), *Daemonologie*, Edinburgh, 1597 (e-book)

Sturgess, Keith, *Jacobean Private Theatre*, Routledge and Kegan Paul, London, 1987

Tearle, Christian, *Rambles with an American*, Dutton, New York, 1920 (https://archive.org/stream/rambleswithameri00jaqu#page/n7/mode/2up)

Thomson, Peter, *Shakespeare's Theatre*, Routledge, London and New York, 1992

Virgil, *The Aeneid*

Walker, Julia (ed.), *Dissing Elizabeth: Negative Representations of Gloriana*, Duke University Press, 1998

Walsh, Brian, *Shakespeare, the Queen's Men, and the Elizabethan Performance of History*, Cambridge University Press, Cambridge, 2009

Wymer, Rowland, *Suicide and Despair in the Jacobean Drama*, Harvester, Brighton, 1986

Picture Acknowledgements

The author and publishers would like to thank the following copyright-holders for permission to reproduce images in this book:

© The Trustees of the British Museum: p. 20, 187
© Rex Features: p. 21
© iStockphoto: p. 37
© Mary Evans Picture Library: p. 46, 89, 100, 117, 131, 150, 180, 207
© Shakespeare's Globe: p. 271

The author and publishers have made all reasonable efforts to contact copyright-holders for permission, and apologise for any omissions or errors in the form of credits given. Corrections may be made for future printings.

Notes

CHAPTER ONE

1. See *A Midsummer Night's Dream*, Act 3 Scene 1
2. See Byrne, *Elizabethan Life in Town and Country,* p. 59
3. Ibid., p. 45
4. See *Oxford Book of English Verse*, p. 26
5. See Byrne, op. cit., p. 60
6. See Platter, Thomas, *Thomas Platter's Travels in England 1599*, p. 154
7. See Byrne, op. cit., p. 65
8. Ibid., p. 62
9. Ibid., p. 63
10. See Byrne, op. cit., p. 72
11. Ibid., p. 73
12. Ibid., p. 74
13. Ibid., p. 75
14. Ibid., p. 76

CHAPTER TWO

1. See *The Taming of the Shrew,* Induction
2. Ibid.
3. Ibid.
4. Ibid.
5. Ibid.
6. See *A Midsummer Night's Dream*, Act 1 Scene 2
7. See *The Winter's Tale*, Act 4 Scene 4

8.   See *The Two Gentlemen of Verona*, Act 4 Scene 4
9.   See Dover Wilson, *Life in Shakespeare's England*, p. 50
10. See Stopes, *Burbage and Shakespeare's Stage*, p. 7
11. Ibid., p. 8
12. Ibid.
13. Ibid., p. 9
14. Ibid.
15. Ibid., p. 13
16. Ibid., p. 8
17. See Chambers, *The Elizabethan Stage*, volume 2, p. 355
18. See *The Merry Wives of Windsor*, Act 1 Scene 1
19. See *Macbeth*, Act 5 Scene 7
20. See Holmes, *Elizabethan London*, p. 77
21. See Gurr, *The Shakespearean Stage 1574–1642*, p. 185
22. See Platter, Thomas, *Thomas Platter's Travels in England*, p. 166
23. Ibid.
24. See Byrne, Elizabethan Life in Town and Country., p. 210
25. Ibid.
26. See *King Lear*, Act 1 Scene 4
27. See *As You Like It*, Act 1 Scene 2
28. See Gurr, op. cit., p. 185
29. See Chambers, op. cit., pp. 379–80
30. Ibid., p. 381
31. See Stopes, op. cit., p. 146
32. Defoe, *A Journal of the Plague Year*, p. 227
33. See Stopes, op. cit., p. 146
34. Ibid., p. 17
35. See *A Midsummer Night's Dream*, Act 2 Scene 1
36. See Stopes, op. cit., p. 17
37. See Byrne, op. cit., p. 218
38. Ibid.
39. See *Love's Labour's Lost*, Act 5 Scene 2
40. See Byrne, op. cit., p. 220.
41. Ibid.
42. Ibid.

CHAPTER THREE

1.   See Stopes, *Burbage and Shakespeare's Stage*, p. 19

2. See *The Merchant of Venice*, Act 1 Scene 1

3. See Holmes, *Elizabethan London*, p. 52

4. Ibid., p. 55

5. Ibid.

6. See *King John*, Act 2 Scene 1

7. See Bradbrook, Muriel, *The Living Monument: Shakespeare and the Theatre of His Time*, p. 3

8. See Stopes, op. cit., p. 70

9. Ibid., p. 26

10. See Chambers, *The Elizabethan Stage*, volume 2, p. 405

11. See Stopes, op. cit., p. 15

12. See Chambers, op. cit., p. 400

13. See Stopes, op. cit., pp. 24–25

14. See Chambers, op. cit., p. 388

15. See Stopes, op. cit., p. 30

16. Ibid., p. 31

17. Ibid.

18. See Chambers, op. cit., p. 397

19. Ibid.

20. See Stopes, op. cit., p. 35

21. Ibid., p. 38

22. Ibid.

23. Ibid., p. 36

24. See *Hamlet*, Act 3 Scene 1

25. See Chambers, op. cit., p. 105

26. See Stopes, op. cit., p. 38

27. See Harrison, *Elizabethan Plays and Players* p. 43

28. See Stopes, op. cit., p. 39

29. Ibid., pp. 39–40

30. Ibid., p. 44

31. See Duncan-Jones, *Shakespeare: An Ungentle Life*, p. 32

32. See Stopes, op. cit., p. 46

33. See Ackroyd, Peter, *Shakespeare, the Biography*, p. 163

34. See Chambers, op. cit., p. 405

35. See Stopes, op. cit., p. 61

36. See Chambers, op. cit., p. 406

37. See Henslowe, Diaries

38. See Gurr, *The Shakespearean Stage 1574–1642*, p. 187

CHAPTER FOUR

1. See Harrison, *Elizabethan Plays and Players*, p. 108
2. Ibid., p. 109
3. See Eliot, *Elizabethan Essays,* p. 155
4. See *Hamlet*, Act 5 Scene 1
5. See Chambers, *Shakespeare: A Study of Facts and Problems*, volume 2, pp. 252–3
6. Ibid., volume 1, p. 265
7. Ibid., p. 288
8. Ibid., p. 296
9. Ibid., p. 253
10. See Harrison, op. cit., p. 44
11. Ibid., p. 45
12. See *Hamlet*, Act 5 Scene 1
13. See Ackroyd, Peter, *Shakespeare, the Biography*, p. 162
14. See *Hamlet*, Act 2 Scene 1
15. See *Henry IV Part 2*, Act 4 Scene 3
16. See Dover Wilson, *Life In Shakespeare's England*, p. 140
17. See Ackroyd, op. cit., p. 162
18. Thomas Fuller, *English Worthies,* 1660 in Chambers, *Shakespeare: A Study of Facts and Problems*, volume 2, p. 211
19. See Harrison, op. cit., p. 63
20. http://www.luminarium.org/renlit/kydbio.htm
21. See Harrison, op. cit., pp. 46–47
22. See *The Spanish Tragedie* by Thomas Kyd, http://www.gutenberg.org/files/6043/6043-h/6043-h.htm
23. Ibid.
24. See *A Concordance to the Works of Christopher Marlowe,* ed. Ule, p. 294
25. See Harrison, op. cit., p. 69
26. See Nashe, Thomas, *Preface to Menaphon*
27. See Marlowe, Christopher, *Tamburlaine the Great*
28. Ibid.
29. Ibid.
30. See Harrison, op. cit., p. 71
31. See Marlowe, Christopher, op. cit.
32. See Harrison, op. cit., p. 108
33. See Marlowe, Christopher, *The Jew of Malta Act, 1 lines 22-23*
34. See Chambers, *The Elizabethan Stage*, volume 2, p. 105

35. See *Love's Labour's Lost*, Act 4 Scene 3 (some texts give the quote as 'suit of night')
36. See Harrison, op. cit., p. 78
37. Ibid., p. 90
38. Ibid., p. 113
39. Ibid., p. 131
40. Ibid., p. 133
41. See Nashe, Thomas, *In Time of Pestilence, The Oxford Book of English Verse*, p. 207
42. See Harrison, op. cit., p. 105
43. Ibid., p. 110
44. See *A Midsummer Night's Dream*, Act 5 Scene 1
45. See Marlowe, Christopher, *Dr Faustus*
46. Ibid.
47. Ibid.
48. See Burgess, *Shakespeare*, p. 103
49. See Ackroyd, Peter, *Shakespeare, the Biography*, p. 188
50. See Harrison, op. cit., p. 117
51. Ibid., pp. 119, 120, 124
52. Ibid., p. 124
53. Ibid., p. 125
54. See *As You Like It*, Act 3 Scene 3
55. See *Romeo and Juliet*, Act 2 Scene 6
56. See *A Midsummer Night's Dream*, Act 1 Scene 1

CHAPTER FIVE

1. See *Richard II*, Act 3 Scene 2
2. See *King Lear*, Act 3 Scene 6
3. See Raleigh, Sir Walter, *The History of the World*, http://www.bartleby.com/39/16.html
4. See *Richard III*, Act 4 Scene 4
5. See *Henry VI Part 1*, Act 1 Scene 1
6. See *Richard II*, Act 3 Scene 4
7. See Walsh, *Shakespeare, the Queen's Men and the Elizabethan Performance of History*, pp. 16–17
8. See Dover Wilson, *Life in Shakespeare's England*, p. 182
9. See Walsh, op. cit., p. 37
10. Ibid.

11. See Chambers, *The Elizabethan Stage*, volume 2, p. 396
12. See *The Oxford Dictionary of Quotations*, 2nd edition, p. 27
13. See *Richard III*, Act 3 Scene 4
14. See Gurr, *Playgoing in Shakespeare's London*, pp. 136–7
15. See Jorgensen, *Shakespeare's Military World*, p. 1
16. Ibid., p. 130
17. See *Henry VI Part 2*, Act 3 Scene 1
18. See *The Cambridge History of English and American Literature*, volume 5, 'The Army and Navy in Elizabeth's Time'
19. See *Henry VI Part 2*, Act 4 Scene 8
20. See *The Cambridge History of English and American Literature,* op. cit.
21. See *Henry IV Part 1*, Act 4 Scene 2
22. Ibid.
23. Ibid., Act 5 Scene 1
24. See Bate, *Being Shakespeare* (DVD)
25. See Gurr, op. cit., p. 227
26. See Ross, Charles, *Richard III*, p. 7
27. See *Henry VI Part 1*, Act 2 Scene 4
28. See *Henry VI Part 2*, Act 4 Scene 4
29. Ibid., Act 4 Scene 2
30. Ibid., Act 4 Scene 4
31. Ibid., Act 4 Scene 7
32. Ibid., Act 4 Scene 8
33. See *Henry VI Part 3*, Act 2 Scene 5
34. Ibid., Act 5 Scene 6
35. See Brown, Ivor, *How Shakespeare Spent the Day*, p. 20
36. See Hammond P. W., (ed.), *Richard III*, p. 71
37. See *Henry VI Part 3*, Act 3 Scene 2
38. See Hammond, op. cit., p. 342
39. See *Richard III*, Act 2 Scene 4
40. See *Henry VI Part 3*, Act 5 Scene 6
41. See *Richard III*, various scenes
42. See More, op. cit., pp. 73–74
43. Ibid., p. 76
44. See *Henry VI Part 3*, Act 1 Scene 4
45. See More, http://www.thomasmorestudies.org/docs/Thomas%20More%20Reader%20IV%203.pdf
46. See *Richard III*, Act 5 Scene 4
47. See *Richard II*, Act 3 Scene 2

48. Ibid., Act 2 Scene 1
49. See *Henry IV Part 1*, Act 1 Scene 3
50. Ibid., Act 3 Scene 2
51. See *Richard II*, Act 2 Scene 1
52. Ibid., Act 5 Scene 3
53. See *Henry IV Part 2*, Act 5 Scene 5
54. Ibid., Act 4 Scene 5
55. See *Richard II*, Act 3 Scene 2
56. Ibid.

CHAPTER SIX

1. See Platter, Thomas, *Thomas Platter's Travels in England*, p. 153
2. See *Henry IV Part 1*, Act 2 Scene 4
3. See Stopes, *Burbage and Shakespeare's Stage*, p. 65
4. Ibid., p. 15
5. See *Love's Labour's Lost*, Act 4 Scene 2
6. Ibid., Act 5 Scene 2
7. See Hales, 'Shakespeare and the Jews', *English Historical Review* (1894)
8. See http://www.jewishencyclopedia.com/articles/10109-lopez-rodrigo
9. See *The Merchant of Venice*, Act 3 Scene 1
10. Ibid.
11. See Stopes, op. cit., p. 69
12. Ibid.
13. See Mulryne and Shewring, *Theatre and Government Under the Early Stuarts*, p. 56
14. See Harrison, *Elizabethan Plays and Players*, p. 166
15. Ibid.
16. See Stopes, op. cit.
17. Ibid.
18. Ibid.
19. Ibid., p. 71
20. Ibid.
21. See *The Merry Wives of Windsor*, Act 1 Scene 1
22. See *Romeo and Juliet*, Act 2 Scene 4
23. Ibid., Act 3 Scene 1
24. See Stopes, op. cit., p. 150

25. The 'benefit of clergy' law or *privilegium clericale* originally permitted clergymen to claim they were outside the jurisdiction of the secular courts and could only be tried under canon law. By Jonson's day, it had become a mechanism by which any literate first-time offenders could obtain a more lenient sentence.
26. See Harrison, op. cit.
27. See Stopes, op. cit., p. 70
28. Ibid.

CHAPTER SEVEN

1. See Stopes, *Burbage and Shakespeare's Stage,* p. 78
2. Ibid., p. 221
3. Ibid., p. 75
4. Ibid., p. 111
5. See Gurr, *Shakespeare's Globe,* p. 18
6. Ibid.
7. This description is based on Johannes De Witte's observations of decorations at the Swan Theatre *c.*1596, see Nagler, *A Source Book in Theatrical History*, p. 117
8. See *The Merchant of Venice*, Act 5 Scene 1
9. See *Hamlet*, Act 2 Scene 2
10. See Ackroyd, Peter, *Shakespeare, the Biography*, p. 327
11. See *As You Like It*, Act 2 Scene 7
12. See Stopes, op. cit., p. 121
13. Ibid.
14. See *A Midsummer Night's Dream*, Act 1 Scene 2
15. See *Hamlet*, Act 3 Scene 2
16. See *Troilus and Cressida*, Act 1 Scene 3
17. See *Richard III*, Act 3 Scene 5
18. See Herbert, *The History of the Twelve Great Livery Companies of London*, p. 322
19. See Gurr, *Playgoing in Shakespeare's London*, p. 136
20. See *Henry V*, Chorus to Act 2
21. See *Henry IV Part 1*, Act 4 Scene 1
22. See *Henry V*, Act 3 Scene 3
23. Ibid., Chorus to Act 4
24. See *Henry V*, Act 3 Scene 1
25. Ibid., Act 4 Scene 7

26. Ibid., Act 1 Scene 2
27. See Stopes, op. cit., p. 123
28. See Brown, Ivor, *How Shakespeare Spent the Day,* p. 77
29. See *Henry V*, Chorus to Act 1
30. Ibid.
31. Ibid., Chorus to Act 3
32. Ibid., Chorus to Act 4
33. Ibid.
34. Ibid., Chorus to Act 5
35. Ibid.
36. See *Romeo and Juliet,* Prologue
37. See Gurr, *Playgoing in Shakespeare's London*, p. 138
38. See Bullen, A. H., (ed.), *The Works of John Marston,* 1887
39. See Jonson, Ben, *Bartholomew Fair,* Induction
40. See *A Midsummer Night's Dream*, Act 5 Scene 1
41. See Brown, op. cit., p. 82
42. See *Coriolanus*, Act 5 Scene 3
43. See *A Midsummer Night's Dream*, Act 4 Scene 2
44. See Platter, Thomas, *Thomas Platter's Travels in England*, p. 155
45. See Dover Wilson, *Life in Shakespeare's England*, p. 86
46. See Gurr, op. cit., p. 46
47. See Gurr, op. cit., p. 42
48. See *Julius Caesar*, Act 2 Scene 1
49. See Platter, op. cit., p. 155

CHAPTER EIGHT

1. See *Hamlet*, Act 2 Scene 2
2. See *Richard II*, Act 3 Scene 2
3. See *Henry V*, Chorus to Act 5
4. See Harrison, *Elizabethan Plays and Players*, p. 237
5. See Simpson, *The Reign of Elizabeth*, p. 120
6. See Highley, in *Dissing Elizabeth*, ed. Walker, p. 72
7. See Harrison, *Shakespeare at Work 1592–1603*, p. 217
8. Ibid., p. 233
9. See Forker Charles R., (ed.), *Richard II*, p. 12
10. Ibid., p. 5
11. See *Richard II*, Act 2 Scene 1
12. Ibid.

13. See Forker, op. cit., p. 14
14. See Kinney (ed.), *A Companion to Renaissance Drama*, p. 229
15. See Forker, op. cit., p. 14
16. Ibid., p. 10
17. Ibid.
18. See Chambers, *Shakespeare: A Study of Facts and Problems*, volume 2, p. 323
19. See Harrison, *Shakespeare at Work 1592–1603*, p. 235
20. Ibid.
21. Ibid.
22. Ibid., pp. 236–7
23. Ibid., p. 239–40
24. Ibid., p. 238
25. See *Henry VI Part 1*, Act 1 Scene 1
26. See Black, J. B., *The Reign of Elizabeth 1558–1603*, p. 120
27. See Forker, op. cit., p. 10
28. See *Macbeth*, Act 1 Scene 3
29. See Stopes, *Burbage and Shakespeare's Stage*, p. 89
30. See *The Return from Parnassus*, Act 4 Scene 3
31. Ibid., Act 1 Scene 1
32. Ibid., Act 4 Scene 3
33. Ibid.
34. Ibid.
35. See *Hamlet*, Act 2 Scene 2
36. Ibid.
37. See Stopes, op. cit., p. 92
38. Ibid., p. 89
39. See Harrison, *Shakespeare at Work*, p. 216
40. See Stopes, op. cit., p. 89
41. See Bednarz, *Shakespeare and the Poets' War*, p. 161
42. See Brown, Ivor, *How Shakespeare Spent the Day*, p. 80
43. See Bednarz, op. cit.
44. See *Hamlet*, Act 2 Scene 2
45. See Burgess, *Shakespeare,* p. 204
46. See Dekker, Thomas, *The Wonderful Year* (1603), https://cms.grcc. edu/sites/default/files/docs/shakespeare/historical/thomas_ dekker_selections_from_two_pamphlets.pdf
47. See Burgess, op. cit.
48. See Stopes, op. cit., p. 96
49. Ibid.

50. See *To the Maiestie of King James, Minor Poems of Michael Drayton,* ed. Brett, Cyril, http://www.gutenberg.org/files/17873/17873-h/17873-h.htm

51. See Stopes, op. cit., p. 97

52. Ibid.

53. Ibid., p. 99

54. Ibid.

55. Ibid., p. 102

56. Ibid., pp. 102–103

57. Ibid., p. 108

58. See Chambers, *The Elizabethan Stage*, volume 2, p. 212

59. See Salmon, *A complete collection of state-trials and proceedings for high-treason*, volume 1, p. 244

60. See Muir, Kenneth, (ed.), *Macbeth*, p. xx

61. See Fraser, *The Gunpowder Plot*, p. 283

62. See Muir, Kenneth, op. cit., p. xxi

63. See *Macbeth*, Act 4 Scene 1

64. Ibid., Act 1 Scene 7

65. See Ankarloo, *Witchcraft in Europe*, p. 79

66. See Stuart, *Newes from Scotland – declaring the damnable life and death of Dr. John Fian* (link available at http://en.wikipedia.org/wiki/Newes_from_Scotland)

67. Ibid.

68. Ibid.

69. See Smout, *A History of the Scottish People 1560–1830*, pp. 198–207

70. See *Daemonologie, by King of England James I*, 'Preface to the Reader' (http://www.gutenberg.org/catalog/world/readfile?fk_files=845529)

71. See *Macbeth*, Act 1 Scene 3

72. See *Daemonologie*, p. 19

73. See Shakespeare's Globe, http://blog.shakespearesglobe.com/the-gunpowder-plot-and-shakespeares-macbeth/

74. See *Macbeth*, Act 2 Scene 3

75. See Muir, op cit., pp. 60–61

76. See *Macbeth*, Act 2 Scene 3

CHAPTER NINE

1. See *Antony and Cleopatra*, Act 5 Scene 2

2. See *Cymbeline*, Act 4 Scene 2

3. *Lacrimae rerum* or 'there are tears for things'; see Virgil, *The Aeneid,* book 1, line 462

4. See Kohn, *Encyclopedia of Plague and Pestilence: From Ancient Times to the Present*, p. 477

5. See *Newton Rebels*, http://www.newtonrebels.org.uk/rebels/history.htm

6. Ibid.

7. See *Coriolanus*, Act 1 Scene 1

8. See Lee, Alexander, 'Making a Famine where Abundance Lies: Shakespeare the Hoarder', *History Today*, 3 April 2013

9. See *King John*, Act 3 Scene 4

10. See Stopes, *Burbage and Shakespeare's Stage*, p. 105

11. See *Eastward Ho*, Act 3 Scene 3

12. See Chambers, *The Elizabethan Stage*, volume 3, pp. 257–8

13. See Stopes, op. cit., p. 105

14. See Ackroyd, Peter, *Shakespeare, the Biography*, p. 506

15. See *A Midsummer Night's Dream*, Act 3 Scene 2

16. See Burgess, *Shakespeare*, p. 215

17. Ibid., p. 216

18. See *The Winter's Tale*, Act 4 Scene 3

19. See Kermode, Frank (ed.), *The Tempest*, pp. xxv, xxix

20. See Burgess, op. cit., p. 253

21. See *The Tempest*, Act 2 Scene 2

22. Ibid., Act 1 Scene 2

23. Ibid., Act 3 Scene 2

24. Ibid., Act 5 Scene 1

25. Ibid.

26. See Bate and Thornton, *Shakespeare, Staging the World*, p. 256

27. See Ackroyd, op. cit., p. 466

28. See Burgess, op. cit., p. 251

29. Ibid.

30. http://www.bardstage.org/globe-theatre-fire.htm

31. See Stopes, op. cit., p. 116

32. Ibid.

33. See http://www.bardstage.org/globe-theatre-fire.htm

34. See Stopes, op. cit., p. 117

35. See *The Tempest*, Act 4 Scene 1

36. See Stopes, op. cit., p. 111

37. Ibid., p. 113

38. See Ackroyd, op. cit., p. 482

39. See *Henry V*, Act 2 Scene 3
40. See Ackroyd, op. cit., p. 482
41. See Burgess, op. cit., p. 259
42. See Jonson, Ben, *Preface*, First Folio, 1623
43. See Stopes, op. cit., p. 116
44. See Jonson, op. cit.
45. See Stopes, op. cit.
46. Ibid., pp. 117–18
47. Ibid., p. 118
48. Ibid., p. 117
49. Ibid., p. 118
50. Ibid., p. 116
51. Ibid., p. 126
52. See Donaldson, Ian, 'Benjamin Jonson (1572–1637)', *Oxford Dictionary of National Biography*
53. See Stopes, op. cit., p. 127
54. Ibid.
55. Ibid.
56. Ibid., p. 131
57. Ibid.
58. Ibid., p. 132
59. Ibid.
60. Ibid.
61. Ibid., p. 133
62. Ibid.
63. Ibid.
64. Ibid.
65. See Burford, *Bawds and Lodgings*, p. 181
66. See *Twelfth Night*, Act 5 Scene 1

CHAPTER TEN

1. See Tearle, Christian, *Rambles with an American*, p. 87
2. See Watson, Nicola, 'Shakespeare on the Tourist Trail', in *The Cambridge Companion to Shakespeare and Popular Culture*, p. 217
3. See Tearle, op. cit., p. 37
4. Ibid.
5. Ibid., p. 50; the quote is from Sonnet 54
6. Ibid., p. 52

7. Ibid., p. 55
8. See Watson, op. cit., p. 219
9. From Shakespeare's Globe papers
10. See Grogan, David, 'Shakespeare's Globe Theatre Will Rise to Glow Again—Thanks to "Uncle Sam" Wanamaker', *People* magazine, 18 August 1986
11. See Chaney, Edward, 'Sam Wanamaker's Global Legacy', *Salisbury Review*, June 1995, pp. 38–40
12. According to Polly Hope, widow of Theo Crosby, on *The Reunion – Shakespeare's Globe,* BBC Radio 4, 22 April 2012
13. See Shakespeare's Globe papers
14. Ibid.
15. Ibid.
16. See *The Reunion*, op. cit.
17. Ibid.
18. See Shakespeare's Globe papers
19. Ibid.
20. See Grogan, op. cit.
21. See Shakespeare's Globe papers
22. See *The Reunion*, op. cit.
23. See Shakespeare's Globe papers
24. See *The Reunion*, op. cit.
25. See Shakespeare's Globe papers
26. Ibid.
27. Ibid.
28. See *The Reunion*, op. cit.
29. Ibid.
30. Ibid.
31. See Gurr, *Shakespeare's Globe,* p. 27
32. Ibid.
33. Ibid.
34. Shakespeare's Globe papers
35. See Folkart, Burt, 'Sam Wanamaker; Actor Led Globe Theater Effort', *Los Angeles Times*, 19 December 1993
36. See Dromgoole, 'Shakespeare's Globe – the next stage', *The Guardian*, 11 January 2014
37. See *The Reunion*, op. cit.
38. Ibid.
39. See Dromgoole, op. cit.
40. Ibid.

41. Ibid.
42. See Moore, 'Sam Wanamaker Playhouse – review', *The Observer*, 12 January 2014
43. Ibid.
44. Dickson, Andrew, 'New Globe playhouse draws us inside Shakespeare's inner space', *The Guardian*, 7 January 2014
45. See Moore, op. cit.
46. See Dromgoole, op. cit.
47. Ibid.
48. From interview with Dominic Dromgoole, 14 September 2013
49. See *Twelfth Night*, Act 5 Scene 1
50. See *A Midsummer Night's Dream*, Act 5 Scene 1

Index

(The initials CB refer to Cuthbert Burbage, JB to James Burbage, RB to Richard Burbage, WS to William Shakespeare. Page numbers in italics refer to illustrations.)

actors' companies:
   Admiral's Men, 84, 109, 110, 165
     Jonson signs up to, 163
   cheats and tricksters among, 37
   Children of the Chapel Royal, 65, 151,
     212, 213, 214
     banned, 233
   Children of the Queen's Revels, 232
   Earl of Leicester's Men, 39, 41 4
     disbanded, 107
     in Kenilworth, 56–7
     plague forces return to touring by, 75
     Queen entertained by, 56–7
     and Queen's disfavour, 80
     royal-command Christmas and
      Shrove Tuesday performances
      by, 59
     settled in the Theatre, see Theatre
   Earl of Pembroke's Men, 103, 110, 163,
     166
   Earl of Warwick's Men, 39
   Earl of Worcester's Men, 38–9
   grim conditions for, 36
   King's Men (formerly Lord
     Chamberlain's Men, q.v.), 216–19
     Blackfriars gives new lease of life to,
      233
     and Civil War, 255
     enhanced status of, 217–18
     old players pass from, 251
     and plague, 218
     royal wedding entertainment
      provided by, 242
     and Spanish Ambassador, 219
   Lord Chamberlain's Men (later King's
     Men, q.v.), 1, 70, 152, 161

     capacity audiences drawn by, 153
     and Essex's rebellion, 208
     Globe opened by, 1, 180–1
     and *Hamlet*, 211
     indoor theatre contemplated by,
      231–2
     King chooses, as own company,
      216–17
     most successful troupe, 188
     name change of, to King's Men, 216
     and *Parnassus*, 209–10
     prosecution escaped by, 208
     and Queen's death, 216
     and *Richard II* revival, 203–4, 208
     Scottish tour of, 208–9
     Theatre transported by, 173–4
   Lord Hunsdon's Men, 152
   Lord Strange's Men, 39, 103, 109, 110,
     118
   old legends inspire, 37
   patronage for, 38–9
   in players' inns, 51–6
   proclamation against, 42
   proclamation to license, 45
   and Puritanism, prejudice and social
     control, 42
   Queen's Men:
     continuing popularity of, 109
     Curtain performances of, 83
     extensive touring of, 77–8, 80–1
     formed, 77
     plea of, to Lord Mayor, 79–80
   and Roman Catholic spies, 38
   romantic view of, *37*
   women not represented among, 38
Acts and Monuments (Foxe), 127

Admiral's Men, 84, 109, 110, 165
  Jonson signs up to, 163
Agincourt, Battle of, 129, 183
Allen, William, 255
Alleyn, Edward 'Ned', 3, 7, 169, 178
  Dulwich College founded by, 8, 118
  as Faustus, 8, 116
  first giant of English drama, 8
  Hieronimo role of, 101
  JB's falling-out with, 83, 109–10
  letter of, to wife, re plague, 113
  Marlowe as ideal vehicle for, 106
  WS's tragic characters brought to life by,
    107
Alleyn, Giles, 64, 81–2, 152, 171
  and Burbages' scheme to demolish
    Theatre, 172–3
Alleyn (née Henslowe), Joan, 3, 109
  and plague, 113
Alleyn, Sir William, 71
Anatomie of Abuses (Stubbes), 76, 97
animal-baiting, 46–9
Anjou, Duke of, 4
Anne of Denmark, see Anne, Queen
Anne, Queen, 219, 223, 232
  death of, 249
  in masque, 236
  postponed funeral of, 249
  and son Henry death, 238
Antony and Cleopatra (Shakespeare), 231, 264
  modern production of, 264
Appletree, Thomas, 63–4
archery, 62
Armin, Robert, 220
Artillery Yard, 63
As You Like It (Shakespeare), 50, 121, 178
  lines from, 16
Aubrey, John, 7, 16, 71, 92
  WS described by, 93, 94, 97

Bacon, Anthony, 52
Bacon, Sir Francis, 11, 127, 134
  on justice, 129
Bains, Richard, 119
Bale, John, 37
Ball, Em, 114
Bankside Globe Developments, 263
Barber, Thomas, 81
Barbican Centre, 264
Barclay Perkins, 258
Bardi, Giovanni, 50
Barrow (preacher), 119
Bartholomew Fair, 39
Bartholomew Fair (Jonson), 188
Bassano brothers, 45

Bate, Jonathan, 134
bear-baiting, 46–8, 46, 74, 84
Bear Gardens Museum and Arts Centre, 264
Beaumont, Francis, 2, 62, 98, 247
Beeston, Christopher, 110, 220
Bell Savage, 51, 52
Benfield, Robert, 253
Bentley, John, 78, 81
Bermuda Pamphlets, The, 238
Blackfriars, 149–51
Blackfriars Theatre, 211–13, 232
  actors demand shares in, 253–4
  Burbages take control of, 231
  coaches banned from waiting at, 252
  demolition of, 256
  King's men given new lease of life by,
    233
  modern reconstruction of, 264
  more elaborate masques in, 235
  non-survival of, into modern times, 258
  Privy Council attempts to close, 251–2
  RB administers, 161
  RB takes lease of, 233
  replica of, 272
  Tire Man (wardrobe master) at, 190
  valuation of, 252
  and War of the Theatres, 213–14
Blackfriars Theatre (first), 150–1
Blackfriars Theatre (second), 151–3
Blount, Sir Christopher, 200, 203–4
  death sentence on, 206
Boar's Head, 51, 144, 181, 258
Book Holder, 189
Bosworth, Battle of, 141
Bradley, William, 108
Braidwood, Emily, 266
Brayne, Ellen, see Burbage, Ellen
Brayne, John, 45, 52, 61, 66
  chaotic affairs of, 82
  death of, 82
  JB's dispute with, 72
  'unlawful assemblies' charges against, 73
Brayne, Margaret, 82–3, 109
Bremer Shakespeare Company, 269
Brend, Sir Matthew, 246, 252–3
Brend, Nicholas, 172, 246
Breton, Nicholas, 58
Brown, Ivor, 138
Browne, Henry, 78
'Brush Up Your Shakespeare' campaign, 265
bubonic plague, 5, 54–5, 71–2, 75, 110, 112–13,
  118, 218, 229
  Globe closed by, 231
  Tarlton succumbs to, 107
bull-baiting, 47

Bull, Eleanor, 120
Bull Inn, 51, 52
Burbage, Alice, birth of, 62
Burbage, Cuthbert, 45, 76
    actors demand Blackfriars shares from, 253–4
    and Alleyn's intentions for Theatre, 171–2
    death and burial of, 255
    father supported by, 85
    and father's death, 161
    in Hemmings's will, 251
    indoor theatre contemplated by, 231–2
    landlord problems of, 252–3
    and Queen's demolition order, 165
    Theatre demolition scheme of, 172–3
    Theatre given to, 161
    Theatre transported by, 173–4
    see also Globe Theatre
Burbage, Elizabeth, 255
Burbage, Ellen (JB's daughter), death of, 152
Burbage (née Brayne), Ellen (JB's wife), 45, 75
Burbage, James:
    Alleyn's falling-out with, 83, 109–10
    becomes tragic figure, 160–1
    birth of, 41
    Blackfriars land purchased by, 151
    Blackfriars Theatre established by, 151–3
    Brayne's dispute with, 72
    and Cobham's appointment as Lord Chamberlain, 152
    death of, 161
    debts of, 148
    earthquake blamed on, 74
    as executor of Phillips's will, 220
    indoor theatre contemplated by, 231–2
    jealousy attracted by, 70
    in Kenilworth, 56
    and licence proclamation, 45
    Lord Mayor orders arrest of, 79
    new premises sought by, 149
    ownership of Blackfriars by, 252, 253
    plague increases debts of, 75
        see also bubonic plague
    plea of, to Dudley, 43–4
    Rose's relationships with, 85
    royal-command Christmas and Shrove Tuesday performances by, 59
    and Russell's petition, 152–3
    shrewd and ambitious, 41
    signs up to Earl of Leicester's Men, 41–2
    sister-in-law's action against, 82–3
    sons born to, 45
    Theatre conceived and built by, 61–2, 64–6

    see also Theatre
    Theatre mortgaged to Hyde by, 73
    Theatre's lease extended by, 81–2
    and Theatre's ongoing success, 148
    travelling company joined by, 35–6
    'unlawful assemblies' charges against, 73
    WS meets, 86
Burbage, James (CB's son), 161
Burbage, John, 41
Burbage, Richard:
    acting career begun by, 75–6
    and Alleyn's intentions for Theatre, 171–2
    bequests of, 250–1
    birth of, 45
    Blackfriars Theatre administered by, 161
    Blackfriars Theatre lease surrendered to, 233
    death and burial of, 249
    epitaphs for, 249–50
    extraordinary range of characters portrayed by, 178
    father supported by, 85
    and father's death, 161
    greatest tragedian, 41
    and investiture pageant, 220
    'kingdom for a horse' catchphrase of, 141
    and Margaret Brayne, 83
    in Parnassus, 209–10
    Phillips's bequest to, 220
    as Richard III, 141
    subtlety and range demonstrated by, 8
    Theatre demolition scheme of, 172–3
    Theatre transported by, 173–4
    WS's tragic characters brought to life by, 107
    see also Globe Theatre
Burbage, William, 249, 251
    actors demand Blackfriars shares from, 253–4
    ownership of Blackfriars by, 252, 253
Burbage, Winifred, 250, 253

Cade, Jack, 131, 132
Camden, William, 4, 127, 159, 250
Cardenio (Shakespeare, Fletcher), 240–1
Carey, Henry, see Hunsdon, 1st Baron
Catesby, Sir Robert, 222, 227
Cecil, Lord, 199, 200, 205
Cecil, Sir Robert, 201–2
Chapman, George, 69, 233
    and Eastward Ho scandal, 232
    plays for children written by, 212–13, 232–3
Chariclea, 67

Charles I, 251
Chettle, Henry, 69, 88, 115, 216
Children of the Chapel Royal, 65, 151, 212, 213, 214
    banned, 233
Children of the Queen's Revels, 232
Cholmley, John, 84
Christmas, 57–8
Cicero, 127
Clarke, Thomas, 43
Clerkenwell Pump, 51
Clifton, Thomas, 212
Cobham, Lord, 144, 152
cock-fighting, 49
Cockpit Theatre, 256
    replica of, 264
Coleridge, Samuel Taylor, 257
Comedy of Errors, The (Shakespeare), 153, 155, 156
commedia dell'arte, 38, 154
commedia eruditia, 154
common land, enclosure of, 229–30
Communist Party, 104
Condell, Henry, 110, 220, 248, 254
    death of, 251
conscription, 131, 133
Cooke, Alexander, 220
Coriolanus (Shakespeare), 2, 230
    lines from, 189
Cowley, Richard, 220
Cox, Charlie, 266
Crosby, Sir John, 26
Crosby, Theo, 262–3, 264, 265, 268
    death of, 269
Cross Keys, 51, 52
cudgel-play, 50
Curtain Theatre, 70–1, 109
    Lord Mayor seeks suppression and
        demolition of, 78
    Queen demands closure and demolition
        of, 164–5
    Queen's Men perform at, 83
Cymbeline (Shakespeare), 234
    lines from, 13, 228
Cynthia's Revels (Jonson), 213

Daemonologie (James VI/I), 225
Damon and Pythias (tr. Edwards), 67–8
Dankworth Johnny, 265
Daughter of Time, The (Tey), 12
De Witte, Johannes, 150
Dee, Dr John, 242
Dekker, Thomas, 158, 192
    and Queen's death, 216
    and War of the Theatres, 213–14

Dench, Dame Judi, 266
Derrick, Thomas, 208
Description of England, The (Harrison), 132
Devlin, Diana, 263, 270
Dickson, Andrew, 273
Dido, Queen of Carthage (Marlowe, Nashe), 101–2
Dmytryk, Edward, 261
Dr Faustus (Marlowe), 8, 116–18, *117*
    lines from, 116
Doctor Who, 276
dog-fighting, 49
Drake, Sir Francis, 132
Drayton, Michael, 10, 216, 239
    at WS's birthday supper, 246–7
Dromgoole, Dominic, 10, 270, 271, 272, 274–5
Duchess of Malfi, The (Webster), 10, 13, 229, 273
Dudley, Sir Robert, Earl of Leicester, 41–2, 158
    death of, 106–7
    ill-advised marriage of, 80
    JB's appeal to, 43–4
    Kenilworth country seat of, 56, 235
    see also actors' companies: Earl of
        Leicester's men
Dulwich College, 8, 118

Earl of Leicester's Men, 39, 41–4
    disbanded, 107
    in Kenilworth, 56–7
    plague forces return to touring by, 75
    Queen entertained by, 56–7
    and Queen's disfavour, 80
    royal-command Christmas and Shrove
        Tuesday performances by, 59
    settled in the Theatre, *see* Theatre
Earl of Pembroke's Men, 103, 110, 163, 166
Earl of Warwick's Men, 39
Earl of Worcester's Men, 38–9
East, Richard, 166
Eastward Ho (Chapman, Jonson, Marston), 232
Edmond Ironside (anon.), 125
Edward I, 158
Edward II (Marlowe), 107
Edwards, Richard, 67–8
Egerton, Sir Thomas, 205
Eliot, T. S., 91
Elizabeth I, Queen:
    and Anjou, Duke of, 4
    anxieties of, over plots, 42–3
    and Appletree's gun, 63–4
    'basely led by flatterers', 201
    death of, 215–16
    Earl of Leicester's Men entertain, 56–7
    Essex's death warrant signed by, 208

Essex's rebellion against, 200, 204–7
Falstaff character delights, 145
grievous taxes imposed by, 202
increasing unpopularity of, 202
Lopez becomes chief physician to, 158
and Marlow's MA, 104
performances for, 2
plot to poison, 158–9
Queen's Men selected by, 76
and second-Armada possibility, 130
seen as unifying force, 130
succession anxieties surrounding, 215
Tarlton admired by, 7, 94
theatre closures demanded by, 164
Tragedy of Byron's reference to, 233
WS's comedies performed before, 153–4
Elizabeth II, Queen, 270
Elizabeth, Princess, 242
Elizabethan Stage Society, 261
enclosure, 229–30
England's Mourning Garment (Chettle), 216
English Civil War, 255–6
Essex, 2nd Earl of, 1, 132, 152, 169, 186, 197, 198–200, 203
death sentence on, 206–7
execution of, 208
house arrest of, 199
Ireland campaign of, *131*, 198–9
knighthoods conferred by, 199
Privy Council imprisoned by, 205
rebellion of, 200, 204–7
and *Richard II* revival, 203–4
Tragedy of Byron's reference to, 233
tried for treason, 206
Evans, Henry, 161, 212, 232
Every Man in his Humour (Jonson), 166, 213
Everyman, 37
Eyre, Richard, 13

Fairbanks, Douglas Jr, 265
Fairfield, James C., 257–60, 276
Falcon Inn, 259
Famous Victories of Henry V, The (anon.), 144
Fawkes, Guido, 1, 221–2
Feake, James, 166–7
fencing matches, 50
Field, Richard, 153
firearms, 63–4
First Folio (1623), 6, 100, 135, 245, 248
Jonson's eulogy in, 248–9
First Part of the Life and Reign of King Henry IV, The (Hayward), 201, 203
Fleetwood, William, 78
Fleming, Abraham, 74
Fletcher, John, 2, 62, 98, 242–3

Fletcher, Lawrence, 208–9, 216–17
Phillips's bequest to, 220
football, 49–50
Fortune Theatre, 256
Foxe, John, 127
Frederick II of Denmark, 236
Frederick V, Count Palatine, 242
Friar Bacon and Friar Bungay (Greene), 89, 111, 118
Friends of Southwark Globe, 266
Frizer, Ingram, 120–1
Fry, Stephen, 14
Fuller, Thomas, 98

Game of Chess, A (Middleton), 158
Gammer Gurton's Needle (Stevenson), 68
Garnet, Fr, 227
Gates, Sir Thomas, 238–9
Gathercole, Sir Toby, 23–5
Gent, P. F., 116
George Inn, 65
Gilburne, Samuel, 220
Giles, Nathaniel, 161, 212
Give Us This Day, 261
Globe Playhouse Trust, 263
insolvency of, 264
Globe Theatre, *180*
absence of lavatories at, 193–4
admission prices at, 192
backstage staff in, 188–9
Blackfriars attracts custom from, 212
Book Holder at, 188–9
burned down, 1, 9, 243–5
daily traffic to, 187
front-of-house staff in, 188
half-size replica of, 261
Henry VIII's magnificent opening at, 242–3
Hercules flag on, 177
Lord Chamberlain's Men open, 1, 180–1
modern reconstruction of, *see* Shakespeare's Globe
modern site of, 258
motto of, 177–8
naming of, 176
non-survival of, into modern times, 258
plague closes, 231
Platter's visit to, 190–6
and *Richard II* revival, 203–4
scale model of, 261
second, *187*
building of, 246
demolition of, 256
Stage Keeper at, 188
successful season embarked on by, 186

Tire Man (wardrobe master) at, 189–90
triumphant opening of, 180–1
Wanamaker's project, *see* Shakespeare's
    Globe
see also Shakespeare's Globe; Theatre
Gloucester Records, 42
Glover, Julian, 264
Goldsmiths' Row, 22
Gorboduc (Sackville, Norton), 67
Great Fire of London, 144, 258
    thatch banned since, 268
Greene, Fortunatus, 114
Greene, Graham, 105
Greene, Robert, 5, 23, 69, 87, 88–90, *89*, 98,
    114–15, 135, 238
    actors disdained by, 95
    death of, 90, 115
    destitution of, 114
    hired to write counterblast against
        'Martin Marprelate', 119
    influence of, on WS's work, 95
    morality play of, 111
    playwriting taken up by, 111
    wife deserts, 114
Greenfield, Jon, 267, 273
Greenwood (preacher), 119
Gresham, Sir Thomas, 25–6
Grey, Lady Jane, 130
Griggs, John, 84
Groatsworth of Wit, A (Greene), 87, 90
Guilpin, Edward, 169–70
Gunpowder Plot, 1, 221–2, 227
Gurr, Prof. Andrew, 130, 264

Hall, Edward, 126, 130, 135
Hall, Dr John, 234
Hall (née Shakespeare), Susanna, 11, 222, 234
Hall's Chronicle, 127, 135
Hamlet (Shakespeare), 2, 7, 8–9, 11, 95, 176,
    211, 235, 237
    length of, 186
    lines from, 3, 9, 179, 214
    modern production of, 263
Harey the Sixth (Shakespeare), *see* works of
    William Shakespeare: *Henry VI*
Harington, Sir John, 199
Harrison, Maj. Gen. Thomas, 255
Harrison, William, 132
Harry Hunks (bear), 47
Hart, Charles, 255
Hathaway, Anne, *see* Shakespeare, Anne
Hawes, James, 53–4
Hayward, Sir John, 201, 203
Hemmings, John, 174, 218, 220, 248, 254
    death and will of, 251

Phillips's bequest to, 220
Henry IV (Shakespeare), 133, 142, 144–5, 181–2
    central theme of, 129
    lines from, 133–4, 182
Henry V, King, 6, 28, 200
Henry V (Shakespeare), 2, 6, 133, 145–7, 180–6
    central theme of, 129
    film of, 261
    Globe opened with, 180–1
    lines from, 61, 171, 181, 183, 184, 185,
        186, 247
    modern production of, 270
Henry VI series (Shakespeare), 91, 110, 111, 118,
    125, 132, 134–8, 141
    central theme of, 129
    as collaborative work, 135
    dates of, 135
    Jonson's sarcasm towards, 184
    lines from, 126, 138
    Nashe on, 128
    theme of, 135
Henry VI (Shakespeare), lines from, 140
Henry VII, King, 44
Henry VIII, King, 44
Henry VIII (Shakespeare, Fletcher), 1, 235,
    240–1, 242–4
    magnificence of, 243
Henry, Prince of Wales, 220, 238
Henslowe, Philip, 3, 7, 84–5, 163, 165–6, 169
    Alleyn moves over to, 109–10
    diary of, 84–5
    Henry VI a big earner for, 125
    Isle of Dogs affair a blow to, 165
    and plague, 113
Herbert, Sir Philip, 253
Hercules, 177–8
Heywood, Thomas, 81
    on Alleyn, 101
Hieronimo is Mad Again (Kyd), *see Spanish
    Tragedy, The*
Historie III (Camden), 4
*Historie of the damnable life and deserved death
    of Dr John Faustus, The*, 116
History of the Collier, The, 67
History of the World (Raleigh), 124
Histriomastix (Marston), 213
Hoefnagel, Georg, 47
Holinshed, Raphael, 127, 143
Hollar, Wenceslaus, *180*
Holywell Priory, 62, 64
Hope, Polly, 265
Hope Theatre, 188
    demolition of, 256
Horestes (tr. Pickering), 68
Howard, Catherine, 215

Hunnis, William, 212
Hunsdon, 1st Baron, 152
Hunsdon, 2nd Baron, 152, 153
  appointed Lord Chamberlain, 161
Hyde, John, 61
  Theatre mortgaged to, 73

Inigo Jones Theatre, *see* Sam Wanamaker
  Playhouse
Ireland, 131, 143, 186
  Essex's campaign in, *131*, 198–9
Isam, Mistress, 115
Isle of Dogs, The (Nashe, Jonson), 4, 149, 155,
  163–4

Jack Drum's Entertainment (Marston), 213
James VI/I, King:
  arrival in London of, 217
  Banquo ancestor of, 226
  becomes King of England, 216
  best claim to throne possessed by, 202
  Essex supported by, 200
  and Fletcher, 209, 216–17
  generosity of, as royal patron, 220
  and Gunpowder Plot, 1, 221–2
  impersonated on stage, 219
  plague halts progress of, 218
  Southampton freed by, 216
  witchcraft preoccupation of, 223–5
Jesuits, 222, 227
Jew of Malta, The (Marlowe), 85, 118, 157, 160
  lines from, 106
Jews, 157–8
  see also Merchant of Venice, The
John of Gaunt, 142
Johnson, Samuel, 16, 92, 257
Johnson, William, 43
Jones, Inigo, 236, 264–5, 273
Jonson, Ben, 10, 71, 97–8, 155, 162–3, 184, 222,
  245
  Admiral's Men joined by, 163
  Aubrey's description of, 7, 162
  'best for tragedy', 166
  blossoming writing talents of, 166
  death and burial of, 251
  and *Eastward Ho* scandal, 232
  eulogy to WS by, 248–9
  execution escaped by, 168–9
  imprisonment of, 4, 164
    and release, 165
  inscription on tomb of, 251
  and *Isle of Dogs* affair, 163–4
  military enlistment of, 163
  murder charge against, 168
  Nashe play completed by, 4

plays for children written by, 212–13,
  232–3
referred to in *Parnassus*, 209
satirising of, 213
Spenser killed by, 168
Spenser's bitter feud with, 166
Spenser's duel with, 5, 167–8
and War of the Theatres, 213–14
at WS's birthday supper, 247
Julius Caesar (Shakespeare), 143, 194–5, 231

Kemp, Will, 5, 112, 155, 174
  dancing bet accepted by, 7–8
  in *Parnassus*, 209–10
Kenilworth Castle, 56, 235
Keyes, Robert, 222
King John (Bale), 37
King John (Shakespeare), lines from, 230
King Lear (Shakespeare), 2, 8, 12, 50
King's Men (formerly Lord Chamberlain's
  Men, *q.v.*), 216–19
  Blackfriars gives new lease of life to, 233
  and Civil War, 255
  enhanced status of, 217–18
  old players pass from, 251
  and plague, 218
  royal wedding entertainment provided
    by, 242
  and Spanish Ambassador, 219
Knack to Know a Knave, A (Kemp), 5, 112, 204
Knell, William, 81
Knight Marshal's men, 111–12
Knight of the Burning Pestle, The (Beaumont,
  Fletcher), 62–3
Knollys, Lady Lettice, *see* Lettice, Countess of
  Leicester
Knollys, Sir William, 205
Kyd, Thomas, 45, 95, 99–100, 178
  arrest of, 119
  bar for drama raised by, 106
  death of, 122
  and divinity of Christ, 119
  facility with language demonstrated by,
    99
  influence of, on WS's work, 95
  other authors praise, 100
  release of, 122
  WS influenced by, 102

'Lady in the Lake, The', 56
Laine, Cleo, 265
Lambard, William, 201, 202–3
Laneham, John, 43, 57, 81
Lanman, Henry, 83
Laurie, Hugh, 14

Lee, Capt. Thomas, 206
Lefèvre de la Boderie, Antoine, 233
Lettice, Countess of Leicester, 80
Litany in Time of Plague, A (Nashe), 229
   lines from, 113–14
Lodge, Thomas, 69, 102–3, 135
   Greene's warning to, 88, 90, 115
   morality play of, 111
London, 16–32
   animal-baiting rings used as theatres in,
      46–7, *46*
   apprentices' riots in, 112
   Artillery Yard, 63
   Bartholomew Fair in, 39
   Bear Gardens Museum and Arts Centre,
      264
   Bell Savage, 51, 52
   Blackfriars, 149–51
   Boar's Head, 51, 144, 181, 258
   booksellers in, 23
   Bull Inn, 51, 52
   busy daily life in, 18
   ceremonial jousts in, 128
   Clerkenwell Pump, 51
   Cross Keys, 51, 52
   Dulwich College, 8, 118
   earthquakes hit, 73–4, 200
   Falcon Inn, 259
   first theatre in, *see* Theatre
   George Inn, 65
   Goldsmiths' Row, 22
   Great Fire of, 144, 258
      thatch banned since, 268
   Holywell Priory, 62, 64
   JB's theatre project in (the Theatre), *see*
      Theatre
   Knight Marshal's men in, 111–12
   London Bridge, 19–20, *20*
   Lord Mayor's Show in, 39
   Marshalsea gaol, 4, 111, 164
   Mermaid Tavern, 98, 222, 258
   Newington Butts Playhouse, 70
   Paris Garden, 48, 74
   plague in, 5, 54–5, 71–2, 75, 112–13, 118
   players' inns in, 51–6
      fire risk in, 55–6
      proclamations against, 53–4
      and risk to life and limb, 54
      see also actors' companies
   population dynamics in, 53
   public executions in, 128–9
   public performances banned in, 56
   Red Lion, 52, 56
   religious tensions in, 118–19
   Royal Exchange, 25–7
   and Russell's petition, 151–3
   St Leonard's Church, Shoreditch, 107
   St Paul's Cathedral, 19, 20
   Saracen's Head, 51
   second theatre in, 70
   Shoreditch, 45, 95–6
      WS takes inspiration from, 96
   St Paul's Walk, 21
   street violence in, 128
   Thames freezes in, 229
   thatch banned in, 268
   Theatre (first playhouse), *see* Theatre
   theatre boom in, 148–9
   theatres in:
      Charles I's attempts to close, 251–2
      and fire risk, 190
      Lord Mayor's damning letter of
         complaint against, 161–2
      Parliament orders destruction of, 256
      Queen demands closure and demoli-
         tion of, 164–5
      see also Barbican Centre; Blackfriars
         Theatre; Cockpit Theatre;
         Curtain Theatre; Fortune
         Theatre; Globe Theatre; Hope
         Theatre; National Theatre; Rose
         Theatre; Sam Wanamaker
         Playhouse; Shakespeare's Globe;
         Swan Theatre; Theatre
   Tower of, 6, 63, 129, 201, *207*
      princes in, 140
   Westminster Abbey, 28
   wherries used in, 190–1
   WS's first experience of, 16–30
   WS's inextricable link to, 1
   young people in, as proportion of popu-
      lation, 53
London Bridge, 19–20, *20*
London Fire Brigade, 273
Long, Maurice, 71
Looking Glass for London, A (Greene, Lodge),
   111
Lopez, Dr Rodrigo, 158–9
Lord Chamberlain's Men (later King's Men,
   q.v.), 1, 70, 152, 161
   capacity audiences drawn by, 153
   and Essex's rebellion, 208
   Globe opened by, 1, 180–1
   and *Hamlet*, 211
   indoor theatre contemplated by, 231–2
   King chooses, as own company, 216–17
   most successful troupe, 188
   name change of, to King's Men, 216
   and *Parnassus*, 209–10
   prosecution escaped by, 208

and Queen's death, 216
and *Richard II* revival, 203–4, 208
Scottish tour of, 208–9
Theatre transported by, 173–4
Lord Hunsdon's Men, 152
Lord Mayor's Show, 39
Lord of Misrule, 40
Lord Strange's Men, 39, 103, 109, 110, 118
L'Orfeo (Moneverdi), 237
Love's Labour's Lost (Shakespeare), 154–5, 156, 219
Lucy, Sir Thomas, 16, 92
Lyly, John, 69, 98
    commedia eruditia of, 154

Macbeth (Shakespeare), 48, 208, 225–7
    inspiration for, 220
    lines from, 197, 226–7
    witches in, 225–6
McCurdy, Peter, 267
Machiavelli, Niccolò, 139
McKellen, Sir Ian, 139
Malone, Edmond, 93
Manners, Edward, Earl of Rutland, 46, 62, 64, 187, 205
Manningham, John, 215
Marlowe, Christopher 'Kit', 1, 45, 69, 95, 101, 103–8
    bar for drama raised by, 106
    birth and education of, 104
    burial of, 121
    Catholic sympathies of, 104
    Greene's warning to, 88, 90, 115
    heresy accusations against, 119–20
    influence of, on WS's work, 95
    in Newgate Gaol, 108
    and Raleigh, 108
    self-mythologising, 6–7
    spectacular ascent of, 103
    spy status of, 105
    stabbed to death, 5, 120–1
    as street fighter, 108
    'that atheist', 105
    and writing of *Dr Faustus*, 116–18
Marshalsea gaol, 4, 111, 164
Marston, John, 187
    and *Eastward Ho* scandal, 232
    plays for children written by, 212–13, 232–3
    and War of the Theatres, 213–14
'Martin Marprelate' controversy, 118–19
Martin, Millicent, 265
Mary I, 130
Mary, Queen of Scots, 99
Masque of Blackness, The (Jonson), 236

masques, 56–7, 59, 213, 231, 235–6
Massacre at Paris, The (Marlowe), 118
Master of the Revels, 44, 58, 189
May Day, 39
Measure for Measure (Shakespeare), 143
Menaphon (Greene), 102
Merchant of Venice, The (Shakespeare), 134, 156, 157–60
    lines from, 62, 159
Meres, Francis, 100, 166
Mermaid Tavern, 98, 222, 258
Merry Wives of Windsor, The (Shakespeare):
    Falstaff 'resurrected' in, 145
    lines from, 47
Meyrick, Sir Gilly, 203
    death sentence on, 206
Michell, Keith, 263
Middleton, Thomas, 158, 249
Midsummer Night's Dream, A (Shakespeare), 5–6, 8, 38, 56–7, 134, 156, 223, 276
    lines from, 57, 190
    performed at Court, 153–4
    reference to Greene in, 116
    rude mechanicals' play within, 38, 155, 235
Mills, Toby, 81
Monday, Anthony, 220
Monnox, Will, 115
Monteagle, Lord, 204, 205
Monteverdi, Claudio, 237
Montgomery, Earl of, 248
Moore, Rowan, 273
More, Thomas, 126, 139
More, Sir William, 151
Much Ado About Nothing (Shakespeare), 156
Mulcaster, Richard, 99
Museum of Shakespearean Stage, 263
Myles, Robert, 64, 152
mystery plays, 51, 53

Nashe, Thomas, 69, 96, 101, 113–14, 115, 135, 152
    on Alleyn, 101
    clerks disdained by, 102
    commedia eruditia of, 154
    epitaph for, 210
    fleas London, 164
    Greene pitied by, 115
    Greene's warning to, 88, 90, 115
    on *Henry VI*, 127
    hired to write counterblast against 'Martin Marprelate', 119
    imprisonment of, 4
National Theatre, 264
Nestor, King, 44

Neville, John, 13
Newes from Scotland, 224
Newington Butts Playhouse, 70
Nicholl, Charles, 104, 121
Nicholson, Andy, 273
Norden, John, 267
Norton, Thomas, 67

Of Well Penn'd Plays (Marston), 187
Oldcastle, Sir John, 144, 152
Olivier, Sir Laurence, 139, 261
On the death of that great Master . . . R Burbage
    (Middleton), 249
O'Neill, Hugh (Earl of Tyrone), *131*, 186, 198–9
Orlando Furioso (Greene), 89, 111
Orrell, John, 264
Osborne, Sir Edward, 76–7
Othello (Shakespeare), 8, 157, 237
Owen, Dame Alice, 62

Page, William, 4
Pandosto (Greene), 88, 238
Paris Garden, 48, 74
Parry, William, 239
Pasco, Richard, 13
Paston, Sir William, 78
Peele, George, 69
Pembroke, Earl of, 110, 248
    RB's death devastates, 250
    see also actors' companies: Earl of
        Pembroke's Men
Percy, Sir Charles, 200, 203–4
Percy, Harry 'Hotspur', 200
Pericles, Prince of Tyre (Shakespeare, Wilkins),
    231, 234–5
Perkin, John, 43
Philemon and Philecia, 67
Philip, Prince, Duke of Edinburgh, 265, 266,
    270
Phillips, Augustine, 174, 208
    death and bequests of, 220–1
plague, 5, 54–5, 71–2, 75, 110, 112–13, 118, 218,
    229
    Globe closed by, 231
    Tarlton succumbs to, 107
Platter, Dr Thomas, 48, 190–6
Plautus, 36, 68
players' inns, 51–6
    fire risk in, 55–6
    proclamations against, 53–4
    and risk to life and limb, 54
    see also actors' companies
Poel, William, 261
Poetaster, The (Jonson), 214
Poley, Robert, 120

political correctness, lack of, 160
Pollard, Thomas, 253
Polyolbion (Drayton), 239
Pope, Thomas, 174
'Pouch, Captain' (John Reynolds), *see* Reynolds,
    John
Preface to Britannia (Camden), 127
princes in the Tower, 140
Puritanism, 42, 48, 69, 119, 162, 199–200
    and Queen's tolerance of Catholics, 202
Puttenham, George, 127

Queen's Men:
    continuing popularity of, 109
    Curtain performances of, 83
    extensive touring of, 77–8, 80–1
    formed, 77
    plea of, to Lord Mayor, 79–80

Raleigh, Sir Walter, 107–8, 122, 124, 132, 200,
    208
Ralph Roister Doister (Udall), 37, 68
Rambles with an American (Tearle), 258
Rape of Lucrece, The (Shakespeare), 153
Reckoning, The (Nicholl), 104, 121
Red Lion, 52, 56
Redgrave, Vanessa, 264
Report of Sundry Broiles in Whitsontide, 78
Restoration, 257
Return from Parnassus, The, 209–10
Reunion: The Globe Theatre, The, 263, 265
Revenger's Tragedy, The (Middleton), 229
Reynolds, John, 229–30
Rice, John, 220
Richard II, King, 28, 201–2
    sexuality of, 142
    starves to death, 143
Richard II (Shakespeare), 13, 123–4, 142–4, 201
    central theme of, 129
    and Elizabethan politics, 142–3
    Essex commissions revival of, 203–4
    lines from, 123, 142, 146
    WS's best speeches in, 143
Richard III, King, 12, 129
    and princes in the Tower, 140
Richard III (Shakespeare), 2, 8, 9, 125–6, 136,
    139–42, 179–80
    length of, 186
    lines from, 126, 180
    as Tudor propaganda, 12, 140
Ritchie, Tony, 265
Robbins, William, 255
Robinson, James, 212
Romeo and Juliet (Shakespeare), 8, 154, 167–8,
    235

lines from, 167
spoofed in *Dream*, 155
Rookwood, Ambrose, 222
Rose Theatre, 3, 7, 83–5
    Alleyn moves over to, 109–10
    and apprentices' riots, 112
    Henry VI packs, 111
    Jonson signs contract with, 163
    Marlowe's first play produced at, 105
    non-survival of, into modern times, 258
    plague closes, 88–9, 111
    remains of, 266–7
    success of, 149
Rowe, Nicholas, 92
Royal Exchange, 25–7
Royal Shakespeare Theatre, 12
Russell, Lady Elizabeth (Dowager), 152–3
Rutland, Earl of, *see* Manners, Edward, Earl
    of Rutland
Rylance, Mark, 269, 270

Sackerson (bear), 47
Sackville, Thomas, 67
St Leonard's Church, Shoreditch, 107
St Paul's Cathedral, 19, 20
Sam Wanamaker Playhouse, 10, 264, 272–4
    fire safety at, 273
Sampson, Agnes, 222–5
Sands, James, 221
Sandys, Lord, 205
Saracen's Head, 51
Satiromastix (Dekker), 214
Selimus (Greene), 125
Seneca, 36, 68, 99
Shakespeare (née Hathaway), Anne, 26
Shakespeare, Edmund, 230, 231
Shakespeare Globe Centres, 264, 267
Shakespeare Globe Trust, 265
Shakespeare, Hamnet, 230
Shakespeare Institute, 262
Shakespeare, John, 41, 92
Shakespeare, Mary, 230, 231
Shakespeare Reading Society, 260
Shakespeare, Susanna, *see* Hall, Susanna
Shakespeare, William:
    abstemious character of, 97
    Aubrey's descriptions of, 93, 94, 97
    battle of sexes as major theme used by,
        156
    battles brought to life by, 130
    birthday supper hosted by, 246–7
    Burbage family's link with, 41
    burial of, 10, 247–8
    consultant role of, 234
    Curtain Old Church window in honour

        of, 260
    death of, 9–10, 247
    deer-poaching myth concerning, 92
    education of, 11
    epitaph for, 248
    facility with language demonstrated by,
        98
    first documented mention of, as part of
        London scene, 91
    Greene's rant against, 5
    history plays of, as war plays, 129
    indoor theatre contemplated by, 231–2
    JB meets, 86
    Kyd's influence on, 102
    London arrival of, 17, 91–3
    London's inextricable link to, 1
    Marlowe inspires, 122
    Parkinson's suspected in, 234, 247
    Phillips's bequest to, 220
    plaques in honour of, 260
    plays and poetry of, *see* works of
        William Shakespeare
    and political correctness, lack of, 160
    poor health of, 247
    preserved in national consciousness, 257
    RB names son after, 249
    referred to in *Parnassus*, 209
    'on the run' myth concerning, 16
    at school, 69
    signature of, *21*
    Southwark Cathedral statue of, 260
    teacher background of, speculated, 92
    and Theatre's transportation and
        rebuilding, 174
    turns to poetry, 114
    unforgettable characters of, 6
    'upstart crow', 89, 90–1
    virtuoso skills of, 154
    will of, 247
    without rival as playwright, 153
    works of, *see* works of William
        Shakespeare
Shakespeare's Globe, 10, 262–76, *271*
    building work begins on, 266
    debts of, 267
    evolution of, 272
    fireproofing of, 268
    first production in shell of, 269
    foundation posts donated to, 266
    gala opening of first full season at, 270
    international recognition of, 272
    lease signed for, 266
    opening ceremony for, 270
    opposition to, 266, 270
    'Prologue Season' in, 270

and Rose remains, 267
self-build scheme for, 267
Southwark Council unsympathetic
    towards, 265
stage construction in, 268
staunch support for, 266
thatched roof of, 268
ticket queues for, 270
work begins on, 266
Shaw, Robert:
    imprisonment of, 164
    release of, 165
Sher, Sir Anthony, 139
Sheres, Nicholas, 120
Shirley, Sir Anthony, 239
Shoreditch, 45, 95–6
    WS takes inspiration from, 96
Shrove Tuesday, 39, 59, 154
Sidney, Sir Philip, 99, 127
Sinclaire, John, 110
Singer, John, 78
Sir Thomas More (Shakespeare, Munday,
    Chettle), 240–1
Skialetheia (Guilpin), 169–70
Sly, Christopher, 34, 35
Sly, William, 220
'Smith, William', 172
Smyth, Sheriff, 205
Somers, Sir George, 239
Southampton, Earl of, 114, 169, 187, 200, 204,
    205, 216
    King's Men protected by, 218
    tried for treason, 206
Spanish Armada, 99
    second, thwarted by weather, 181
Spanish Tragedy, The (Kyd), 8, 95, 100–2, *100*,
    118
    lines from, 101
Spencer, Prof. Terence, 262
Spenser, Gabriel 'Gab', 1, 95
    Feake killed by, 166–7
    imprisonment of, 5, 164
    Jonson kills, 168
    Jonson's bitter feud with, 166
    Jonson's duel with, 5, 167–8
    release of, 165
Spottiswoode, Patrick, 265
St Paul's Walk, 21
Stage Keeper, 189
Stevenson, William, 68
Stewart, Francis, Earl of Bothwell, 223
Still, John, 68
Stockwood, John, 69
Stow, John, 50, 63, 69, 170
Stratford-upon-Avon:

Bear in, 81
commercialisation of, 257–8
New Place, 234, 246
Queen's Men's memorable appearance in,
    81
shrine to all things Shakespearean, 257–8
WS spends more time in, 234, 246
'Stratford-on-Thames', 263
Street, Peter, 172, 173, 174–6
Strype, John, 255
Stubbe, John, 4
Stubbes, Philip, 40, 48, 49, 76, 97
Suffolk, Duke of, 232
Summer's Last Will and Testament (Nashe), 113
Survey of London (Stow), 63, 170
Swan Theatre, 148, 149, *150*
    and Queen's demolition order, 165
    raided, 163–4
Swanston, Eliard, 253, 254, 255–6
Swinton, Tilda, 13
Sylvester, William, 52

Tamburlaine (Marlowe), 7, 105–6, 125
    lines from, 103
Taming of the Shrew, The (Shakespeare), 70,
    110, 134, 156–7
    lines from, 33, 34
    performed at Court, 153–4
TARDIS, 276
Tarlton, Richard, 7, 77, 78, 94–5
    death of, 107
    own brand of comedy developed by,
        98–9
Tearle, Christian, 257–60, 276
Tempest, The (Shakespeare), 231, 234, 238–42
    inspiration for, 238–9
    lines from, 228, 240–1, 245
    modern (tent) production of, 268
    as royal wedding entertainment, 242
Terence, 36, 68
Tey, Josephine, 12
Theatre:
    Alleyn's plan to demolish, 171
    becomes Globe, 176
        see also Globe Theatre
    bubonic plague closes, 71, 75
        see also bubonic plague
    Burbage–Brayne dispute concerning, 72
    Burbage mortgages, to Hyde, 73
    Burbages' scheme to demolish, 172–3
    as 'cause' of plague, 72
    CB takes ownership of, 161
    Curtain as rival to, 70–1
    executions at, 129
    first production in, speculated, 67–8

fundamentalist preachers condemn, 70
immediate success of, 69
interior of, 66–7
JB's conception and building of, 61–2,
    64–6
    see also Burbage, James
lease extended on, 81–2
Lord Chamberlain's Men draw capacity
    audiences to, 153
Lord Mayor attacks, 70
Lord Mayor seeks suppression and
    demolition of, 78
naming of, 66
ongoing success of, 148
opening of, 66
plague closes, 111
Queen demands closure and demolition
    of, 164–5
    CB's stay of execution concerning,
        165
rebuilding of, 174–7
remains 'dark', 169
represented as threat to public safety, 76
Stow's last reference to, 170
transporting of, 173–4
Theatre (first playhouse), see Theatre
Thompson, Emma, 14
Tilney, Sir Edmund, 58
Tire Man (wardrobe master), 189–90
Titus Andronicus (Shakespeare), 70, 102, 110,
    118, 136
Tooley, Nicholas, 110, 220, 251
Topcliffe, Sir Richard, 164
Tower of London, 6, 63, 129, 201, 207
    princes in, 140
Tragedy of Byron (Chapman), 233
Tragedy of Gowrie, The, 219
Troilus and Cressida (Shakespeare), 179
Trojan War, 44
Troublesome Reign of King John, The (anon.),
    125
True Tragedy of Richard III, The (anon.), 125
Tudor interludes, 37
Twelfth Night (Shakespeare), 256
    lines from, 13, 148, 257
Two Gentlemen of Verona, The (Shakespeare),
    39–40, 155, 156
    lines from, 40, 148
    modern production of, 270
    performed at Court, 153–4
Two Noble Kinsmen, The (Shakespeare,
    Fletcher), 240–1
Tyrell, Sir James, 139
Tyrone, Earl of, see O'Neill, Hugh

Udall, Nicholas, 37, 68

Venus and Adonis (Shakespeare), 113–14, 153
Vernon, Elizabeth, 169
Vischer, Claus, 187
Vitruvius, 176

Walsingham, Sir Francis, 76–7, 80, 105, 158,
    202
Wanamaker, Abby, 270
Wanamaker, Charlotte, 263, 270
Wanamaker, Jessica, 270
Wanamaker, Sam, 10, 261–3, 265–6, 267
    death of, 269
    Playhouse named after, 272
Wanamaker, Zoë, 270
War of the Theatres, 213–14
Ward, Ann, 266
Warrants for Payment, 57
Watson, Thomas, 95, 99, 108
Webb, John, 273
Webster, John, 10, 229
Westminster Abbey, 28
What You Will (Marston), 214
wherries, 190–1
White Devil, The (Webster), 229
Whitsuntide, 39
Whore of Babylon (Dekker), 158
Wickham, Prof. Glynne, 262
Wilkins, George, 235
Williamson, Nicol, 266
Wilson, Robert, 43, 77, 81, 95
Winter's Tale, The (Shakespeare), 39, 157, 231,
    234, 237–8
    court performance of, 238
Wintour, Thomas, 222
witchcraft, 140, 222–6
Witter, John, 221
Wonderful Year, The (Dekker), 215
Wood, Alan à, 92
Woodward, Joan, see Alleyn, Joan
Worcester, Earl of, 205
    see also actors' companies: Earl of
        Worcester's men
works of William Shakespeare:
    Antony and Cleopatra, 231
        modern production of, 264
    Cardenio (with Fletcher), 240–1
    Comedy of Errors, The, 153, 155, 156
    comic relief in, 6
    Coriolanus, 2, 230
        lines from, 189
    Cymbeline, 234
        lines from, 13, 228
    First Folio (1623), 6, 100, 135, 245, 248

Jonson's eulogy in, 248–9
Hamlet, 2, 7, 8–9, 11, 95, 176, 211, 235,
    237
    length of, 186
    lines from, 3, 9, 179, 214
    modern production of, 263
Henry IV, 133, 142, 144–5, 181–2
    central theme of, 129
    lines from, 133–4, 182
Henry V, 2, 6, 133, 145–7, 180–6
    central theme of, 129
    film of, 261
    Globe opened with, 180–1
    lines from, 61, 171, 181, 183, 184,
        185, 186, 247
    modern production of, 270
Henry VI series, 91, 110, 111, 118, 125,
    132, 134–8, 141
    central theme of, 129
    as collaborative work, 135
    dates of, 135
    Jonson's sarcasm towards, 184
    lines from, 126, 138
    Nashe on, 128
    theme of, 135
Henry VI, lines from, 140
Henry VIII (with Fletcher), 1, 235, 240–1,
    242–4
    magnificence of, 243
Julius Caesar, 143, 194–5, 231
King John, lines from, 230
King Lear, 2, 8, 12, 50
Love's Labour's Lost, 154–5, 156, 219
Macbeth, 48, 208, 225–7
    inspiration for, 220
    lines from, 197, 226–7
    witches in, 225–6
Measure for Measure, 143
Merchant of Venice, The, 134, 156, 157–60
    lines from, 62, 159
Merry Wives of Windsor, The:
    Falstaff 'resurrected' in, 145
    lines from, 47
Midsummer Night's Dream, A, 5–6, 8, 38,
    56–7, 134, 156, 223, 276
    lines from, 57, 190
    performed at Court, 153–4
    reference to Greene in, 116
    rude mechanicals' play within, 38,
        155, 235
    most famous characters in, 138–9
Much Ado About Nothing, 156
Othello, 8, 157, 237
Pericles, Prince of Tyre (with Wilkins),
    231, 234–5

Rape of Lucrece, The, 153
Richard II, 13, 123–4, 142–4, 201
    central theme of, 129
    and Elizabethan politics, 142–3
    Essex commissions revival of, 203–4
    lines from, 123, 142, 146
    WS's best speeches in, 143
Richard III, 2, 8, 9, 125–6, 136, 139–42,
    179–80
    length of, 186
    lines from, 126, 180
    as Tudor propaganda, 12, 140
Romeo and Juliet, 8, 154, 167–8, 235
    lines from, 167
    spoofed in *Dream*, 155
Sir Thomas More (with Munday and
    Chettle), 240–1
Taming of the Shrew, The, 70, 110, 134,
    156–7
    lines from, 33, 34
    performed at Court, 153–4
Tempest, The, 231, 234, 238–42
    inspiration for, 238–9
    lines from, 228, 240–1, 245
    modern (tent) production of, 268
    as royal wedding entertainment, 242
Titus Andronicus, 70, 102, 110, 118, 136
Troilus and Cressida, 179
Twelfth Night, 256
    lines from, 13, 148, 257
Two Gentlemen of Verona, The, 39–40,
    155, 156
    lines from, 40, 148
    modern production of, 270
    performed at Court, 153–4
Two Noble Kinsmen, The (with Fletcher),
    240–1
Venus and Adonis, 113–14, 153
Winter's Tale, The, 39, 157, 231, 234,
    237–8
    court performance of, 238
As You Like It, 50, 121, 178
    lines from, 16
World Centre for Shakespeare Studies, 263,
    264
World Shakespeare Congress, 263
Wotton, Sir Henry, 243
Wounds of Civil War, The (Lodge), 125
wrestling, 50, 62
Wyatt, Sir Thomas, 130
Wynsdon, Mr, 78

York, Michael, 265